The Political Economy of Latin American Defense Expenditures

The Political Economy of Latin American Defense Expenditures

Case Studies of Venezuela and Argentina

Robert E. Looney
Naval Postgraduate School

Lexington Books
D.C. Heath and Company/Lexington, Massachusetts/Toronto

Library of Congress Cataloging-in-Publication Data

Looney, Robert E.

   The political economy of Latin American defense expenditures.

   Bibliography: p.
   Includes index.
   1. Latin America—Defenses. 2. Latin America—Armed Forces—Appropriations and expenditures. 3. Venezuela—Defenses. 4. Venezuela—Armed Forces—Appropriations and expenditures. 5. Argentina—Defenses. 6. Argentina—Armed Forces—Appropriations and expenditures. I. Title.
UA602.3.L66 1986   355.6'22'098   85-46043
ISBN 0-669-12928-3 (alk. paper)

Copyright © 1986 by D.C. Heath and Company

All rights reserved. No part of this publication may be reproduced or transmitted in any form or by any means, electronic or mechanical, including photocopy, recording, or any information storage or retrieval system, without permission in writing from the publisher.

Published simultaneously in Canada
Printed in the United States of America
International Standard Book Number: 0-669-12928-3
Library of Congress Catalog Card Number: 85-46043

The paper used in this publication meets the minimum requirements of American National Standard for Information Sciences—Permanence of Paper for Printed Library Materials, ANSI Z39.48-1984.
∞ ™

For Pam

Contents

List of Tables xi

Foreword xix

Preface xxi

Acknowledgments xxiii

Part I Cross-Sectional Analysis 1

1. **Determinants of Third World Defense Burdens 3**

   Factor and Discriminant Analysis 4
   Analysis of per Capita Military Expenditures 12
   Conclusions 27

2. **Economic Environments Conducive to Indigenous Third World Arms Production 31**

   Methodology 32
   Results 35
   Summary of Results for Latin American and Non-Latin American Groupings 43
   Conclusions and Implications 46

3. **Impact of Defense Spending and Indigenous Arms Production on Latin American Growth 51**

   Empirical Tests 52
   Conclusions 56

4. **Defense Expenditures and the Budgetary Process in Latin America 59**

   The Budgetary Process 59
   Empirical Tests 60

viii · Latin American Defense Expenditures

Defense Expenditures as a Tool for Stabilization   67
Conclusions   69

5. **Patterns of Defense and Socioeconomic Budgetary Trade-offs in Latin America   71**

   Trade-off Literature   71
   Methodology   78
   Empirical Results   80
   Conclusion   97

Part II   Venezuela   105

6. **Austerity and Military Expenditures in Venezuela   107**

   Patterns of Austerity   107
   The Venezuelan Case   111
   Conclusions   115

7. **Factors Underlying Venezuelan Defense Expenditures, 1950-83   117**

   Analysis of Trends in Venezuelan Defense Expenditures   118
   Historical Defense-Macroeconomic Patterns   130
   Impact of Military Expenditures in Other Latin American Countries   140
   Determinants of the Deviation from Trends in Real Military Expenditures   142
   Conclusions   146

8. **Determinants of Venezuelan Budgetary Patterns: Possible Trade-offs between Defense and Nondefense Expenditures   151**

   Conceptual Issues   151
   Empirical Tests   154
   Longer-Term Determinants of Nondefense Allocations   163
   Defense   164
   Nondefense Sectors   166
   Conclusions   173

9. **An Optimal Control Forecast of Venezuelan Defense and Socioeconomic Budgetary Expenditures   179**

   Economic Priorities and Constraints   179
   Description of the Model   182

Structural Equation Estimates 188
The Model's Use in Forecasting 196
Preliminary Optimal Control Simulations 198
Final Optimal Control Forecasts 199
Conclusions 205

Part III Argentina 209

10. **The Impact of Recent Developments on Argentinian Military Expenditures 211**

    Initial Reforms 211
    The Cost of the Malvinas War 213
    Alfonsin's Record 214
    Conclusions 217

11. **Impact of Regime Type on Argentinian Central Government Budgetary Priorities, 1961-82: A Test of the O'Donnell Thesis 219**

    The O'Donnell Thesis 219
    Previous Empirical Examinations of Regime Type and
       Budgetary Priorities 222
    Empirical Evidence for Argentina 226
    Conclusions 243

12. **Consequences of Military Rule in Argentina: An Analysis of Central Government Budgetary Trade-offs, 1961-82 247**

    Theory of Budgetary Trade-offs 247
    Empirical Tests 250
    Conclusions 259

13. **Impact of Increased External Debt Servicing on Government Budgetary Priorities in Argentina 261**

    Empirical Testing 261
    Conclusions 267

14. **The Future Demand for Military Expenditures in Argentina 277**

    Methodology 277
    The Macroeconomic Model 278
    Policy Design 290
    Forecasts of the Economy: 1984-90 292

Conclusions 307

Bibliography 309

Index 315

About the Author 327

List of Tables

1-1. Orthogonally Rotated Factor Pattern: (Loadings) Economic Variables   7

1-2. Discriminant Analysis of Countries in Total Sample Based on Economic Factor Analysis High Loadings   10

1-3. Means of Discriminant Analysis Variables   11

1-4. Oblique Factor Pattern: Economic Variables, Military Expenditures per Capita, Total Country Sample   13

1-5. Oblique Factor Pattern: Economic Variables, Military Expenditures per Capita, Group I Countries   16

1-6. Oblique Factor Pattern: Economic Variables, Military Expenditures per Capita, Group II Countries   20

1-7. Determinants of Military Expenditures per Capita, 1981, Total Country Sample, Economic Variables   22

1-8. Military Expenditures per Capita, Group II Countries   23

1-9. Determinants of Military Expenditures per Capita, 1981, Group I Countries, Economic Variables   24

1-10. Determinants of Military Expenditures per Capita, Group II Countries, Economic Variables   25

1-11. Determinants of Military Expenditures per Capita, Latin American Countries, Economic Variables   26

1-12. Determinants of Military Expenditures per Capita, Non-Latin American Countries, Economic Variables   28

2-1. Means of Structural, Performance, and Defense Expenditure Variables for Third World Military and Non-Military Producers 33

2-2. Discriminant Analysis, Total Country Sample for Arms-Producing and Non-Arms-Producing Nations 36

2-3. Discriminant Analysis, Non-Latin American Arms-Producing and Non-Arms-Producing Nations 40

2-4. Means of Discriminating Variables for Non-Latin American Arms Producers and Non-Arms Producers 42

2-5. Discriminant Analysis, Latin American Arms-Producing and Non-Arms-Producing Nations 44

4-1. Determinants of Defense Expenditures: Latin American Non-Defense Producers 62

4-2. Determinants of Military Expenditure: Latin American Defense Producers 63

4-3. Determinants of Public Consumption's Share in GDP: Latin American Arms Producers 65

4-4. Determinants of Public Consumption's Share in GDP: Latin American Total Country Supply, Non-Arms Producers 66

5-1. Venezuela: Defense Expenditures–Budgetary Trade-offs, 1972–83 84

5-2. Brazil: Defense Expenditures–Budgetary Trade-offs, 1972–82 85

5-3. Argentina: Defense Expenditures–Budgetary Trade-offs, 1972–82 86

5-4. Chile: Defense Expenditures–Budgetary Trade-offs, 1973–82 87

5-5. Ecuador: Defense Expenditures–Budgetary Trade-offs, 1973–82 88

5-6. Dominican Republic: Defense Expenditures–Budgetary Trade-offs, 1973–82 89

5-7. Mexico: Defense Expenditures–Budgetary Trade-offs, 1973–82 90

List of Tables · xiii

5-8. Peru: Defense Expenditures–Budgetary Trade-offs, 1973–81   91

5-9. Bolivia: Defense Expenditures–Budgetary Trade-offs, 1972–82   92

5-10. Paraguay: Defense Expenditures–Budgetary Trade-offs, 1972–82   93

5-11. Costa Rica: Defense Expenditures–Budgetary Trade-offs, 1972–82   94

5-12. Uruguay: Defense Expenditures–Budgetary Trade-offs, 1973–83   95

5-13. El Salvador: Defense Expenditures–Budgetary Trade-offs, 1973–83   96

5-14. Alternative Classifications of Latin American Countries by Ideology and Level of State Economic Intervention, 1970s   98

5-15. Alternative Classifications of Latin American Countries by Types of Regime, Economic Management, and Alliances to Major Power Blocs (1978)   99

5-16. Latin American Arms Producers' and Non–Arms Producers' Defense Expenditures–Budgetary Trade-offs   100

6-1. Impact of Reduction in Government Expenditures   110

6-2. Patterns of Venezuelan Military Expenditures, 1950–1983   112

7-1. Venezuela: Time Series Analysis of Defense Expenditures as a Percentage of Government Revenues, 1950–82   120

7-2. Venezuela: Trend Analysis of Military Expenditures as a Percentage of Government Expenditures, 1950–82   124

7-3. Venezuelan Defense Expenditures, Trend-Structural Analysis, 1950–83   126

7-4. Venezuelan Real Defense Expenditures: Trend Analysis, Residuals (Actual–Estimated)   128

7-5. Determinants of Venezuelan Military Expenditures, 1950–82 132

7-6. Determinants of Venezuelan Military Expenditures, 1950–65 134

7-7. Determinants of Venezuelan Military Expenditures, 1966–82 135

7-8. Venezuelan Military Expenditure Elasticities, 1950–82 137

7-9. Venezuelan Military Expenditure Elasticities, 1950–65 138

7-10. Venezuelan Military Expenditure Elasticities, 1966–82 139

7-11. Venezuelan Defense Expenditures' Response to Defense Expenditures in Selected Latin American Countries, 1955–82 141

7-12. Determinants of Military Expenditures, Trend Analysis for Selected Latin American Countries, 1955–83 143

7-13. Venezuelan Government Revenue Determinants of the Deviations from the Historical Trend in Defense Expenditures, 1950–82 147

7-14. Venezuelan Government Expenditures and GNP: Determinants of the Deviations from the Historical Trend in Defense Expenditures, 1950–82 148

8-1. Venezuela: Budget Analysis, 1973–82 158

8-2. Venezuela: Determinants of Public Expenditures on Defense: Distributed Lag Estimates, 1973–83 165

8-3. Venezuela: Determinants of Public Expenditures on General Public Services: Distributed Lag Estimates, 1973–83 167

8-4. Venezuela: Determinants of Public Expenditures on Education: Distributed Lag Estimates, 1973–83 168

8-5. Venezuela: Determinants of Public Expenditures on Health: Distributed Lag Estimates, 1973–83 170

8-6. Venezuela: Determinants of Public Expenditures on Social Security and Welfare: Distributed Lag Estimates, 1973–83 171

List of Tables · xv

8-7. Venezuela: Determinants of Public Expenditures on Housing: Distributed Lag Estimates, 1973-83   172

8-8. Venezuela: Determinants of Public Expenditures on Other Community and Social Services: Distributed Lag Estimates, 1973-83   174

8-9. Venezuela: Determinants of Public Expenditures on Economic Services: Distributed Lag Estimates, 1973-83   175

8-10. Venezuela: Determinants of Public Expenditures on Miscellaneous Items: Distributed Lag Estimates, 1973-83   176

9-1. Venezuela: Major Macroeconomic Trends, 1979-83   180

9-2. Venezuela: Macroeconomic Forecasting Model   183

9-3. Venezuela: Final Macroeconomic Defense Expenditures Forecast, 1984-90   200

9-4. Venezuela: Final Forecast of Major Budgetary Items, 1990   201

9-5. Venezuela: Time Profile of Major Macroeconomic Variables and Defense Expenditures, 1983-90   204

11-1. Argentinian Political Dummy Variables, 1961-82   227

11-2. Argentina: Impact of Political Change on the Level of Defense Expenditures: Shift Analysis, 1961-82   229

11-3. Argentina: Impact of Political Change on the Level of Defense Expenditures: Modification Analysis, 1961-82   231

11-4. Argentina: Impact of Political Change on the Level of Defense Expenditures: Shift and Modification Analysis, 1961-82   233

11-5. Argentina: Impact of Political Change on the Share of Defense Expenditures in the Total Central Government Budget: Shift Analysis, 1961-82   234

11-6. Argentina: Impact of Political Change on the Share of Defense Expenditures in the Total Central Government Budget: Modification Analysis, 1961-82   236

11-7. Argentina: Impact of Political Change on the Share of Defense Expenditures in the Total Central Government Budget: Shift and Modification Analysis, 1961–82   238

11-8. Argentina: Impact of Political Change on the Share of Defense Expenditures in the Non–Debt Service Central Government Budgetary Items: Shift Analysis, 1961–82   240

11-9. Argentina: Impact of Political Change on the Share of Defense Expenditures in the Non–Debt Service Central Government Budgetary Items: Modification Analysis, 1961–82   241

11-10. Argentina: Impact of Political Change on the Share of Defense Expenditures in the Non–Debt Service Central Government Budgetary Items: Shift and Modification Analysis, 1961–82   242

12-1. Argentina: Impact of Political Change on Budgetary Trade-offs between Defense and Nondefense Expenditures, 1961–82   252

12-2. Argentina: Impact of Political Change on Budgetary Trade-offs between Defense and Nondefense Expenditures, 1961–75   254

12-3. Argentina: Impact of Political Change on Budgetary Trade-offs between Defense and Nondefense Expenditures, 1966–82   255

13-1. Argentina: Impact of Public Sector Debt Service Allocations on Major Budgetary Items, 1961–82   262

13-2. Argentina: Impact of Public Sector Debt Service Allocations on Major Budgetary Items, 1961–75   268

13-3. Argentina: Impact of Public Sector Debt Service Allocations on Major Budgetary Items, 1966–82   273

14-1. Argentina: Macroeconomic Forecasting Model   279

14-2. Argentina: Macroeconomic Forecasts, Moderate Austerity Program I: Non-Peronist Regime, 1984–90   294

14-3. Argentina: Macroeconomic Forecasts, Moderate Austerity Program II: Non-Peronist Regime, 1984–90   295

List of Tables · xvii

14-4. Argentina: Macroeconomic Forecasts, Moderate Austerity Program III: Non-Peronist Regime, 1984–90   296

14-5. Argentina: Macroeconomic Forecasts, Mild Austerity Program I: Non-Peronist Regime, 1984–90   298

14-6. Argentina: Macroeconomic Forecasts, Severe Austerity Program I: Non-Peronist Regime, 1984–90   299

14-7. Argentina: Macroeconomic Forecasts, Non-Peronist Regime, 1990 Values   301

14-8. Argentina: Budgetary Forecasts, Moderate Austerity Model I, with Nominal External Public Debt Held Constant: Non-Peronist Regime, 1984–90   302

14-9. Argentina: Budgetary Forecasts, Moderate Austerity Model II, with Nominal External Public Debt Increasing 5 Percent per Annum: Non-Peronist Regime, 1984–90   303

14-10. Argentina: Budgetary Forecasts, Moderate Austerity Model III, with Nominal External Public Debt Declining 5 Percent per Annum: Non-Peronist Regime, 1984–90   304

14-11. Argentina: Forecast of Military Expenditures at Three Annual Growth Rates for External Debt, 1984–90   305

14-12. Argentina: Forecast of Military Expenditures in Falklands Type Cases at Three Annual Growth Rates for External Debt, 1983–90   306

Foreword

Martin C. Needler
Professor of Political Science and
Director of the Division of
Inter-American Affairs,
University of New Mexico

One cannot hope to arrive at an understanding of Latin America today or in the recent past without paying the closest attention to the military institution. Military officers continue today, as they have done during the entire history of the region, to play a central role in domestic politics and policy. In doing this they act, as we all do, in pursuit of their own institutional and personal interests. However, at the same time they usually act in the service of other interests. Sometimes these are the interests of the public at large; often, however, they are the interests of a particular limited sector of society, usually a priviledged class or clique. And sometimes, of course, they act on behalf of the interests of the United States, the hegemonic power in much of the region, as these interests are interpreted by departments and agencies of the United States government, and at their instigation.

Because of this, the various roles played by the armed forces in the countries of Latin America are very much a matter of political controversy. No doubt the readers of this book, like most North Americans, share the commitment of the present writer to the cause of responsible democratic government in Latin America and thus deplore the all too frequent cases in which the actions of Latin American military forces constitute a setback for that cause.

Ideological commitment should not, however, mean that scholarship is anything but dispassionate and objective. In this admirable work, Professor Robert Looney has made a significant contribution to our knowledge of military expenditures in Latin America. His conceptual clarity and methodological sophistication have illuminated a topic of very great complexity. Professor Looney has shown that several widely accepted interpretations of the relations between military intervention in politics and economic policy lack empirical substantiation. He has performed the valuable function of subjecting some items of generally accepted dogma to confrontation with the best available data (sometimes, to be sure, far from perfect) and found them lacking, thus both showing the need and preparing the way for a new generation of subtler and more discriminating theorizing.

Preface

Currently the world is expending vast amounts of resources, both physical and human, on its military efforts. Although in total the bulk of this effort is accounted for by the industrialized countries, over the past twenty years military expenditure has grown more rapidly in the Third World than in the NATO or Warsaw Pact countries. In many less-developed nations this has produced high military burdens either in per capita terms or in terms of the share of defense expenditure in national income. The Third World is also the major market for weapons exported by the industrialized countries. As might be imagined, financing these arms purchases has imposed considerable costs in terms of scarce foreign exchange and increased external indebtedness.

The factoral dimensions of defense spending are revealing and they demonstrate that the problem is important. In 1973, the non-oil developing countries spent $28,518 million (in constant 1980 prices and exchange rates) on defense, while the OPEC countries spent $15,707 million. A decade later in 1982, these figures had risen to $50,810 millions and $52,903 million respectively. The Third World as a whole had doubled its total defense spending within ten years, a rate of growth far in excess of the major western and eastern alliances.

The foreign exchange cost of weapons acquisition has been reduced somewhat by the use of countertrade (barter), which is becoming more prevalent in this market, particularly for French sales. More important is the fact that some less-developed countries have established indigenous arms industries. The initial motivation for establishing an arms industry is often said to be strategic: to gain independence from suppliers. The application of President Carter's human rights policy is said to have been a major incentive for a number of Latin American countries to develop their own weapons. In any case, as production expanded, economic factors increased in importance, and weapons manufacture has come to play a role in both import-substituting and export-promoting strategies of industrilization. It is estimated that by 1979-80 about twenty-six countries in the Third World were producing armaments of one level of sophistication or another, while nine Latin American countries have begun production.

A number of scholars have decried the worldwide tendency for nations to devote significant and increasing proportions of their national resources to military expenditures. These arguments are usually phrased in terms of opportunity costs of other public priorities foregone or of the direct deleterious effects of military spending on other social and economic goals. Support for this perspective has been heightened by growing concern for problems of population growth, environmental decay, and ecological balance—especially when seen in the context of global resource constraints. Despite this widespread concern over military spending, research on the determinants of military spending levels in confined largely to the NATO or Warsaw Pact nations. Consequently, few attempts have been made to understand the environments in which Third World countries in general—and Latin American nations in particular—allocate resources for defense and defense-related activities.

The purpose of this book is to make a first attempt at understanding the political economy of Latin American defense expenditures by two means. The first is through testing alternative hypotheses for the bulk of Third World nations and, especially, for Latin America. The second is through a detailed case study of two contrasting Latin American countries: Venezuela, a small military spender and minor arms producer, and Argentina, a major military force on the South American continent and a leading Third World arms producer.

The results of this analysis provide empirical evidence on the relative importance of the role of economic variables in constraining allocations to the defense sector and of the critical trade-offs among budgetary choices usually opted for by the Latin American countries. As the case studies show, the general results and conclusions derived from the cross-section analysis provide a suitable framework for assessing the political economy of both Venezuelan and Argentinian defense expenditures.

Research of this type appears crucial for a better understanding of the process and constraints that operate to affect Latin American military expenditures. Moreover it provides a basis for forecasting future patterns of developments in the area's defense spending.

Acknowledgments

This book is an outgrowth of a research project on the effects of arms transfers to developing countries sponsored by the Research Foundation of the Naval Postgraduate School. I am grateful to the Foundation for its financial support and, just as important, its encouragement to pursue this broader study.

Many people at the Naval Postgraduate School aided in making this book a reality. Peter Frederiksen provided particularly valuable insights as to the nature of the overall impacts of military expenditures in Latin America. Paul Buchanan was of considerable assistance in guiding me through the subtleties of the assorted types of Argentinian regimes. Librarians Roger Martin and Gordon Greeson were especially helpful in providing exhaustive literature searches on Venezuela and Argentina. Many thanks also go to Albertine Potter for her typing of the tables included in the book. And, finally, Dean Lindsey deserves much of the credit for this book for his patience and tolerance concerning my computer excesses.

Most of all, I am indebted to may wife, Pam, who not only prepared and edited the final manuscript and many of the rough drafts that preceeded it, but also provided the moral support necessary for an undertaking of this scope.

Part I
Cross-Sectional Analysis

The cross-sectional analysis developed in part I is intended to serve as a springboard to the case studies of Venezuela and Argentina which follow in parts II and III. In broad terms, this section attempts to establish a framework for analyzing the political economy of defense allocations in Third World countries.

Clearly, Third World countries cannot be treated as a homogenous group for purposes of analyzing this or any other policy issue. It is a question, then, of determining the theoretical formulation most useful in analyzing the various aspects of military expenditure in Third World countries, in general, and in Latin America, in particular.

Chapter 1 attempts to determine the most appropriate environmental basis for examining the factors affecting Third World defense burdens (and presumably other military-related issues). Are regional groupings of countries (based on common strategic needs) the most appropriate basis for analysis, or is the overall economic environment more appropriate in predicting the level of per capita military expenditures in any particular country?

The analysis in chapter 1 indicates that Third World countries can be grouped into essentially two categories—countries with relatively severe resource constraints and countries whose external situation provides a larger degree of budgetary freedom. Based on these groupings, an accurate prediction of the defense burden of any one particular country can be made. Such predictions are much more accurate than those obtained by examining Third World countries either as a whole or by region.

Since the focus of this book is Latin America, the next question is the appropriate framework for analyzing military expenditures within this group of countries: is the relative resource scarcity approach superior to alternative profiles for this regional study, as well?

2 · Cross-Sectional Analysis

Chapter 2 shows that Latin American military producers and nonproducers can also be delineated on the basis of several economic variables unique to the region and that, in fact, there is a high correlation between relative resource availability (particularly the availability of external resources) and whether or not a Latin American country possesses an indigenous arms industry.

In short, chapters 1 and 2 establish that the most appropriate framework for analyzing Latin American defense is based, as for the total sample of Third World countries, on whether or not an individual country has relatively easy access to foreign exchange. Arms producers in Latin America do, nonproducers do not.

Chapters 3, 4, and 5 confirm this dual image approach by demonstrating the marked difference in the impact of defense spending on economic performance, the budgetary process, and military/nonmilitary budgetary trade-offs for Latin American arms producers and nonproducers.

Part I of this book, therefore, is intended to prove the appropriateness of economic variables in examining defense issues. It demonstrates that whether or not a country is a producer of armaments is largely a function of its relative resource position. It also shows that the production or nonproduction of armaments has a major influence on the budgetary process and allocation trade-offs between defense and nondefense expenditures.

1
Determinants of Third World Defense Burdens

A large descriptive literature on the burden of military expenditures in developing countries has accumulated over the past several years. Understandably, the main thrust of most of this analysis concerns the loss in social welfare associated with increases in military expenditure per capita, that is, that social expenditures in lieu of military expenditure would have provided more tangible improvements in the quality of life of large groups of individuals in developing countries. Without questioning this view, the following analysis attempts to determine the major factors underlying military expenditure per capita in developing countries.

Surprisingly, no previous studies have attempted to determine whether or not per capita military expenditures are related to anything except per capita income. The usual presumption is that military expenditures are in large part a function of political or strategic factors, with economic variables playing at most a tangential role.

The departure of this chapter is four fold:

1. It attempts to verify the validity of Wagner's Law, which states that military expenditures per capita increase with increased per capita income.
2. It examines the impact of public external debt on military expenditures in developing countries. Specifically, did the rapid increase in LDC external borrowing in the 1970s play a significant role?
3. It tests the uniformity of military expenditures in developing countries to see whether developing countries as a group experience the same underlying factors that contribute to military expenditures or whether certain patterns of military expenditures are unique to particular subgroupings of countries.

4. It tests the degree to which economic variables alone can account for the differences in per capita military expenditures across a wide group of diverse developing countries.

Hopefully, answers to these questions will provide new information as to the real burdens of military expenditures in developing countries and the mechanisms through which military expenditures are likely to increase in the future.

Factor and Discriminant Analysis

With reference to the third question posed above, several studies have indicated that developing countries may lack homogeneity with regard to the impact that defense expenditures have on the overall economic growth of the country.[1] With regard to the impact of defense expenditures on economic growth, Peter Frederiksen and Robert Looney contend that:

> One can argue that under certain circumstances defense spending can help growth while, under a different set of circumstances, it can hinder growth. Indeed, both propositions are likely to be true for the same country at different points in time.
> On the positive side, defense spending may contribute to the growth of the civilian economy by: (1) feeding, clothing and housing a number of people who would otherwise have to be fed, housed and clothed by the civilian economy, (2) providing education and medical care as well as vocational and technical training, (3) engaging in a variety of public works—roads, dams, river improvements, airports, communication networks, etc.—that may in part serve civilian uses, and (4) engaging in scientific and technical specialties which would otherwise have to be performed by civilian personnel.[2]

They add that on the negative side:

> There are at least three different types of possible effects. The first, named the "income shift" by Benoit, is that increases in defense expenditures will reduce the civilian GDP and will thus tend to decrease growth proportionately. Second, it is possible that defense spending adversely affects growth since the government sector for the most part exhibits "negligible rates of measurable productivity increases." Finally, growth can suffer since increased spending on defense uses resources which could have been better employed as civilian investment.[3]

Frederiksen and Looney note that while these arguments make intuitive sense, the crucial determinant of the impact of defense expenditures on economic growth is the country's financial resource constraint.[4] According to them, a country that is severely resource constrained (that is, faces some combination of lagging taxes, reduced private and government savings, reduced borrowing power overseas, export shortfalls, and so forth) will probably face budget cuts. In order to maintain defense programs, the high growth development programs will be sacrificed:

> This is likely for two reasons. First, it is usually more politically acceptable to curtail capital investment (on infrastructure, for example) than expenditures on the current account. Second, given that a well-established military establishment already exists, there will be the obvious pressure to maintain the status quo. These special interest groups might have included high ranking officers, military contractors, and certain political groups. As budgets are reduced, the military share is frozen and the brunt of the deflationary policy is borne by development projects which we assume are relatively productive. In short, defense expenditures are likely to be asymmetric—difficult to cut back but easily expanded. Thus, for resource-constrained countries, we should expect a negative relationship between defense spending the economic growth.[5]

The authors contend that the opposite is likely to hold for countries with a relative abundance of financial resources—an elastic supply of tax revenues, a high inflow of foreign exchange, and the like:

> These countries can more easily afford the capital investment programs necessary for economic growth while maintaining or even increasing defense programs.[6]

They conclude that:

> If this thesis is correct, one can see why previous authors have failed to find any consistency between economic growth and defense. Using a model based on resource constraints, however, it is easy to see why developing countries with identical levels of defense spending can experience very different growth levels: richer countries are apparently able to invest in development programs while, on the other hand, poorer countries have had to sacrifice these programs to pay for defense.[7]

Since their hypothesized relationship between defense and economic growth depended on financial resource constraints, their sample of developing countries was separated into either a resource-constrained or non–resource-constrained group by means of cluster analysis. While a large number of conceivable proxy measures could be used to indicate the relative abundance or scarcity of financial resources, the selection of those used in the cluster analysis was based on the ratios of gross domestic investment to Gross Domestic Product (GDP) in 1960 and 1978 and the ratios of gross domestic savings to GDP in 1960 and 1978. (Data are taken from the World Bank's 1980 *World Development Report*.) The cluster analysis produced two distinct groups, one having high ratios of savings and investment to GDP, the other having low ratios of savings and investment to GDP.

Linear regression equations were estimated for each group.

> The most striking result and one that supports our hypothesis, is that the coefficient of the defense variable was positive and statistically significant at the 99 percent level for the richer group. While the coefficient for the defense variables for the poorer group was negative (as hypothesized) it was not statistically different from zero.[8]

Based on these results it makes sense to split the sample of developing countries into groups based on some measure of resource constraint. Presumably, those countries who have either more domestic resources (savings and investment) or more access to foreign capital (everything else such as gross national product, being equal) will be able to support a higher level of defense expenditures. On the other hand, those countries with a lower level of domestic resources or less access to international capital will (everything else being equal) not have as high a level of defense expenditures.

Using factor analysis with a number of measures of debt and capital flows (table 1-1), the main trends in the data were identified and a discriminant analysis was then performed using as variables those with the highest loading on each one of the individual factors.[9] The orthogonal rotation assures that each variable selected had a relatively low degree of correlation with the others in the sample. The variables thus selected for splitting the two groups were:

Gross inflow of public loans/exports, 1982,

Total public external debt, 1982,

Gross international reserves, 1982,

Public external debt as a percentage of GDP, 1982,

Table 1-1
Orthogonally Rotated Factor Pattern: (Loadings) Economic Variables

	Factors						
	1	2	3	4	5	6	7
Variables	Factors Facilitating Public Consumption	Factors Contributing to 1982 External Debt	Gross International Reserves	Share of 1982 Public External Debt in GDP	Growth in Exports	External Debt Service 1982	Public External Debt 1970
Gross inflow of public loans/exports, 1982	97*	0	-14	8	2	-9	5
Public debt/exports, 1982	96*	3	-13	2	-4	-13	-6
Resource balance as a percentage of GDP, 1982	94*	11	1	-14	7	7	7
Growth in public consumption, 1970–82	92*	3	-5	4	26	-7	2
Public external borrowing commitments/exports, 1982	91*	-4	-13	8	12	-11	23
Gross inflow of public loans/GDP, 1982	86*	7	-8	-2	-11	-13	-25
Public consumption as a percentage of GDP, 1982	63*	-5	-9	55	-13	-5	27
Growth in private consumption, 1970–82	62*	12	10	1	48	8	2
Private consumption as a percentage of GDP, 1960	-72*	7	-15	-16	1	-13	-44
Private consumption as a percentage of GDP, 1982	-82*	-15	-16	-28	-11	-19	-10
Terms of trade, 1982	-83*	21	21	9	10	17	-5

Table 1-1 continued

	Factors						
	1	2	3	4	5	6	7
Variables	Factors Facilitating Public Consumption	Factors Contributing to 1982 External Debt	Gross International Reserves	Share of 1982 Public External Debt in GDP	Growth in Exports	External Debt Service 1982	Public External Debt 1970
Total public external debt, 1982	0	94*	11	0	20	20	-4
Gross inflow of public loans, 1970	14	92*	20	-7	-18	-7	9
Interest payments on external debt, 1970	9	90*	13	-16	-20	2	-10
Repayment of principal on public loans, 1982	4	89*	10	-11	-15	12	-17
Gross inflow of public loans, 1982	-5	86*	10	1	29	28	-11
Public external borrowing commitments, 1982	-6	85*	14	-4*	34	18	-4
Interest payments on external debt, 1982	-6	82*	6	2	30	38	-8
Total public external debt, 1970	15	80*	19	-14	-23	-30	10
Net inflow of public external loans, 1970	19	77*	23	-2	-17	-19	25
Repayment of principal on external loans, 1982	-4	73*	21	5	31	37	7
Growth in exports, 1970–82	-2	39*	25	3	5	-8	-36
Current account balance, 1970	15	-80*	-1	-6	-29	1	10

Variable							
Gross international reserves, 1982	-8	19	89*	-11	9	-7	9
Gross international reserves, 1970	-8	29	85*	-5	-7	1	-6
Average maturity of public external debt	23	-18	-48*	5	-11	-43	23
Current account balance, 1982	13	-26	-59*	10	-22	0	21
Public external debt as a percentage of GDP, 1982	9	-9	-29	76*	-15	12	17
Exports as a percentage of GDP, 1982	-8	-8	7	76*	4	22	5
Growth in exports, 1960–70	8	2	-6	67*	7	-27	-24
Public consumption as a percentage of GDP, 1960	47	-11	-12	55*	20	-18	37
Growth in imports, 1970–82	36	-18	19	-1	71*	-6	1
External debt service as a percentage of GDP, 1982	-8	27	-7	5	-6	59*	7
Public external debt as a percentage of GDP, 1970	50	0	-23	20	5	-1	55*

Notes: All military variables together with Gross Domestic Product and per capita income are omitted.
*Indicates high correlation of variable with respective factor.

Growth in imports, 1970–1982,

External debt service as a percentage of GDP, 1982, and

Public external debt as a percentage of GDP, 1970.

The results of the discriminant analysis (table 1-2) show a high degree of probability of correct placement in each group. (That is, the

Table 1-2
Discriminant Analysis of Countries in Total Sample Based on Economic Factor Analysis High Loadings

Group I		Group II	
Country	Probability of Correct Placement	Country	Probability of Correct Placement
1. Israel	69.34	1. Greece	57.78
2. Honduras	83.48	2. India	84.91
3. Cameroon	60.73	3. Nigeria	89.07
4. Sudan	66.47	4. Indonesia	90.67
5. Costa Rica	92.64	5. Egypt	68.20
6. Bolivia	86.27	6. Korea	89.95
7. Somalia	86.46	7. Rwanda	69.08
8. Tunisia	68.31	8. Turkey	66.95
9. Morocco	73.06	9. Spain	51.89
10. Guatemala	54.91	10. Venezuela	80.26
11. Malawi	91.40	11. Mexico	99.69
12. El Salvador	65.90	12. Brazil	99.02
13. Mali	97.12	13. Algeria	76.44
14. Pakistan	86.98	14. Philippines	55.78
15. Paraguay	60.02	15. Libya	75.69
16. Ecuador	56.61	16. Colombia	54.63
17. Dominican Republic	74.12	17. Thailand	60.95
18. Liberia	94.77	18. Malaysia	65.16
19. Ivory Coast	84.42	19. Argentina	66.09
20. Mauritania	96.04	20. Saudi Arabia	94.65
21. Sierra Leone	86.05	21. Kuwait	81.31
22. Panama	94.37	22. Syria	63.95
23. Chile	70.09	23. Jordan	50.81
24. Chad	87.18		
25. Uruguay	67.87		
26. Tanzania	79.87		
27. Uganda	88.76		
28. Ethiopia	70.24		
29. Central African Republic	76.89		
30. Ghana	78.72		
31. Burma	82.91		
32. Sri Lanka	75.39		
33. Jamaica	90.66		
34. Trinidad	77.62		
35. Zambia	95.88		
36. Peru	71.67		
37. Zimbabwe	85.68		
38. Kenya	86.61		

discriminating variables selected from the factor analysis are able to split the sample countries into two fairly distinct groupings based largely on the external debt situation facing each set of countries.) The Group II countries consist of several major oil exporters and several of the more dynamic newly industrializing nations, such as Mexico, Greece, India, Korea, Spain, Algeria, and Malaysia. Group I countries in general seem to be the poorer, less economically dynamic nations, this group being heavily weighted with African and poorer Latin American countries.

Further insight into the two groups can be gained by examining the means of the variables used in the discriminant analysis (table 1–3):

1. Group 1 countries resorted to a 3.6 times higher inflow of external public loans in 1982 relative to their exports (*ECIBE*) that year.

Table 1-3
Means of Discriminant Analysis Variables

Variable	Total Sample	Group I	Group II	Non-Latin America	Latin America
Discriminating Variables					
ECIBE	0.70	0.94	0.26	0.46	0.80
PDB	5932.00	2629.30	11786.90	8041.90	3860.10
GIRB	2587.20	583.80	6138.80	2024.30	2411.70
PDPB	35.30	44.30	19.20	35.90	37.47
ZB	4.10	1.09	9.50	2.10	5.10
DSEB	14.10	15.00	12.50	18.30	10.60
PDPA	17.30	21.20	10.40	14.70	38.40
Other Variables					
MEY	4.20	3.60	5.10	2.12	6.31
GNPPER	1793.20	1066.70	3048.20	1861.40	1971.60
MEP	117.90	57.70	223.30	39.70	179.20
GEDB	14.10	13.40	15.30	9.90	18.10
ME	1318.10	389.10	2943.90	571.20	1541.90

Notes:
ECIBE = Gross inflow of public loans, 1982, divided by exports, 1982.
PDB = External public debt, 1982.
GIRB = Gross international reserves, 1982.
PDPB = External public debt as a percentage of gross domestic product, 1982.
ZB = Average annual growth in imports, 1970–82.
DSEB = Debt service as a percentage of exports, 1982.
PDPA = External public debt as a percentage of gross domestic product, 1970.
MEY = Military expenditures as a percentage of gross national product, 1981.
GNPPER = Per capita gross national product, 1982.
MEP = Military expenditures per capita, 1981.
GEDB = Defense expenditures as a percentage of total government expenditure, 1981.
ME = Total military expenditures, 1981.

2. On the other hand, the overall level of total public external debt (*PDB*) in 1982 averages nearly four and one-half times as much for Group II countries as for Group I countries.
3. The level of international reserves (*GIRB*) is also much higher for Group II countries—nearly 10 times the average for Group I countries.
4. With regard to debt as a percentage of gross domestic product (*PDPB*) however, Group I countries have much higher levels of attainment, averaging nearly twice as much as Group II countries in both 1970 and 1982. The debt service ratio to exports is correspondingly higher for Group I countries.
5. The rate of growth of imports (*ZB*) was nearly nine times higher over the 1970–82 period for Group II countries.

In terms of profiles, therefore, the Group II countries are considerably larger, more affluent, and less reliant on external debt as a percentage of gross domestic product. They tend to spend relatively large amounts on military activities, but not necessarily significantly greater amounts of their overall budgets.

Analysis of per Capita Military Expenditures

The per capita military expenditure measure also confirmed the splitting of the developing-country sample into two groups based on common economic environment. Table 1–4's factor analysis of the total sample of countries showed that per capita military expenditure loaded only moderately on one factor, Factor 7 (simply referred to as per capita military expenditure) containing just a single variable, public external debt as a percent of gross domestic product in 1970. In sharp contrast, a factor analysis of Group I countries produced a loading of 100 on the factor depicting various measures of external public debt (table 1–5). In a similar manner, Group II countries loaded fairly heavily on a factor other than that obtained in the total sample and one that did not represent external public debt in the 1980s. As seen in table 1–6, military expenditures per capita for Group II loaded relatively high at 57 on a factor representing the balance of payments, exports, and public consumption, suggesting that the better the export position of the country and the more expansive the public sector in increasing its consumption, the greater the level of military expenditure per capita.

Table 1-4
Oblique Factor Pattern (Standard Regression Coefficients): Economic Variables, Military Expenditures per Capita, Total Country Sample

Variables	Factors						
	1 Factors Affecting Total External Debt, 1982	2 Public Consumption's Share of GDP, 1982	3 International Reserves	4 External Debt/Exports, 1982	5 Growth in Consumption	6 Debt Service as a percentage of Exports, 1981	7 Military Expenditures per Capita, 1981
Repayment of principal on public external loans, 1970	100*	-1	-5	0	-26	9	-10
Interest payments on external debt, 1970	100*	-7	-3	5	-23	1	-4
Gross inflow of public loans, 1970	94*	-4	1	3	-6	1	29
Total external debt, 1982	94*	2	-1	3	11	16	3
Gross inflow of external loans, 1982	89*	6	-3	1	14	17	-13
Public external borrowing commitments, 1982	85*	0	-4	6	26	7	-8
Total public external debt, 1970	83*	-9	-3	6	-8	-17	34
Interest payments on external debt, 1982	82*	3	0	0	11	29	-11
Net inflow of public external loans, 1970	73*	-6	7	4	9	-4	54
Repayment of principal on public external loans, 1982	60*	0	15	-3	27	37	13
Gross Domestic Product, 1982	56*	-11	39	-1	8	-27	-19
Growth of exports, 1970–82	43*	22	3	-38	-18	-14	-4
Current account balance, 1970	-86*	-13	14	8	-8	0	-10
Growth in exports, 1960–70	15	89*	-16	-9	5	-43	-9

Table 1-4 continued

Variables	1 Factors Affecting Total External Debt, 1982	2 Public Consumption's Share of GDP, 1982	3 International Reserves	Factors 4 External Debt/Exports, 1982	5 Growth in Consumption	6 Debt Service as a percentage of Exports, 1981	7 Military Expenditures per Capita, 1981
Gross inflow of public loans—GDP, 1982	6	84*	0	26	-2	0	-10
Public consumption as a percentage of GDP, 1982	-1	79*	20	0	-19	5	21
External public debt as a percentage of GDP, 1982	4	76*	-12	15	-8	14	8
Exports as a percentage of GDP, 1982	-10	72*	20	-9	8	21	0
Public consumption as a percentage of GDP, 1960	-10	67*	-5	-11	16	-10	36
Resource balance as a percentage of GDP, 1982	21	-55*	12	-23	-9	56	-3
Gross National Product per capita, 1982	-7	6	86*	0	-13	14	10
Gross international reserves, 1982	-4	-14	84*	-1	16	-23	5
Gross international reserves, 1970	17	0	77*	-10	-10	-21	-17
Current account balance, 1982	-19	0	-46*	8	-13	27	27
Private consumption as a percentage of GDP, 1960	22	-9	-62*	-5	5	-27	-6

Determinants of Third World Defense Burdens · 15

Average maturity of public external debt, 1982	-2	4	-67*	-9	0	-25	28
Public external borrowing commitments/exports, 1982	2	2	-2	95*	3	-18	-10
Gross inflow of public external loans/exports, 1982	5	14	11	88*	-7	3	-13
Total public external debt/exports, 1982	5	1	-6	88*	-2	-3	7
Growth in private consumption, 1970-82	-12	-12	8	21	87*	8	14
Growth in imports, 1970-82	10	-3	-2	-10	80*	-20	-9
Growth in public consumption, 1970-82	0	8	-25	-20	67*	1	-16
Terms of trade, 1982	23	18	24	6	49*	7	18
Debt service as a percentage of exports, 1982	20	-2	-4	-3	-2	73*	22
Private consumption as a percentage of GDP, 1982	-12	-35	-35	4	-24	-38*	-4
Public external debt as a percentage of GDP, 1970	-4	3	-26	-3	6	31	63*
Military expenditures per capita, 1981	7	30	35	-10	-17	9	54*

Note: *Indicates a high correlation of variables with respective factor.

Table 1-5
Oblique Factor Pattern (Standard Regression Coefficients): Economic Variables, Military Expenditures per Capita, Group I Countries

	Factors						
	1	2	3	4	5	6	7
Variables	Determinants of Military Expenditures per Capita, 1981	Public Consumption as a Percentage of GDP	Repayment of Public External Debt, 1970	Public Debt/Exports, 1982	Growth in Public Consumption	Growth in Private Consumption	Public External Debt as a Percentage of GDP, 1970
Military expenditures per capita, 1981	100*	7	-35	-2	-11	0	2
Net inflow of public external loans, 1970	96*	8	10	2	-9	-1	27
Total public external debt, 1982	94*	-2	-6	14	10	12	2
Gross international reserves, 1982	92*	-4	5	-11	-14	6	-10
Gross National Product per capita, 1982	89*	-13	-12	14	5	-4	0
Total public external debt, 1970	86*	4	36	-3	-10	-5	26
Gross inflow of public loans, 1970	83*	8	41	2	-7	-1	27
Interest payments on external debt, 1982	82*	-3	6	1	34	7	-2
Repayment of principal on public external loans, 1982	78*	-3	4	0	28	13	-22
Gross international reserves, 1970	75*	-9	12	-18	0	-12	-30
Gross inflow of public external loans, 1982	71*	2	24	12	15	5	-25
Public external borrowing commitments, 1982	69*	0	23	10	9	9	-32
Gross domestic product, 1982	53*	-33	27	-6	-7	-14	-1

Current account balance, 1982	-10*	0	-28	5	7	-8	14
Current account balance, 1970	-87*	0	51	3	2	14	-17
Growth in exports, 1960–70	-22	95*	8	-4	-5	1	3
Gross inflow of public external loans/GDP, 1982	-13	85*	19	19	16	-5	-17
Public debt as a percentage of GDP, 1982	-12	83*	7	10	26	-6	7
Public consumption as a percentage of GDP, 1960	10	82*	-12	-10	-22	20	-1
Public consumption as a percentage of GDP, 1982	42	68*	-10	4	15	-21	-2
Exports as a percentage of GDP, 1982	5	65*	3	0	49	-20	0
Resource balance as a percentage of GDP, 1982	0	-71*	12	-16	53	-12	16
Repayment of principal on public external loans, 1970	17	5	99*	1	0	-1	15
Interest payments on public external debt, 1970	21	3	95*	-1	-3	-7	15
Average maturity of public external debt, 1982	-10	11	45*	-26	-23	0	13
Public debt/exports, 1982	4	1	0	94*	-15	10	23
Public borrowing commitments/exports, 1982	2	6	4	93*	-26	11	-17
Gross inflow of public external loans/exports, 1982	0	8	11	89*	1	-4	-4

Table 1–5 continued

Variables	Factors						
	1 Determinants of Military Expenditures per Capita, 1981	2 Public Consumption as a Percentage of GDP	3 Repayment of Public External Debt, 1970	4 Public Debt/Exports, 1982	5 Growth in Public Consumption	6 Growth in Private Consumption	7 Public External Debt as a Percentage of GDP, 1970
Growth of exports, 1970–82	36	14	22	-41*	-16	19	-9
Growth of public consumption, 1970–82	-32	9	-11	-21	70*	24	9
Public external debt service as a percentage of exports, 1982	17	-3	16	-16	69*	21	-4
Private consumption as a percentage of GDP, 1982	-13	-29	2	-2	-79*	-3	-8
Growth of exports, 1970–82	0	5	14	-9	14	85*	23
Growth of private consumption, 1970–82	13	-14	-21	30	15	82*	22
Terms of trade, 1982	6	49	-13	-4	28	47*	3
Private consumption as a percentage of GDP, 1960	-33	-18	21	9	3	24	72*
Public external debt as a percentage of GDP, 1970	38	7	3	-5	15	24	59*

Note: *Indicates a high correlation of variable with respective factor.

Regressions on per capita military expenditure in 1981 using the total sample (table 1-7) indicated that three variables–gross national product per capita (*GNPPER*), the current account in 1982 (*CAB*), and the share of public consumption in gross domestic product for 1982 (*PCB*) account for over 83 percent of the fluctuations in that measure of military expenditure. Net capital inflows (*ECNIA*) in 1970 are also statistically significant and positive, as is the external public debt in 1982 (*PDB*). However, while the overall regression results appear satisfactory, in terms of the r^2, the *F*-statistic, and *t*-statistic on individual independent variables, the best regression equation (equation 4, table 1-7) was able to predict only Saudi Arabia's per capita military expenditures within 5 percent of the actual value (table 1-8).

In contrast, the results for Group I countries (table 1-9) show a pattern much different from that obtained from the total sample. In addition to gross national product per capita (*GNPPER*), the government deficit (*GDB*) as a percent of GDP in 1982 is highly significant but negative. Countries in the Group I environment have large government deficits apparently used in part to increase military expenditures. The share of defense (*GEDB*) in the overall government budget is, however, positive and statistically significant, as are the net capital flows (*ECNIA*) in 1970 and the public debt in 1982 (*PDB*). Interestingly, the current account of the balance of payments (*CAB*) is statistically significant but in contrast to Group II countries, the sign is negative.

One can only speculate at this point, but it appears that Group I countries' external borrowings are in part used to finance military expenditures, as are government deficits, while any improvement in the current account of the balance of payments is appropriated by the private sector for non–defense-related expenditures, and/or by the public sector for external debt servicing or non–military-related imports.

Group II countries also follow a pattern considerably different from that of the sample whole (table 1-10). Two variables, the gross national product per capita (*GNPPER*) and the current account of the balance of payments (*CAB*) account for over 92 percent of the fluctuation in the per capita military expenditure. The government budget surplus as a percent of GNP in 1982 (*GDB*) together with the share of public consumption in 1982 (*PCB*) also contribute positively to the regression equation. In addition to gross national product per capita, these two variables account for over 95 percent of the fluctuation in per capita military expenditures. The high correlation between the current account balance (*CAB*) and government budget

Table 1-6
Oblique Factor Pattern (Standard Regression Coefficients): Economic Variables, Military Expenditures per Capita, Group II Countries

Variables	Factors					
	1 Determinants of External Debt, 1982	2 Public External Borrowing Commitments, 1982	3 Determinants of Military Expenditures per Capita, 1981	4 Growth in Public Consumption	5 Public External Debt, 1970	6 Growth in Exports
Interest payments on external public debt, 1982	100*	-6	2	10	-15	-4
Gross inflow of public loans, 1982	100*	0	2	17	-5	7
Total public external debt, 1982	94*	-1	3	4	15	4
Public external borrowing commitments, 1982	93*	2	-3	34	7	1
Repayment of principal on public external debt, 1970	76*	3	-4	-38	15	15
Interest payments on external public debt, 1970	69*	3	-14	-36	26	7
Repayment of principal on public external debt, 1982	69*	-13	35	20	20	-11
Debt service on external debt as a percentage of exports, 1982	69*	9	30	-13	-5	-32
Resource balance as a percentage of GDP, 1982	58*	-35	9	-19	16	-14
Current account balance, 1970	-88*	-4	11	-12	-5	-28
Public external borrowing commitments/exports, 1982	0	82*	-21	-1	1	-15
Average maturity of public external debt, 1982	-42	77*	-8	1	29	9
Public external debt/exports, 1982	27	69*	-1	-45	19	-13
Gross inflow of public loans/exports, 1982	51	66*	8	-33	-12	-9
Terms of trade, 1982	43	-51*	2	26	22	-18
Gross Domestic Product, 1982	45	-59*	-48	-10	17	9

Determinants of Third World Defense Burdens

GNP per capita, 1982	3	-71*	18	-36	-28	-1
Gross international reserves, 1982	-32	-73*	-13	-14	29	-24
Gross international reserves, 1970	0	-77*	-16	-39	1	9
Public consumption as a percentage of GDP, 1960	-26	-8	30*	17	34	17
Public external debt as a percentage of GDP, 1970	47	26	77*	0	6	0
Exports as a percentage of GDP, 1982	3	-23	68*	31	-9	28
Gross inflow of public external loans/GDP, 1982	38	21	66*	14	-17	14
Public consumption as a percentage of GDP, 1982	-19	6	60*	-23	-25	12
Military expenditures per capita, 1981	-9	-31	57*	-39	-14	32
Current account balance, 1982	-23	44	48*	-9	43	-2
Private consumption as a percentage of GDP, 1982	-21	20	-71*	4	-9	22
Growth in imports, 1970-82	17	6	-13	88*	-8	-4
Public consumption growth, 1970-82	-2	35	0	81*	7	0
Private consumption growth, 1970-82	14	-12	37	71*	12	-19
Net inflow of public external loans, 1970	20	1	0	3	90*	1
Total public external loans, 1970	19	6	-18	-18	75*	11
Public external debt as a percentage of GDP, 1970	8	11	35	32	70*	10
Gross inflow of public external loans, 1970	52	2	-2	-17	63*	8
Growth in exports, 1960-70	-7	-6	24	1	12	84*
Growth in exports, 1970-82	21	-7	20	-34	1	82*
Private consumption as a percentage of GDP, 1982	13	29	-47*	18	3	59*

Note: *Indicates high loading of variable on respective factor.

Table 1-7
Determinants of Military Expenditures per Capita, 1981, Total Country Sample, Economic Variables
(standardized estimates)

	Independent Variables										Statistics		
GNPPER	CAB	PCB	ECNIA	PDPB	EGB	GDPB	GEDB	GDB	PDB		r^2	F	df
0.32 (4.42)	0.75 (10.15)										.730	67.84	52
0.29 (4.60)	0.75 (12.06)	0.21 (3.41)									.834	72.12	46
0.28 (4.98)	0.79 (13.82)	0.22 (3.84)	0.19 (3.38)								.869	70.06	46
0.23 (3.94)	0.76 (13.47)	0.31 (4.39)	0.17 (3.21)	-0.14 (-2.06)							.882	61.22	46
0.26 (4.52)	0.77 (14.27)	0.29 (4.40)	0.14 (2.66)	-0.12 (-1.86)	0.12 (2.29)						.896	57.19	46
0.28 (4.78)	0.78 (12.20)	0.22 (3.23)	0.17 (2.41)			0.03 (0.43)					.870	55.08	46
0.63 (7.71)		0.29 (3.09)					0.33 (3.66)				.787	40.83	36
0.83 (4.91)		0.30 (2.56)						-0.28 (-1.66)			.697	27.71	39
0.28 (4.67)	0.78 (12.71)	0.22 (3.69)							0.13 (2.11)		.850	59.51	46
0.22 (3.61)	0.75 (12.51)	0.33 (4.43)		-0.17 (-2.26)					0.12 (2.13)		.866	53.36	46

Notes: See text for definition of variables.
( ) = t statistic.
r^2 = correlation coefficient.
F = F statistic.
df = degrees of freedom.

Table 1-8
Military Expenditures per Capita, Group II Countries

Country	Actual Expenditures	Predicted Expenditures	Actual Expenditures/ Predicted Expenditures	Placement
Rwanda	3.962	164.274	.0241	Below
India	7.360	64.386	.1143	Below
Colombia	13.759	110.325	.1247	Below
Indonesia	18.581	147.319	.1261	Below
Mexico	16.634	110.519	.1505	Below
Thailand	27.413	136.867	.2003	Below
Philippines	16.792	52.817	.3179	Below
Algeria	91.959	222.219	.4138	Below
Venezuela	62.663	130.375	.4806	Below
Spain	96.693	133.193	.7260	Below
Argentina	111.010	127.112	.8733	Below
Kuwait	836.000	870.248	.9606	
Korea (South)	103.666	105.488	.9827	
Saudi Arabia	2110.000	1956.000	1.0787	Above
Malaysia	101.119	74.901	1.3500	Above
Greece	265.773	194.039	1.3697	Above
Jordan	273.125	189.901	1.4382	Above
Syria	267.802	183.639	1.4583	Above

Notes: Based on regression equation: $MEP81 = 0.21\,GNPPER + 0.91\,CAB$.
(3.15) (13.35)

Below = countries whose actual expenditures are less than 95 percent of predicted value.
Above = countries whose actual expenditures are greater than 105 percent of predicted value.

position (GDB) precluded including both variables in the regression equation. Nevertheless, a clear contrast appears between this group and Group I. Group II countries appear to maintain much stronger balance of payments positions and are in a position to expand military expenditures when either the current account or the government budget improves. These countries do not necessarily have to resort to external loans or inflows of capital to increase expenditures in defense-related activities. All measures of external debt—absolute totals or debt as a proportion of GNP—were statistically insignificant in accounting for fluctuations in military expenditures per capita.

Examining countries on a regional basis also provides further insights as to the relative importance of economic variables in affecting per capita military expenditures. For example, an analysis of the Latin American sample (table 1-11) indicates that gross national product per capita ($GNPPER$), the share of public consumption in GDP (PCB), the share of military expenditures in the total government budget ($GEDB$), together with the public external debt in 1970

Table 1-9
Determinants of Military Expenditures per Capita, 1981, Group I Countries, Economic Variables
(standardized estimates)

	Independent Variables										Statistics		
GNPPER	GDB	PCB	GEDB	ECNIA	PDB	ECNIB	CAB	PBCB	GDP		r^2	F	df
0.54 (3.63)											.291	13.14	33
0.58 (4.22)	-0.46 (-3.39)										.505	13.28	28
0.74 (6.43)	-0.24 (-2.93)	0.09 (0.64)									.782	26.34	25
0.56 (5.99)	-0.44 (-4.65)		0.46 (4.87)								.807	30.75	25
0.38 (4.39)	-0.30 (-3.44)		0.32 (3.74)	0.40 (3.77)							.885	40.64	25
0.45 (4.63)	-0.31 (-3.10)		0.37 (3.94)		0.29 (2.45)						.850	29.82	25
0.37 (4.36)	-0.30 (-3.64)		0.31 (3.72)	0.48 (4.09)		-0.13 (-1.64)					.896	34.56	25
0.44 (3.13)							-0.38 (-2.64)				.424	11.05	32
0.25 (2.65)	-0.22 (-2.14)			0.67 (4.67)				-0.04 (-0.35)			.788	22.32	28
0.52 (3.94)	-0.47 (-3.65)								0.28 (2.11)		.580	11.52	28

Notes: See text for definition of variables.
( ) = t statistic.
r^2 = correlation coefficient.
F = F statistic.
df = degrees of freedom.

Table 1-10
Determinants of Military Expenditures per Capita, Group II Countries, Economic Variables
(standardized estimates)

Equation	\multicolumn{8}{c}{Independent Variables}								Statistics		
	GNPPER	CAB	PCB	PDB	GEDB	GDB	ECNIA	GDP	r^2	F	df
1 MEP81 =	0.21 (3.15)	0.90 (13.35)							.923	102.05	19
2	0.19 (4.73)	0.91 (22.30)	0.08 (1.80)						.979	215.33	17
3	0.19 (4.48)	0.91 (21.31)	0.07 (1.53)	-0.02 (-0.38)					.979	151.10	17
4	0.80 (8.37)		0.43 (4.54)		0.01 (0.11)				.921	35.14	12
5	0.56 (3.17)		0.34 (4.34)			0.29 (2.74)			.953	68.13	13
6			0.43 (4.54)		0.01 (0.11)	0.80 (8.37)		.921	35.14		12
7	0.19 (4.48)	0.91 (21.82)	0.06 (1.28)				-0.03 (-0.73)		.979	156.26	17
8	0.19 (4.67)	0.89 (19.34)	0.10 (2.03)					0.04 (0.95)	.980	160.67	17

Notes: See text for definition of variables.
( ) = t statistic.
r^2 = correlation coefficient.
F = F statistic.
df = degrees of freedom.

Table 1-11
Determinants of Military Expenditures per Capita, Latin American Countries, Economic Variables
(standardized estimates)

Equation	Independent Variables								Statistics		
	GNPPER	PCB	GEDB	GDP	PDB	PDA	EB	CAB	r^2	F	df
1 MEP=81	0.89 (4.23)	0.46 (2.65)	0.66 (3.16)						.726	7.96	12
2	0.88 (5.42)	0.43 (3.35)	0.91 (4.88)	−5.00 (−3.16)	4.65 (3.11)				.887	11.08	12
3	0.91 (4.80)	0.38 (4.47)	0.49 (2.46)	−0.75 (−2.15)		0.69 (2.23)			.843	7.54	12
4	1.71 (6.20)	0.38 (3.78)	0.76 (4.93)	−4.66 (−3.81)	3.87 (3.24)	0.50 (2.42)			.943	16.63	12
5	1.62 (6.66)	0.40 (4.57)	0.58 (3.46)	−4.51 (−4.24)	3.60 (3.45)	0.55 (3.02)	−0.20 (−1.73)		.964	19.41	12
6	1.91 (5.93)	0.28 (2.47)	1.00 (5.28)	−6.81 (−3.69)				−0.41 (−1.60)	.726	7.96	12

Notes: See text for definition of variables.
( ) = t statistic.
r^2 = correlation coefficient.
F = F statistic.
df = degrees of freedom.

(*PDA*) and 1982 (*PDB*) are all positively related to this measure of military expenditure and statistically significant. Gross domestic product (GDP) was, however, negatively related to per capita military expenditures.

In contrast, the non–Latin American countries (table 1-12) followed a pattern similar to the total sample, except that government budget surplus/deficit (*GDB*) had a negative sign, indicating that this group of countries resorts more to budget deficits as a means of increasing military expenditure.

In summary, the basic regression equation for total military expenditures per capita shows the following differences by sample group.

	GNPPER	CAB	PCB	PDB	GDB	GEDB	PDA
Total Sample	+	+	+	+	o	+	o
Group I	+	–	o	+	–	+	o
Group II	+	+	o	o	+	o	o
Latin America	+	o	+	+	o	+	+
Non-Latin America	+	+	+	+	–	+	o

GNPPER = per capita gross national product, 1982; *CAB* = current account balance, 1982; *PCB* = government consumption as a percent of GDP, 1982; *PDB* = total public external debt, 1982; *GDB* = government deficit or surplus as a percent of *GNP*, 1981; *GEDB* = share of military expenditure in total government budget, 1981; and *PDA* = public external debt in 1970.

Conclusions

While only a first step in examining the determinants of Third World defense burdens, the above analysis throws considerable light on the four questions posed at the beginning of the chapter:

1. Wagner's Law (at least on a cross-sectional basis) appears to be valid for developing countries; that is, per capita military expenditures tend to increase in line with increases in per capita income. This result appears valid whether developing countries are examined as a whole, on a broad regional basis (Latin America and non–Latin America), or by degree of resource constraint (relatively financially constrained or unconstrained). On the

Table 1-12
Determinants of Military Expenditures per Capita, Non-Latin American Countries, Economic Variables
(standardized estimates)

Equation	Independent Variables								Statistics		
	GNPPER	PCB	GEDB	PDB	CAB	ECNIA	GDP	GDB	r^2	F	df
1 MEP81 =	0.66 (6.59)								.441	43.48	56
2	0.65 (6.34)	0.30 (2.71)	0.23 (2.13)						.716	22.74	30
3	0.67 (6.67)	0.35 (3.14)	0.13 (1.10)	0.18 (2.62)					.742	18.74	31
4	0.32 (5.34)	0.20 (3.25)		0.20 (3.30)	0.80 (12.73)				.862	58.22	41
5	0.32 (5.05)	0.19 (2.92)			0.78 (12.03)	0.18 (2.90)			.857	52.73	39
6	0.31 (4.61)	0.22 (3.14)			0.71 (9.97)		0.15 (2.07)		.841	48.89	41
7	1.03 (5.78)	0.21 (1.77)						−0.45 (−2.51)	.738	26.29	31

Notes: See text for definition of variables.
( ) = t statistic.
r^2 = correlation coefficient.
F = F statistic.
df = degrees of freedom.

other hand, per capita income tends to account for only a relatively small proportion of the observed fluctuations in per capita military expenditures irrespective of the group used.

2. Public external debt does appear to have played a significant role in expanding military expenditures per capita, particularly among those countries (Group I) with limited alternative sources of foreign exchange. While not tested here, it may be assumed that, for a number of developing countries, a high proportion of the public external debt accumulated by 1982 had been used to significantly expand military expenditures on a per capita basis.

3. With regard to the uniformity of developing countries, the analysis clearly indicates significant structural differences by country type. Military expenditures in the poorer, less dynamic countries have been to a large extent facilitated by public external borrowing and domestic public deficits, while the more affluent and dynamic LDCs which spent more on military-related activities relied largely on balance of payments and budgetary surpluses to expand their per capita military expenditures.

4. Significant regional differences in military expenditures may exist, but these differences do not appear to be as pronounced as those occurring between the resource-constrained and -unconstrained countries. Because of the small sample size for the Middle East and South Asia, it is impossible to provide a definitive answer as to the usefulness of a regional approach in explaining the observed patterns of military expenditures.

5. Most importantly, the analysis indicates the usefulness of examining the defense burden from an economic perspective. Despite the wide diversity of political and strategic situations in the sample of developing countries, economic variables were shown to account for the bulk of differences in per capita military expenditures across countries.

The above analysis, by demonstrating the importance of economic constraints in affecting the defense burden in the Third World, provides a useful first step in understanding the political economy of defense allocations in Latin America. That is, Latin American defense allocations are not regionally unique nor are they determined by political variables such as regime type. Rather, two different groups of Latin American countries approach the budgetary process from much different perspectives largely molded by the economic constraints they face.

The following chapter attempts to extend this analysis to an issue of major current importance to the political economy of Latin American defense: the development of indigenous arms industries. Are political variables, such as the desire to achieve autonomy from major arms suppliers, the key to understanding the creation of domestic arms capabilities? Or is a dual grouping of countries based on contrasting economic environments (a grouping similar to that developed in chapter 1) a more insightful way of explaining the existing pattern of military production in Latin America?

Notes

1. See P.C. Frederiksen and R.E. Looney, "Defense Expenditures and Economic Growth in Developing Countries: Some Further Empirical Evidence," *Journal of Economic Development* (July 1982), pp. 113–25; P.C. Frederiksen and R.E. Looney, "Defense Expenditures and Economic Growth in Developing Countries," *Armed Forces and Society* (Summer 1983), pp. 633–45; P.C. Frederiksen and R.E. Looney, "Another Look at Defense Spending and Development Hypothesis," *Defense Analysis* (September 1985), pp. 205–10; and P.C. Frederiksen and R.E. Looney, "Defense Expenditures and Economic Growth in Developing Countries: A Reply," *Armed Forces and Society* (Winter 1985), pp. 298–301.

2. P.C. Frederiksen and R.E. Looney, "Defense Expenditures and Economic Growth in Developing Countries: Some Further Empirical Evidence," *op. cit.*, p. 117.

3. *Ibid.*

4. *Ibid.*, p. 118.

5. *Ibid.*

6. *Ibid.*

7. *Ibid.*, p. 124.

8. *Ibid.*

9. Cf. Statistical Analysis System (SAS), *User's Guide: Statistics, 1982 Edition* (Cary, North Carolina: SAS Institute, 1982), pp. 381–396 for a description of this program. The sample countries were initially assigned an arbitrary one or zero so that placement could be made into two groups. A three-group division of countries did not produce a clear split between the means of the groups (that is, there was not a high probability of correct placement for each country in one of the three groups).

2
Economic Environments Conducive to Indigenous Third World Arms Production

Despite the heated debate over the presumed high opportunity cost associated with domestic production of armaments in Third World countries, remarkably little empirical attention has been devoted to the socioeconomic sources of national military industrial capabilities.[1]

Recently, Stephanie Neuman has raised the question of "why, for example, do some states produce arms while others do not? What explains why some producing states support large and diversified military industries while others do not?"[2] Neuman is, in fact, one of the few researchers who has attempted to determine the critical characteristics that set Third World arms producers apart from those countries that have not developed domestic arms industries.[3]

Her general hypothesis and regression results indicate that:

> What emerges within the Third World from these data is a hierarchically shaped arms production system based largely on factors of scale. In each region, the largest defense producers are generally also those countries with the biggest militaries and GNPs which dwarf quantitatively, if not always qualitatively, the capabilities of their smaller, poorer neighbors.[4]

Clearly, however, Neuman's results and conclusions apply only in a general sort of way, given numerous smaller countries—Ecuador, Peru, Chile, and Dominican Republic, for example—whose arms industries would not be anticipated in light of their small economic size and relatively limited level of military expenditures.[5]

The purpose of this chapter is to determine whether the possession of a limited number of economic characteristics is necessary and sufficient to predict with a high degree of probability whether or not a Third World country is likely to possess a domestic arms industry. More specifically, is there a unique combination of economic characteristics that sets apart the Third World arms producers from the nonproducers? What benefits do the factors associated with these characteristics convey to indigenous arms producers?

The following analysis indicates that the conditions associated with Third World arms production can be identified, but that these conditions are regional, specific, and multidimensional in nature, with surprisingly the size of the military and the size of the economy (economy of scale factors) playing little or no role.

Methodology

The data set used for the analysis contained a variety of socioeconomic and political indicators for ninety-six developing countries.[6] Neuman classified twenty-eight of these as military producers, that is, producers of at least one major weapons system in the 1979–80 period.[7] Due to missing observations for several countries, most of the analysis dealt with forty-nine countries, nineteen of which were arms producers and thirty of which were not.[8]

To determine the extent to which socioeconomic variables could correctly classify arms producers and nonproducers, several sets of variables were first examined to see if their mean values for the producer and nonproducer countries were significantly different. The variables selected were representative of broad structural-, performance-, and defense-related differences between developing countries:

1. External balance of payments variables,
2. External debt variables,
3. Fiscal savings variables,
4. Composition of GNP variables,
5. Defense variables,
6. Performance variables, and
7. Size variables.

The examination of the means of the arms and non–arms producers in table 2–1 indicates that:

1. As noted by Neuman, arms producers do in fact tend to have larger areas, higher GDP, and larger populations, armed forces, and military expenditures.
2. Interestingly enough, the arms and non–arms producers have nearly the same per capita incomes.

Table 2-1
Means of Structural, Performance, and Defense Expenditure Variables for Third World Military and Non-Military Producers

Symbol	Variable	Arms Producers	Nonproducers	Total Sample
External Balance of Payments Variables				
RBB	Resource balance, 1982	-5.1	-12.2	-10.2
ZGA	Growth in imports, 1960-70	5.4	6.0	5.8
ZGB	Growth in imports, 1970-82	5.7	3.8	4.3
EGA	Growth in exports, 1960-70	5.7	9.6	8.5
EGB	Growth in exports, 1970-82	5.0	-0.3	1.1
CAA	Current account balance, 1970	-353.5	-22.0	-127.7
CAB	Current account balance, 1982	-2964.8	837.8	-340.5
External Debt Variables				
PDA	External public debt, 1970	1670.7	240.2	620.5
PDB	External public debt, 1982	13299.1	1941.3	4960.5
PDP	External public debt as a percentage of GDP, 1970	15.5	39.9	33.3
PDPB	External public debt as a percentage of GDP, 1980	26.9	4.7	37.8
PBCB	Public external borrowing commitments, 1982	3798.7	377.0	510.3
PBCBE	Public external borrowing commitments, to exports, 1982	1.0	0.5	0.7
ECNIB	Net inflow of publicly guaranteed external capital, 1982	1582.2	173.2	547.7
Fiscal and Savings Variables				
AS	Average national savings, 1970-81	20.2	15.4	16.7
MS	Average marginal savings, 1970-81	19.7	9.9	12.5
PCB	Government consumption as a percentage of GDP, 1982	—	—	—
GDIB	Gross domestic investment as a percentage of GDP, 1982	14.0	17.2	16.2
Composition of GDP				
AB	Share of agriculture in GDP, 1982	17.4	28.1	25.1
MB	Share of manufacturing in GDP, 1982	18.8	10.8	13.1
EB	Share of exports in GDP, 1982	30.0	26.7	27.6
Defense Expenditure Variables				
ME	Military expenditures, 1981	1863.7	1013.1	1247.0
AF	Armed forces, 1981	240.7	71.1	116.5
MEY	Military expenditures' share of GDP, 1981	4.0	5.8	5.4
MEP	Military expenditures per capita	112.1	158.4	145.7
Performance Variables				
EI	Export instability index, 1967-71	8.6	10.8	10.2
GDPGA	Growth in GDP, 1960-70	5.8	5.4	5.5
GDPGB	Growth in GDP, 1970-80	5.5	3.9	4.3
GIRA	Gross international reserves, 1970	536.4	141.9	253.2
GIRB	Gross international reserves, 1982	3869.9	1495.6	2148.5
GNPPER	Per capita income	1862.3	1886.6	1879.9
Size Variables				
AREA	Area	1280.2	502.8	695.0
GDDB	Gross Domestic Product, 1982	59203.2	10387.5	23981.8
POP	Population, 1982	73.2	11.3	26.6

3. Arms producers tend to have less export instability, a stronger growth in imports, a higher percentage of exports in GDP, and, in recent years, a better export performance.
4. Due to their larger size, the arms producers undoubtedly have accumulated higher volumes of external indebtedness but lower overall debt burdens (in terms of debt as a percentage of GDP) than the nonproducers.
5. The savings performance of the arms producers is distinctly superior to that of the nonproducers, but the degree of government involvement in the economy (measured in terms of either revenues or expenditures) is nearly similar for each group.
6. The arms producers, as might be expected, tend to have a much higher share of manufactures in GDP than the non-arms producers.
7. Although having larger armies and levels of military expenditures than the non-arms producers, the producing countries tend to devote less to defense either as a percentage of GNP or on a per capita basis.
8. While the overall economic performances of the arms and the non-arms producers are fairly similar (with the arms producers experiencing higher overall rates of growth), the level of international reserves accumulated by the defense producers considerably outweighs that of the non-arms producers.

In short, the arms producers are larger and more open to external trade, while having more external debt, higher savings, and more dynamic import and export performances than the nonproducers.

Given these diverse characteristics associated with arms and non-arms producing countries, it seemed likely that no one single underlying factor was necessary and sufficient for the establishment of an indigenous arms industry in the Third World. Instead, arms production is likely to be multidimensional.

One analytical approach to identify which combination of these factors is critical for arms production is multiple discriminant function analysis (MDA).[9] Numerous applications of MDA to identification problems based on profile data exist.[10] In past research, MDA has been used primarily as a method of studying profile relationships among several groups and for classifying individual entities into groups. This book, however, makes use of a specific aspect of MDA which is frequently ignored: its ability to provide the best statistical basis (in a least squares sense) for computing estimates of the specific probabilities of a Third World country achieving the status of arms producer.

Results

To determine the relative importance of these broad factors in differentiating the producers from the nonproducers, a stepwise discriminant analysis was first performed using the variables in table 2-1 as independent discriminating variables. As might be anticipated, in table 2-2, total military expenditures (*ME*) was the variable most significant in differentiating arms from non-arms producers. Following military expenditures in order of importance were (1) public external borrowing commitments in 1982 (*PBCB*), (2) public external debt in 1982 (*PDB*), (3) public external borrowing commitments in 1982 as a percentage of exports (*PBCBE*), (4) gross international reserves in 1970 (*GIRA*), (5) growth in public sector consumption, 1970-82 (*PCGB*), (6) area (*AREA*), and (7) the current account balance, 1982 (*CAB*).

Contrary to Neuman's analysis, variables such as gross national product, population, and size of the armed forces were not statistically significant for purposes of differentiating arms and non-arms producers. Furthermore, by itself total military expenditures provided little discriminating power between arms and non-arms producers. Using this variable, ten of the nineteen arms producers were classified incorrectly, as were two of the thirty arms producers. The overall probability of correct placement was also very low (50 percent) for most countries in each group.

A clear improvement in delineation between the groups was made by adding the next three variables: public external borrowing commitments, 1982 (*PBCB*); public external debt, 1982 (*PDB*); and public external borrowing commitments as a percentage of exports, 1982 (*PBCBE*). With these four variables, all of the nonproducers were correctly classified with an average correct classification rate of 85.0 percent.

Four of the producing countries were, however, incorrectly classified, with the overall average probability of correct placement only 64 percent. Clearly, a limited number of discriminating variables are much superior at predicting the conditions under which Third World arms production is not likely to occur than predicting the countries in which arms production has actually been established.

36 · Cross-Sectional Analysis

Table 2-2
Discriminant Analysis, Total Country Sample for Arms-Producing and Non-Arms-Producing Nations
(probability of correct classification)

Arms Producer	Discriminating Variables			Nonproducer	Discriminating Variables		
	I	II	III		I	II	III
	ME	ME PBCB PDB PBCBE	ME PRCB PDB PBCBE	GIRA PCGB AREA CAB		ME	ME PBCB PDB PBCBE	ME PRCB PDB PBCBE	GIRA PCGB AREA CAB
Israel	58.4	65.5		100.0	Cameroon	54.1	87.0	99.1
India	60.6	92.2		100.0	Sudan	53.4	80.1	100.0
Nigeria	52.0	85.8		100.0	Costa Rica	54.3	89.1	99.6
Indonesia	54.1	99.6		99.2	Bolivia	53.8	90.9	99.9
Korea, South	57.8	91.0		100.0	Togo	54.3	91.6	99.8
Singapore	47.7*	15.7*		98.8	Tunisia	53.7	84.5	99.2
Pakistan	50.8	73.9		99.9	Rwanda	54.2	88.5	99.7
Venezuela	48.8*	67.9		99.9	Guatemala	54.0	89.0	99.0
Mexico	49.2*	100.0		99.8	Malawi	54.2	90.8	99.7
Brazil	51.1	100.0		100.0	El Salvador	54.0	85.7	97.3
Philippines	48.2*	58.8		91.1	Turkey	46.1*	71.9	63.2
Ecuador	46.5*	11.8*		2.4*	Paraguay	54.1	82.7	98.7
Colombia	46.7*	74.0		70.9	Algeria	49.1*	57.8	99.8
Thailand	49.6*	65.5		99.7	Libya	54.2	91.2	93.9
Malaysia	49.9*	84.8		100.0	Ivory Coast	54.0	67.0	98.7
Dominican Republic	46.0*	15.1*		35.1*	Mauritania	54.2	87.2	99.9
Chile	49.1*	42.0		94.9	Congo	54.3	90.7	99.7
Argentina	55.0	14.2*		17.1*	Sierra Leone	54.3	90.2	96.2
Peru	48.7	84.2		96.2	Panama	54.3	79.5	96.4
					Uruguay	53.3	84.0	92.3
					Madagascar	54.0	88.4	99.2
					Ethiopia	53.1	89.4	99.9
Average	51.1	65.4		84.5				

Central African Republic	54.3	89.0	98.4
Ghana	53.9	91.3	99.7
Zaire	54.1	90.2	100.0
Jamaica	54.3	86.9	97.3
Zimbabwe	53.1	75.2	96.0
Kuwait	50.7	89.4	900.0
Kenya	53.8	83.2	98.3
Jordan	51.8	87.1	93.3
Average	53.4	85.0	97.1

Note: *Represents misclassified country.

Utilizing the full set of eight independent discriminating variables raised the overall probability of correct classification of non-arms producers to 97.1, and arms producers to 84.5. However, in the environment characterized by the variables, three countries—Ecuador, Dominican Republic, and Argentina—were classified as non-arms producers.

A number of political variables were added to the data set to see if further discrimination between arms and non-arms producers could be obtained. The results were not, however, an improvement over those obtained from the eight socioeconomic variables initially selected.

Obviously, the one thing Ecuador, Argentina, and the Dominican Republic have in common is their geographic location. Are the conditions conducive to arms production different in Latin America than in the rest of the world? To test this hypothesis, the sample of developing countries was split into two groupings: Latin American and non-Latin American. As with the total sample, a stepwise discriminant analysis was performed on each geographic group to determine those variables that were statistically significant in delineating producers from nonproducers.

Results: Non-Latin American Countries

For the non-Latin American countries—twenty-nine nonproducers and twelve producers—six variables in table 2-3 were found to be statistically significant in discriminating producers from nonproducers, with the net inflow of public and publicly generated external capital in 1982 (*ECNIB*) by far the most significant discriminating variable.

This variable was followed by: (1) the current account balance in 1970 (*CAA*), (2) gross international reserves in 1970 (*GIRA*), (3) the current account balance in 1982 (*CAB*), (4) public external borrowing commitments in 1982 (*PBCB*), and (5) gross international reserves in 1982 (*GIRB*).

As for the total sample of countries, several discriminant functions were formed for the non-Latin American countries by increasing the number of independent variables in the analysis:

1. By itself, *ECNIB* correctly classified all but two producers and two nonproducers with the average probability of correct placement of nonproducers at over 90 percent and of producers at 77.7 percent.

2. Adding the current account balance in 1970 resulted in a correct placement of all producing countries (with an average probability of correct placement at over 94 percent). Two nonproducers—Turkey and Morocco—were, however, incorrectly classified.
3. Utilizing all six statistically significant variables in the discriminant function markedly improved the results with only Egypt (with a probability of correct placement of 69.4), Turkey (with a probability of correct placement of 74.3), and Morocco (with a probability of correct placement of 79.1) falling outside the sharply delineated groupings of producers and nonproducers.

In general, however, whether a non–Latin American country is a producer or nonproducer of arms depends largely on the volume of recent inflows of public and publicly guaranteed external capital. For the most part, the non–Latin American countries not possessing large recent (1982) inflows of external capital are not capable, regardless of their size or level of industrial sophistication, of either justifying or sustaining the ongoing production of at least one major weapons system.

Interestingly enough, military expenditures per se play no role whatsoever in determining whether a non–Latin American country will possess an indigenous arms industry.

Table 2-4 looks at the means of the discriminating and other variables for the non–Latin American producers and nonproducers. It confirms the high level of capital inflows and foreign exchange earnings associated with the producers and the relatively low level of external capital inflows and export earnings associated with the nonproducers. Even though the growth in producers' exports greatly outpaced nonproducers' during 1970-82, producers' current account deficits were significantly higher than the nonproducers'.

Results: Latin American Countries

For the Latin American countries as a group, a completely different picture emerges. For this group of countries, as shown in table 2-5, export growth between 1960 and 1970 (*EGA*) was the most important variable in discriminating between producing and non-producing countries, followed by: (1) public external debt, 1970 (*PDA*), (2) growth of imports between 1960 and 1970 (*ZA*), (3) gross international reserves in 1982 (*GIRB*) and (4) the current account balance in 1970 (*CAA*).

Table 2-3
Discriminant Analysis, Non-Latin American Arms-Producing and Non-Arms-Producing Nations
(probability of correct classification)

Arms Producer	Discriminating Variables				Nonproducer	Discriminating Variables			
	I	II	III			I	II	III	
	ECNIB	ECNIB CAA	ECNIB CAA GIRA CAB	PBCBE GIRB		ECNIB	ECNIB CAA	ECNIB CAA GIRA CAB	PBCBE GIRB
Israel	72.3	100.0	100.0		Cameroon	99.1	99.9	100.0	100.0
India	99.5	100.0	100.0		Sudan	94.4	93.4	100.0	100.0
Nigeria	92.2	99.6	100.0		Somalia	98.6	99.9	100.0	100.0
Indonesia	100.0	100.0	100.0		Togo	99.1	99.9	100.0	100.0
Egypt	90.8	81.7	69.4		Tunisia	95.1	99.3	100.0	100.0
Korea	99.9	100.0	100.0		Morocco	3.9*	11.1*	79.1	
Singapore	1.7*	95.7	100.0		Ruandu	99.1	100.0	100.0	100.0
Pakistan	17.6*	99.9	100.0		Malawi	99.1	99.9	100.0	100.0
Philippines	96.5	66.4	89.4		Turkey	5.5*	45.3*	74.3	
Thailand	84.5	93.9	98.4		Algeria	100.0	100.0	99.9	99.9
Malaysia	100.0	99.9	100.0		Libya	99.3	100.0	100.0	100.0
					Ivory Coast	52.6	93.4	100.0	100.0
Average	77.7	94.3	96.1		Mauritania	97.6	99.9	100.0	100.0
					Sierra Leone	99.0	99.9	100.0	100.0
					Chad	99.3	100.0	100.0	100.0
					Madagascar	97.5	99.9	100.0	100.0
					Tanzania	97.3	99.7	100.0	100.0
					Uganda	99.1	100.0	100.0	100.0
					Ethiopia	98.8	99.9	100.0	100.0
					Car	99.2	99.9	100.0	100.0
					Ghana	99.0	99.8	100.0	100.0
					Burma	94.9	99.2	100.0	100.0
					Zaire	98.6	99.8	100.0	100.0
					Zambia	97.4	100.0	100.0	100.0

Order	Symbol for Discriminating Variables	F Statistic	Wilks's Lambda	Saudi Arabia	Kenya	Syria	Jordan	South Yemen	Average	Discriminating Variable
1	ECNIB	46.8	0.33	99.3	100.0				90.1	Net inflow of publicly guaranteed external capital, 1982
2	CAA	12.6	0.21	97.5	99.7					Current account balance, 1970
3	GIRA	13.2	0.13	98.4	99.7					Gross international reserves, 1970
4	CAB	7.6	0.09	97.0	99.8					Current account balance, 1982
5	PBCBE	7.0	0.07	98.4	99.9					Public external borrowing commitments/exports, 1982
									91.0	
6	GIRB	1.5	0.06	100.0	100.0	100.0	100.0	100.0	98.4	Gross international reserves, 1982
1	ME	37.1	0.50							
2	PCB	12.5	0.37							
3	PDB	11.7	0.28							
4	PBCBE	9.8	0.22							
5	GIRA	3.8	0.19							
6	PCGB	5.5	0.17							
7	AREA	8.3	0.13							
8	CAB	5.0	0.11							

Notes: *Represents incorrect classification.
ME   = Military expenditures, 1981.
PCB   = Public consumption share in GDP, 1982.
PDP   = Public external debt, 1982.
PBCBE = Public external borrowing commitments/exports, 1982.
GIRA = Gross international reserves, 1982.
PCGB = Growth in public consumption, 1970–82.
AREA = Area, 1982.
CAB   = Current account balance, 1982.

Table 2-4
Means of Discriminating Variables for Non-Latin American Arms Producers and Non-Arms Producers

Symbol	Variable	Arms Producers	Nonproducers
ECNIB	Net inflow of publicly guaranteed external capital, 1982	1659.0	117.6
CAA	Current account balance, 1970	-357.1	8.2
GIRA	Gross internal reserves, 1970	500.0	180.8
CAB	Current account balance, 1982	-2699.4	-25.6
PBCB	Public external borrowing commitments, 1982	2925.4	444.1
GIRB	Gross international reserves, 1982	3939.8	1177.3
EGB	Export growth, 1970-82	6.9	-0.3
ZGB	Import growth, 1970-82	6.8	3.9
PDA	Public external debt, 1970	2142.1	190.4
PDB	Public external debt, 1982	1236.1	1994.9
PBCBE	Public external borrowing commitments share of exports, 1982	1.5	0.5

Note that other than *GIRB* and *CAA*, the variables statistically significant in discriminating Latin American arms from non-arms producers are different than those for the non-Latin American countries. Furthermore, whereas *CAA* is second in importance in delineating non-Latin American countries, it is last for the Latin American sample. *GIRB* is tangential to both groups.

The results for the Latin American sample show that:

1. Using only export growth in the 1960s (*EGA*), all but four countries are correctly classified. This increases to all but one when the public external debt in 1970 (*PDA*) is added to the discriminant function.

2. Latin American arms producers and non-arms producers can be correctly classified (with an average probability of correct placement of 98.9 percent for both) with only three variables—export and import growth, 1960-70 (*EGA* and *ZGA*) and the accumulated public external debt in 1970 (*PDA*).

Third World Arms Production · 43

3. More significantly, a sharp delineation takes place between producers and nonproducers with 96.9 the lowest probability of correct placement.

Looking at the means of the discriminating variables in table 2-5, the Latin American producers achieved lower growth in exports and imports in the 1960s than did the nonproducers, although the producers' external public debt was significantly higher, as were their current account deficit in 1970 and their level of reserves in 1982. On the other hand, the producers' export and import growth rates were considerably higher in the 1970s.

It appears that the Latin American defense industries are largely the result of import substitution policies with undoubtedly high levels of protectionism in the 1960s. The industries survived in the 1970s largely due to rapid increases in foreign exchange inflows stemming from relatively high rates of export growth and increased public external indebtedness.

Summary of Results for Latin American and Non-Latin American Groupings

In sum, there is a sharp contrast between the environments in which Latin American arms production takes place and the conditions under which it is present in the rest of the world:

1. The conditions facilitating Latin American arms production seem to have been established largely in the 1960s and involved the creation, through export growth and external borrowing, of a high import capacity. Presumably, this import capacity was necessary to facilitate the high level of technology transfer, capital equipment, and so on needed to establish an indigenous arms industry.

2. It should be noted that the only new Latin American arms producers between 1969–70 and 1979–80 were Mexico, Ecuador, and Venezuela, all of which were oil exporters whose access to foreign exchange was enhanced during the period.

3. The non-Latin American arms producers appear to be highly dependent on a steady infusion of public external borrowed funds. Overall export and import performance does not appear to be critical in the establishment or maintenance of an indigenous arms industry. Instead, the ability to finance existing current

Table 2-5
Discriminant Analysis, Latin American Arms-Producing and Non-Arms-Producing Nations
(probability of correct classification)

	Discriminating Variables			
	I	II	III	IV
Arms Producers	EGA	EGA PDA	EGA PDA ZGA	EGA PDA ZGA GIRB CAA
Venezuela	96.1	98.7	99.4	100.0
Mexico	78.1	100.0	100.0	100.0
Brazil	41.8*	100.0	100.0	100.0
Ecuador	85.4	57.5	97.9	99.1
Colombia	87.4	99.0	98.3	100.0
Dominican Republic	00.7	99.8	100.0	100.0
Chile	97.2	100.0	100.0	100.0
Argentina	71.8	99.5	97.4	100.0
Peru	91.4	97.3	96.9	100.0
Average	83.2	85.3	98.9	99.9

	Discriminating Variables			
	I	II	III	IV
Nonproducers	EGA	EGA PDA	EGA PDA ZGA	EGA PDA ZGA GIRB CAA
Nicaragua	98.5	100.0*	100.0	100.0
Honduras	99.4	100.0	100.0	100.0
Costa Rica	98.1	99.9	100.0	100.0
Bolivia	98.3	100.0	100.0	100.0
Guatemala	97.6	98.9	99.8	100.0
El Salvador	74.8	96.7	98.3	100.0
Paraguay	60.2	100.0	100.0	100.0
Panama	99.0	37.8*	99.3	100.0
Uruguay	14.5*	94.2	99.7	100.0
Jamaica	49.8*	92.7	98.9	100.0
Trinidad	49.8*			
Average	76.2	92.7	98.9	100.0

Order	Symbol	F statistic	Wilks's Lambda	Variable
1	EGA	19.7	0.46	Growth in exports, 1960–70
2	PDA	14.5	0.24	External public debt, 1970
3	ZGA	3.5	0.20	Growth in imports, 1960–70
4	GIRB	3.9	0.15	Gross international reserves, 1982
5	CAA	4.4	0.11	Current account balance, 1970

	Means	
	Producers	Nonproducers
Growth in exports, 1960–70	2.2	7.4
Growth in imports, 1960–70	5.4	7.0
Growth in exports, 1970–82	4.2	0.7
Growth in imports, 1970–82	4.6	0.3
External public debt, 1970	1521.3	172.7
External public debt, 1982	16619.8	1608.7
External public debt as a percentage of GDP, 1970	12.9	16.2
External public debt as a percentage of GDP, 1982	24.8	40.5
Gross international reserves, 1982	3896.2	793.4
Current account balance, 1970	−285.4	−50.6

Note: *Represents incorrect classification.

account deficits through publicly guaranteed loans appears critical. It follows that the non-Latin American arms industries may be less viable than those in Latin America.
4. Interestingly, for both the Latin American and non-Latin American countries, economic size, per capita income, military capabilities, and associated economies of scale in production do not appear to be either necessary or sufficient conditions for undertaking indigenous arms production. Instead, the main factor determining whether arms production will be established and viable over time appears to be access to foreign exchange presumably required to facilitate imported inputs—both technical and material—for actual arms production.
5. Foreign exchange availability by and of itself is a multidimensional factor and not associated with one specific index such as export growth or inflows of external borrowed funds.
6. The above findings are consistent with and reinforce Ron Ayres' analysis of the stages typically associated with domestic arms production, the first several of which are heavily foreign-exchange intensive:
   a. Arms are imported, but are serviced and maintained domestically.
   b. A license to produce arms is acquired and production facilities are built requiring huge technical and personnel assistance from the supplier.
   c. Production starts. To begin with, it involves local assembly of imported subassemblies.
   d. The subassemblies are assembled locally from imported components and sometimes reexported to the licenser.
   e. Components are manufactured locally from imported raw materials.
   f. Raw materials are locally produced.
   g. Complete indigenous production includes design, raw materials, and manufacture.

Ayres notes, however, that even those LDCs such as India which have been pursuing military self-sufficiency for many years have not reached the final two stages.[11]

Conclusions and Implications

One of the main findings of this analysis was that access to relatively high amounts of foreign exchange tends to be a necessary condition for the establishment and survival of a Third World domestic arms industry. No Third World country is currently or is likely to become completely self-sufficient in either the technical or material inputs required for arms production. Instead, the establishment of an indigenous arms industry places high and continuous demands on a country's foreign exchange reserves.[12]

One of Neuman's major concerns was the rapid expansion of Third World arms producers—from five in 1950 up to twenty-one in 1969–70 and twenty-six by 1979–80.[13] Not surprisingly, a number of commentators have specifically cited the proliferation of arms production facilities in the Third World as a major contributing factor to the disintegration of hegemonic power.[14]

> The indigenous weapons production phenomenon is one small dimension of a much larger development: the diffusion of power throughout the international system. This has occurred in the economic and political realm as well as in the military. In each case this has involved the erosion of the incredible concentrations of political, economic, and military power in the hands of a small number of large industrial states.[15]

> In this context, interdependence is a zero-sum pie in which the individual shares are becoming more equal in size. Indigenous arms production capabilities become a symbol not just of the growing self-sufficiency of key Third World producers, but of the erosion of the traditional suppliers' influence as well.[16]

In short, as technology becomes available to developing countries, traditional ties to the super powers for military support become weakened. The underlying impetus is part of a growing international movement for political–military autonomy on the part of the Third World.

What are the prospects that this trend will continue?

1. If the discriminant analysis is correct, there should be no new Latin American arms producers in the foreseeable future. Given the poor export prospects for most of the nonproducers and their high levels of external debt, is extremely unlikely that any of these countries will have sufficient surpluses of foreign exchange to allocate to arms production.

2. The situation may be less clear for the non–Latin American arms producers, since for these continuous access to publicly guaranteed external capital inflows appears to be critical for the establishment and survival of a domestic arms industry. Clearly,

however, if the major arms suppliers wanted to restrict new indigenous production in the Third World, denial of credit at past levels could efficiently accomplish this objective.

The next chapter extends this analysis by examining Latin American arms producers and nonproducers from another perspective: the relative impact which military expenditures have on overall economic performance in the two environments.

Notes

1. The literature is increasing rapidly, however. An interesting attempt incorporating political and power relationships is given in R. Vayrynen, "Semi-Peripheral Countries in the Global Economic and Military Order" in H. Tuomi and R. Vayrynen, eds., *Militarization and Arms Production* (New York: St. Martin's, 1983), pp. 163-92. See also J. Katz, ed., *Arms Production in Developing Countries* (Lexington, Mass: Lexington Books, 1984); and H. Tuomi and R. Vayrynen, eds., *Transnational Corporations, Armaments and Development* (New York: St. Martin's, 1982).
2. Stephanie Neuman "International Stratification of Third World Military Industries," *International Organization* (Winter 1984), p. 181.
3. Others are Herbert Wulf, *Transnational Arms Production Technology* (Hamburg: University of Hamburg Institut fur Friedensforschung und Sicherheitspolitik, 1980); Robert Harkavy, *The Arms Trade and International Systems* (Cambridge, Mass: Ballinger, 1975); and Ilan Peleg "Military Production in Third World Countries: A Political Study" in Patrick J. McGowan and Charles W. Kegley, eds., *Threats, Weapons and Foreign Policy,* (Beverly Hills, Calif.: Sage, 1980), pp. 209-30.
4. Neuman, *op. cit.,* p. 185.
5. Arms producers as defined by Neuman (*op. cit.,* pp. 172-73) are those countries producing at least one major weapon system. For 1979-80, these nations consisted of: Argentina, Brazil, Chile, China, Colombia, Dominican Republic, Fiji, Ecuador, India, Indonesia, Egypt, Israel, India, North Korea, South Korea, Malaysia, Mexico, Nigeria, Pakistan, Peru, Philippines, Singapore, South Africa, Sri Lanka, Taiwan, Thailand, and Venezuela. Her definition of arms producers is used here.
6. Economic and social variables are taken from *World Development Report, 1984* (Washington, D.C.: World Bank, 1984). Military expenditures and defense related variables are taken from *World Military Expenditures and Arms Transfers, 1972-82* (Washington, D.C.: U.S. Arms Control and Disarmament Agency, 1984).
7. Neuman, *op. cit.,* p. 173.
8. The nineteen arms producers included in the study were: Israel, India, Nigeria, Indonesia, South Korea, Singapore, Pakistan, Venezuela, Mexico,

Brazil, Philippines, Ecuador, Colombia, Thailand, Malaysia, Dominican Republic, Chile, Argentina, and Peru.

9. The program used for the analysis was from the Statistical Analysis System statistical package. A description of the program and output is given in *SAS User's Guide: Statistics, 1982 Edition* (Cary, N.C.: SAS Institute, 1982). An excellent description of the analysis is given in C. James Klett, *Applied Multivariate Analysis* (New York: McGraw-Hill, 1972), pp. 243-300.

10. Cf. Randall Jones, "A Model for Predicting Expropriation in Latin America Applied to Jamaica," *Colombia Journal of World Business* (Spring 1980), pp. 74-80.

11. Ron Ayres, "Arms Production as a Form of Import Substituting Industrialization: The Turkish Case," *World Development (1983)*, p. 814.

12. See, for example, P. Terhal, "Foreign Exchange Costs of the Indian Military, 1950-72," *Journal of Peace Research* (1982), pp. 251-59. Terhal estimates that in the late 1960s, one military claim on foreign exchange in India was nearly half of Indian civil imports of machinery and equipment.

13. Neuman, *op. cit.,* pp. 172-73.

14. See Robert Gilpin, *War and Change in World Politics* (Cambridge: Cambridge University Press, 1981) p. 180; and Martin Shibik and Paul Bracken, "Strategic Purpose and the International Economy," *Orbis* (Fall 1983), pp. 567-89.

15. Steven Miller, "Arms and the Third World: Indigenous Weapons Production," PSIS Occasional Paper no. 3 (University of Geneva Programme for Strategic and International Security Studies, December 1980), p. 25.

16. Neuman, *op. cit.,* p. 168.

3
Impact of Defense Spending and Indigenous Arms Production on Latin American Growth

It has been suggested that the supply of arms to developing countries is often largely the result of the political influence that the supplier can exert over the recipient.[1] The initial supply of weapons reflects that supplier's technological, economic, and scientific superiority. Later, this superiority may become a political influence when used as a diplomatic tool to change the behavior of the recipient. Indigenous production may be undertaken to avoid this political influence.

On the other hand, the establishment of a weapons industry in a developing country is based on economic variables as suggested in the preceding discriminant analysis. The question examined in the rest of this section is: Are there any purely economic arguments that can be used by governments to rationalize their establishment of a domestic arms industry, other than the usual arguments made for import-substituting industrialization in Latin America?[2]

At first glance, based on pure cost and comparative advantage considerations, local production would appear suspect. For example, while labor in the developing country may be relatively cheap, the final cost per item is often higher. Unfortunately, while specific data on the cost of domestically produced weapons are usually not available, it appears reasonable to assume that it would be cheaper to import than to produce.[3]

Domestic production may be justified, however, if one considers the total (economy-wide) impact of these industries. Dynamic linkage considerations between the defense and civilian sectors may be enough to offset and even warrant the drain of skilled personnel and foreign exchange into arms production.

In addition, military production and expenditure may provide the government with a powerful tool for stabilizing the economy:

1. Military production and expenditure possess a number of interrelationships with the civil economy. The government might, for example, place weapons production contracts with either state enterprises or private manufacturing firms, and soldiers might be expected to spend their wages in civilian markets.
2. Expenditure on the military sector—in common with most public spending—is inherently inflationary owing to the fact that a proportion of the resources taxed to pay for it would have been saved from income or profits and therefore removed from circulation. A reduction in military production can therefore be a powerful anti-inflationary device.
3. Most significantly, the military sector is the one major area of the economy under the direct control of the central government. Economic expansion can therefore be effected immediately by, say, the ordering of a new weapons system. In contrast, indirect policies such as marginal tax changes would take a much longer period to produce noticeable multiplier effects. Such control is also useful in the possible expansion of the economy as weapons systems can be immediately cancelled or contracted to help deflate the system.[4]

Once this system of regulation has become established, several groups of people will find it economically advantageous to maintain its existence. These groups will include senior soldiers, the owners and managers of private industries with which the government places defense-related contracts, and also politicians whose careers are tied to the defense sector. Together these groups clearly wield considerable economic and political power.[5] In sum, therefore, the three propositions outlined here suggest the maintenance of a strong commitment to military production for purely economic reasons.

The purpose of this chapter is to determine the scope indigenous arms production provides for budgetary stabilization and overall growth.

Empirical Tests

Given these economic arguments supporting and rejecting the possible positive contribution of military-production expenditures to the economy, it is necessary to derive some empirical test of the impact of military production on the Latin American economies. This task is especially difficult because precise figures on military output or value added in producing countries are not available. Other indirect tests are possible, however.

The contribution of overall defense spending (as opposed to just defense production) to economic growth has been the object of close scrutiny over the past few years. One of the earliest studies was completed by Emile Benoit.[6] He concluded that "contrary to my expectations, countries with a heavy defense burden generally had the most rapid rate of growth, and those with the lowest defense burdens tended to show the lowest growth rates." On the question of causality, he noted that while high growth may cause increased defense spending in some instances, on the whole growth was a weak determinant of defense and that "the direct interaction ... seems to run primarily from defense burdens to growth rather than vice versa."[7] Subsequent studies by Mary Kaldor,[8] Alice Amsden,[9] R.D. McKinley and A. S. Cohen,[10] and David Dabelko and James McCormick[11] appeared to either support or negate Benoit's hypothesis.

In a somewhat different vein, Frederiksen and Looney have suggested that these studies might not be an appropriate test of the thesis since they lumped all developing countries into one large group.[12] Hypothesizing that the individual countries' financial resource constraints had been excluded, they split Benoit's original sample of countries into groups depending on the relative financial constraints facing the nation. They then reestimated his regression equations. It was found that defense had a positive and statistically significant effect on growth in the richer countries but a negative effect on growth in the poorer countries. In a later paper, in which the sample was substantially enlarged, it was found that the coefficient of the defense variable was not statistically significant for the entire group, was significant for the relatively unconstrained group, and was negative but not statistically significant for the constrained group.[13]

David Lim suggested that the functional form of the relationship tested by Benoit was inappropriate and proposed a Harrod-Domar type of growth model.[14] He concluded that "defense spending is detrimental to economic growth in LDC's, a conclusion diametrically opposite that reached by Benoit."[15] Frederiksen and Looney tested their resource-constrained hypothesis once again using the functional form suggested by Lim.[16] It was found that defense played a positive role in the growth of countries that are relatively resource unconstrained.

As noted, the question of whether or not military expenditures play a positive or negative role in producer versus non-producer countries has not yet been examined. It is hypothesized that productive spinoffs and linkages from defense production industries should result in total military expenditures having a positive impact (or less of a negative impact) on overall growth in producer countries. Nonproducers cannot, of course, capture the externalities associated with domestic weapons production nor can they obtain as great an economic stabilization effectiveness by altering military expenditures as that obtained in the producer countries.

Along the lines of Benoit, the model used to test this hypothesis was:

$$Y' = f(I', F, ME) \quad (3.1)$$

where Y' is the 1970–82 growth in GDP, I' is the 1970–82 growth in investment, F is a financing variable, and ME is 1981 military expenditures. The financing variables used were PDA and PDB (external public debt for 1970 and 1982, respectively) and GDP (1982 central government fiscal surplus or deficit as a percent of GDP).[17] The estimated regression equations were as follows:

Total Sample

$$Y' = 0.72I' + 0.3PDB - 0.25ME; \; r^2 = 71.9, \; df = 19 \quad (3.2)$$
$$(5.3) \quad\;\;\; (2.3) \quad\;\; (-1.5)$$

Producers

$$Y' = 1.29I' + 0.39GDB + 0.40ME; \; r^2 = 96.7, \; df = 7; \quad (3.3)$$
$$(8.4) \quad\;\;\;\; (2.8) \quad\;\;\;\; (2.6)$$

Nonproducers

$$Y' = 1.02I' + 0.53PDA + 0.02GDB - 0.56ME; \; r^2 = 87.7, \; df = 10 \quad (3.4)$$
$$(3.76) \quad\;\; (2.55) \quad\;\;\;\; (0.05) \quad\;\; (-3.03)$$

$$Y' = 1.05I' + 0.39PDB - 0.35ME; \; r^2 = .82, \; df = 10 \quad (3.5)$$
$$(5.3) \quad\;\;\;\; (1.9) \quad\;\;\; (-2.0)$$

The regression equations confirm the positive role that military expenditures have on economic growth in producer countries. While the coefficient of the military expenditure variable is negative but statistically insignificant for the entire sample (equation 3.2), it is positive and statistically significant for the producing countries (equation 3.3). In addition, the estimated coefficient is negative and statistically significant for the nonproducers (equations 3.4 and 3.5). These results indicate that in the non-producer countries the military expenditures for such things as imported equipment, operations, and maintenance—items with significant opportunity costs—represent a drain on economic growth. Military expenditures in the producing countries contribute to economic growth presumably from spin-offs, other externalities derived from arms production, and the stabilization function that expanding and contracting military production can have on the economy.

In all equations, the coefficient of the investment variable is, as expected, statistically significant. In terms of the financial variable, the results indicate that the producing nations obtain higher rates of growth through fiscal policy (the lower the government deficit as a percentage of GDP, the higher the overall rate of growth). For this group of countries, external public debt as of 1982 did not play a significant role in affecting overall growth.

On the other hand, the non-producing countries have not experienced any correlation between their fiscal surpluses and deficits and overall economic growth. During the 1970-82 period, however, they relied on external public sector borrowing to accelerate their overall rates of growth in real gross domestic product.

These results are quite consistent with the results obtained from the discriminant analysis and examination of means for the producing and non-producing countries. The producing countries have apparently less of a foreign exchange constraint than the non-producing countries and therefore may be relatively more constrained by domestic resources.[18] If this is the case, public savings generated by the budgetary process would raise the growth constraint imposed by domestic resources, thus facilitating higher overall rates of growth. The producing countries, while large external borrowers in the absolute sense, have on the other hand relied less on external funds as a percentage of GDP than the non-producing countries. In short, additional foreign external funds (due to these countries' relatively good foreign exchange earning capabilities) are not as necessary for increasing overall growth as are domestic savings in the form of government surpluses or deficits.

As noted, the government surplus-deficit can also be used as a regulatory device by modifying military procurement and expenditures in the producing countries. The reverse is true for the non-producing countries. These countries' relatively poor foreign exchange earning capabilities mean that augmented sources of foreign exchange in the form of public external borrowing have a much greater impact in raising the foreign exchange constraint on growth than is the case for the producing countries. For the nonproducers, the foreign exchange constraint on growth must be so binding that increased public savings are not capable (due to lack of complementary foreign exchange) of mobilizing resources for higher growth.

Conclusions

Because economists are unable to determine the precise impact military production has on the economy (due to a lack of data on military production), I have had to use indirect tests to determine whether, in the net, military production has an adverse or a positive effect on the Latin American economies.

The empirical results presented in chapters 2 and 3 indicate that:

1. Whether a country in Latin America produces armaments or not can be determined by purely economic considerations largely relating to the relative availability of foreign exchange.
2. The overall impact of total military expenditure in the producing countries tends to produce positive effects on the observed rate of real growth in gross domestic product. In the non-producing countries, the overall impact of total military expenditure was negative with regard to real economic growth.
3. The producer countries were able to use fiscal policy, as measured by the government surplus-deficit as a percent of GDP, to achieve higher rates of growth, that is, reductions in the government deficit were associated with higher rates of growth. The nonproducers, on the other hand, financed higher rates of growth with external borrowing.

It is clear that the producer countries are more capable of obtaining positive benefits from military expenditure than the non-producer countries. As a group, they appear to be able to link their state enterprises to overall fiscal policy and, consequently, obtain a greater impact on growth through their stabilization policies. The nonproducers, on the other hand, apparently lack not only any positive spin-offs from military expenditures, but also the ability to control levels of military expenditure as part of an overall stabilization effort undertaken to facilitate higher rates of overall economic growth.

Beside the political motives for undertaking arms production, certain countries in Latin America (those with relatively abundant foreign exchange as measured by exports and imports) are able to justify military production on purely economic grounds. The benefits of production show up largely in the macro sense and are apparently sufficient to offset the higher cost of domestically producing defense items rather than importing these items.

Given the importance of budgetary surpluses and deficits in affecting overall growth in the producer countries, the next chapter examines the manner in which Latin American arms producers and nonproducers integrate their military expenditures into the budgetary process.

Notes

1. Steven E. Miller, "Arms and the Third World: Indigenous Weapons Production," *PSIS Occasional Paper no. 3* (University of Geneva Program for Strategic and International Studies, December 1980).

2. Cf. Albert O. Hirschman, "The Political Economy of Import Substituting Industrialization in Latin America," *Quarterly Journal of Economics* (February 1968), pp. 1–32.

3. James E. Katz, "Understanding Arms Production in Developing Countries" in J.E. Katz, ed., *Arms Production in Developing Countries* (Lexington, Mass.: Lexington Books, 1984), pp. 5–7.

4. David K. Whynes, *The Economics of Third World Military Expenditure* (London: Macmillan, 1979), pp. 26–27.

5. *Ibid.*, p. 27.

6. Emile Benoit, "Growth and Defense in Developing Countries," *Economic Development and Cultural Change* (January 1978), pp. 271–80.

7. *Ibid.*, p. 279–80.

8. Mary Kaldor, "The Military in Development," *World Development* (June 1976), pp. 459–82.

9. Alice H. Amsden, "Kaldor's 'The Military and Development'—A Comment," *World Development* (August 1977), p. 757.

10. R.D. McKinley and A.S. Cohen, "The Economic Performance of Military Regimes: A Cross-National Aggregate Study," *British Journal of Political Science* (July 1976), pp. 291–310.

11. David Dabelko and James M. McCormick, "Opportunity Costs of Defense: Some Cross-National Evidence," *Journal of Peace Research* (April 1977), pp. 145–54.

12. Cf. P.C. Frederiksen and R.E. Looney, "Defense Expenditures and Economic Growth in Developing Countries," *Armed Forces and Society* (Summer 1983), pp. 633–45; P.C. Frederiksen and R.E. Looney, "Defense Expenditures and Economic Growth in Developing Countries," *Journal of Economic Development* (July 1982), pp. 113–25; and P.C. Frederiksen and

R.E. Looney, "Defense Expenditures and Economic Growth in Developing Countries: A Reply," *Armed Forces and Society* (Winter 1985), pp. 298–301.

13. P.C. Frederiksen and R.E. Looney, "Another Look at Defense Spending and Economic Growth in Less Developed Countries," *Defense Analysis* (September 1985), pp. 205–10.

14. David Lim, "Another Look at Growth and Defense in Less Developed Countries," *Economic Development and Cultural Change* (January 1983), pp. 377–84.

15. *Ibid.*, p. 384.

16. P.C. Frederiksen and R.E. Looney, "Another Look at Defense Spending and Economic Growth in Less Developed Countries," *op. cit.*

17. In Benoit's original work, foreign aid was the second variable in the regression equation. Benoit postulated a positive sign for this variable, assuming that aid facilitated overall growth through loosening the foreign exchange constraint. Since foreign aid has played a relatively minor role over the past decade in Latin America, public external borrowing served as a more appropriate measure of the impact of foreign external savings on overall country growth. Domestic savings efforts on the part of government as proxied by the public sector's surplus or deficit (*GDP*) as a percent of GDP could similarly be assumed to contribute to overall resource availability and thus higher growth. Cf. L. Taylor, *Structuralist Macroeconomics: Applicable Models for the Third World* (New York: Basic Books, 1983), pp. 130–34.

18. The concept of independent binding external (foreign exchange) and internal (domestic savings) constraints on growth was first developed by H. Chenery. For Latin America, see H. Chenery and P. Eckstein, "Development Alternatives for Latin America," *Economic Development Report no. 29* (Cambridge, Mass.: Harvard University, Project for Quantitative Research in Economic Development, 1967). For an empirical estimation of the binding constraint (external or internal) on growth in industrial Latin American countries, see Luis Landau, "Saving Functions for Latin America" in H. Chenery, ed., *Studies in Development Planning* (Cambridge, Mass: Harvard University Press, 1971), pp. 299–321.

4
Defense Expenditures and the Budgetary Process in Latin America

The economic climate in Latin America during the 1970s and into the 1980s has been particularly unstable, not only because of oil price changes but also because of wide-ranging fluctuations in commodity prices and induced changes in patterns of world demand. One of the consequences of this relative economic instability (and resulting stagnation) has been an increasing difficulty for governments to finance their customary budgets.

The purpose of the following analysis is to extend the findings of the previous chapter through an examination of the manner in which the defense section in arms-producing countries is linked to fiscal policy, presumably enabling fluctuations in defense spending to perform as a fairly powerful fiscal tool. Put differently, the purpose of this chapter is to examine whether or not there is a greater tendency and scope for linking defense expenditures to overall government expenditures in arms-producing countries than in non–arms-producing countries.

The Budgetary Process

In the absence of a market mechanism to serve as a means of allocating resources, the defense sector receives its inputs from public funds by means of the budget. In its ideal form, the budgetary process can be thought of as follows:

> Defense budgeting is an organizational routine that reflects the interplay of strategic objectives and national resource constraints. As such, it is a two-tiered exercise in choice: a means of making decisions as to the resources to be given to a state's defense establishment and, on a different level, a way of deciding how these resources will be allocated within the defense establishment.[1]

In most Latin American countries today, the annual defense budget often consists simply of the presentation of estimates to the central government by the senior officials of each of the armed services, and the allocation of this or of an adjusted amount by the treasury department to the service concerned. Such an allocation system clearly gives rise to a number of problems.

For one thing, the traditional method of annual budgeting is said to ignore the problems of military planning. A substantial proportion of military expenditure in the arms-producing countries is oriented toward longer-term investment (for example, the establishment of additional defense manufacturing industries or the expansion of existing ones), so military officials are under constant pressure to insure a continued supply of funds to cover the recurrent costs associated with military production.[2]

Clearly, due to its vested interest in maintaining a viable arms industry, the military in arms-producing nations should have an even greater incentive to overstate its requirements than the military in the non-producing countries. In other words, in the arms-producing countries, additional expenditures (and/or deficits) might be incurred to prevent cancellation of projects which, because of their inadequate initial costings, would otherwise be written off as resource cost.

If this view of the budgeting process is correct, economists should expect to find that military expenditures, because of their ties to domestic arms production, are more closely linked to government expenditures in defense-producing countries than in non-producing countries. In addition, given the producers' strong export positions identified in chapter 2, one should not expect external financing to play a large role in affecting the military expenditures of this group of countries.

Given that the overall needs for defense expenditures may be deferred by slowly changing strategic internal needs, economists would expect relatively fewer linkages between government expenditures (and/or deficits or external borrowing) in the non-arms-producing countries than in the case of the producing countries.

Empirical Tests

To confirm the linkage between defense industries, the public sector, and military expenditures, military expenditures (ME) were regressed on total national armed forces (AF) in 1981, public consumption as a percentage of 1982 GDP (PCB), population (POP), and gross domestic product (GDP) 1982.

The results for the nonproducers in table 4-1 indicate that the size of the armed forces (AF) was largely responsible for explaining military expenditures, followed by GDP (with armed forces not affected by GDP). Strategic security motivation and the size of the country defined military expenditures, with the size of the armed forces defined largely by noneconomic considerations.

In the case of the arms-producing countries, the most significant variable associated with military expenditures was government consumption as a percentage of gross domestic product (PCB), accounting for over 63 percent of the fluctuation in military expenditures. (See table 4-2.) Total population (POP) and government consumption as a percentage of gross domestic product together accounted for slightly over 82 percent of the fluctuation in military expenditure. Size (as measured by population) and overall government involvement in the economy (as measured by the share of public consumption in gross domestic product) therefore account for the bulk of the difference in military expenditures in the arms-producing countries. Note that for these countries, the size of the armed forces was not statistically significant in explaining the overall level of military expenditure, that is, there was no significant link between the perceived need for defense expenditures (as measured by the size of the armed forces) and actual military expenditures. Note also that the overall economic condition of the country (as measured by gross national product) was also insignificant when regressed on total military expenditures, indicating that ability per se to finance higher levels of military expenditure was not necessarily manifested in actual expenditure—with government's relative involvement in the economy a much more significant measure of military spending.

As noted, size (gross domestic product) and population were insignificant in explaining variations between the nonproducers' armed forces. In contrast, several close associations existed in the arms-producing countries between economic variables and the overall size of the armed forces. The overall population of these countries accounted for slightly over 85 percent of the size of the armed forces, with government consumption as a proportion of the gross domestic product statistically significant in explaining intercountry overall differences in armed forces size.

Also, for the producers, the size of the labor force (not shown here) clearly dominates the gross national product in these countries in explaining the overall size of the armed forces. In short, it appears that the armed forces in defense-producing countries might be used as a source of employment, while in non-producing countries employment considerations do not seem to affect the overall size of the armed forces.

Table 4-1
Determinants of Defense Expenditures: Latin American Non-Defense Producers

	Independent Variables						Statistics		
Equation	AF	GDP	PCB	POP	IMFGED	PDB	r^2	F	df
ME =	0.76 (3.61)						0.592	13.04	10
ME =		0.65 (2.58)					0.426	6.69	10
ME =	0.50 (2.19)	0.68 (2.27)	0.23 (0.81)				0.806	6.93	8
AF =		0.28 (0.92)					0.078	0.85	11
AF =				0.26 (0.86)			0.070	0.75	11
AF =					0.68 (2.51)		0.473	6.30	8
AF =						0.43 (1.54)	0.192	2.38	11

Notes: See text for definition of variables.
( ) = t statistic.
r^2 = correlation coefficient.
F = F statistic.
df = degrees of freedom.

Table 4-2
Determinants of Military Expenditure: Latin American Defense Producers

Equation	Independent Variables							Statistics		
	PCB	POP	AF	PDB	PDB75	ECNIB	GDP	r^2	F	df
(1) ME =	0.80 (3.24)							0.637	10.52	7
(2)	0.87 (4.60)	0.44 (2.31)						0.825	11.79	7
(3)	0.57 (2.09)		0.39 (1.42)					0.741	7.16	7
(4)	0.94 (4.71)	1.20 (1.57)		-0.78 (-1.03)				0.861	8.32	7
(5)	0.96 (5.67)	1.47 (2.35)			-1.05 (-1.71)			0.898	11.83	7
(6)	0.84 (4.69)	1.27 (1.90)				-0.86 (-1.28)		0.876	9.44	7
(7)	0.72 (2.43)		0.16 (0.47)				0.31 (1.14)	0.805	5.50	7

Notes: See text for definition of variables.
( ) = t statistic.
r^2 = correlation coefficient.
F = F statistic.
df = degrees of freedom.

Interestingly enough, the arms producer group of countries has, in addition to taxes ($RTCRYB$) financed their public consumption largely out of government deficits (GDB), but not out of public external debt in 1970 or 1982 (PDA or PDB), while the non-producer group has relied on taxes, with government deficits not affecting the overall share of public consumption in gross domestic product. (See tables 4-3 and 4-4.) From this, one might conclude that defense producers have found it expedient to subsidize their defense industries through government deficits due to the contribution that these industries make to meeting the politically determined overall level of military expenditures. This activity has apparently been justified by the positive linkage between military expenditures and the overall rate of economic growth in the producing countries identified in the previous chapter.

The nonproducers have not used government deficits to finance public consumption, apparently because they do not have the need to subsidize state enterprises in the arms area. In other words, they have not been compelled to increase their deficits to maintain arms production (and employment) in state enterprises because these enterprises are clearly not viable in their economies. As noted below, the scope for using countercyclical fiscal policy may be considerably less for this group of countries than for the arms producers.

It might be argued that countries such as the arms producers, with a relatively greater degree of government participation in the economy, are subject to greater spending pressures. The mere fact that their government is large is probably evidence of past spending pressures, with the cumulative effect that the public has come to rely more and more on government for a broad range of goods and services. Under these circumstances, it may be more difficult for a government to restrain expenditures in the face of revenue constraints when the impact on the economy would be substantial.

According to this line of argument, the relative level of government participation in an economy is a structural factor in the sense that increasing government intervention is a very difficult process to reverse. The public learns to depend on the government for services and employment that it provides and places severe pressure on the authorities to run deficits rather than reduce expenditures. If the arms-producing countries as a group had a relatively large public sector involvement in the economy, the empirical patterns observed here between government consumption and military expenditures and between public sector deficits and the overall share of public consumption in gross domestic product might be spurious correlations. In actuality, however, public consumption expenditure as a

Table 4-3
Determinants of Public Consumption's Share in GDP: Latin American Arms Producers

Equation	Independent Variables								Statistics		
	RTCRY	GDB	GNPPER	PDA	PDB	PBCB	PDPB75	IMFGED	r^2	F	df
(1) PCB =	4.22 (3.51)	-2.71 (-3.47)	-2.86 (-3.09)						0.820	4.57	6
(2)	5.29 (9.88)	3.46 (-9.77)	-3.55 (-8.92)	-0.48 (-4.19)					0.982	26.82	6
(3)	4.24 (13.91)	-2.98 (-14.74)	-2.75 (-11.68)		-0.50 (-6.69)				0.992	64.22	6
(4)	4.09 (9.79)	-2.77 (-10.22)	-2.69 (-8.32)			-0.43 (-4.79)			0.985	34.33	6
(5)	5.53 (5.71)	-3.02 (-5.76)	-4.08 (-5.08)				-0.71 (-2.27)		0.950	9.50	6
(6)	0.89 (2.91)	-1.00 (-3.11)						0.80 (3.27)	0.947	6.03	4

Notes: See text for definition of variables.
    ( ) = t statistic.
    r^2 = correlation coefficient.
    F = F statistic.
    df = degrees of freedom.
    PDPB75 = public external debt as percentage of GNP, 1975.

Table 4-4
Determinants of Public Consumption's Share in GDP: Latin America Total Country Supply, Non-Arms Producers

Equation	RTCRYB	GDB	Independent Variables GNPPER	PDA	PDB	r^2	Statistics F	df
Total Sample PCB =								
(1)	0.53 (2.32)					0.278	5.39	15
(2)	0.67 (3.48)	-0.57 (-2.96)				0.581	8.32	14
(3)	1.14 (6.05)	-0.56 (-4.09)	-0.67 (-3.60)			0.808	15.39	14
(4)	1.11 (3.39)	-0.78 (-2.31)		0.35 (0.78)	-0.22 (-0.51)	0.524	4.97	15
Nonproducers								
(5)	0.75 (2.97)					0.558	8.83	8
(6)	0.62 (2.54)	-0.43 (-1.74)				0.722	6.50	7
(7)	1.24 (6.74)	-0.01 (-0.05)	-0.80 (-4.31)			0.951	25.76	7
(8)	1.35 (3.68)		-0.82 (-3.56)	0.25 (1.03)	-0.12 (-0.34)	0.930	13.35	8

Notes: See text for definition of variables.
( ) = t statistic.
r^2 = correlation coefficient.
F = F statistic.
df = degrees of freedom.

percentage of GDP is considerably lower for the arms-producing countries than the non-producing countries (13.0 percent versus 16.1 percent). Also, the average deficit/gross domestic product ratio is considerably higher for the nonproducers than for the arms-producing countries (-5.9 percent versus -3.4 percent).

These patterns would appear to rule out spurious correlation as an explanation for the observed link between increased deficits leading to increased public expenditures leading in turn to increased military expenditures that was found for arms producers by not for non-arms producers.

Defense Expenditures as a Tool for Stabilization

The above analysis does not suggest that the arms-producing countries are able to or do use changing levels of military expenditures as a major tool in stabilizing their respective economies. It merely suggests that, on the whole, given their economies' relative abundance of foreign exchange compared to the nonproducers', these countries have more scope for the use of fiscal policy along the lines adopted by the advanced countries. The regression analysis suggests that they take advantage of this opportunity.

In general, cyclical or short-run instability of overall economic activity may be caused by:

1. Variation in enterprise or household investment;
2. Changes in the volume of exports because of fluctuations in external demand;
3. Changes in terms of international trade;
4. Natural conditions including weather, pests, and plant and animal diseases;
5. Errors in the conduct of fiscal or monetary policies;
6. Political uncertainty or disturbances.

The contrast in the economic structures of less-developed countries suggest that the scope for stabilizing policies and their content will differ considerably from one group to another.[3] In industrial countries, a broadly Keynesian interpretation came to be widely accepted in the years following World War II. According to this view, fluctuations in activity could be reduced by stabilizing aggregate demand. Fiscal measures could compensate for autonomous fluctuations in domestic investment demand and in demand for exports, and thus would prevent the increases in unemployment and excess capacity that would otherwise occur.

The application of fiscal instruments to offset fluctuations in aggregate demand was aptly referred to as "compensatory fiscal policy." Variations in government expenditures and predictable responses of household consumption to changes in tax reductions were central to the policy. Expenditure increases and tax reductions were prescribed when a downturn in activity began, and opposite fiscal actions were called for when aggregate demand threatened to become excessive and to result in rising prices and a balance of payments deficit. The tax changes could be either discretionary or automatic responses to changing activity. Expenditure adjustments depended mainly on discretionary actions, with some form of automaticity in response of transfer payments to economic activity.

In contrast, it is said that developing economies relying more on primary than industrial production when suffering, say, a crop failure cannot compensate for that loss of real income by immediately producing more of other goods and services.[4] Neither can a loss of purchasing power due to a decline in the prices of exports relative to the prices of imports be offset by these countries in the short run by stimulating domestic activity.

If a developing country that experiences such misfortunes has no foreign exchange reserves and no capacity to borrow abroad or obtain additional aid, it will have no alternative to austerity. It will have to avoid a balance of payments deficit by cutting imports. Given these assumptions, the government should follow fiscal policies that will accentuate the decline in incomes. Thus, tax increases and expenditure cuts will be needed rather than the tax reductions and expenditure increases prescribed by the doctrine of compensatory fiscal policy. Usually, quantitative restrictions on imports will be instituted or intensified, but contractionary fiscal measures will be advisable to strengthen them and make them less inefficient. The net result is usually a marked decline in income and employment, rather than the stabilizing impact on these variables produced by fiscal policy in the more industrialized nations.

Given the fact that the arms-producing countries in Latin America have relatively greater access to foreign exchange than do the nonproducers, these countries will have relatively more opportunity to use fiscal policy in a countercyclical manner along the lines adopted in the advanced countries; that is, they can be more concerned with domestic stabilization and less with external stabilization than can the nonproducers, who must be more concerned with stabilizing their balance of payments.

The link between government deficits leading to increases in public consumption leading in turn to increased military expenditures present in the arms-producing countries but absent in the non-arms-producing countries suggests that, first, the former have an environment facilitating countercyclical use of military expenditures to stabilize the economy and, second, that use is made of altered military expenditures to stabilize economic activity. For nonproducers, scope for countercyclical fiscal policy using, in part, altered levels of military expenditures apparently does not exist.

Conclusions

With regard to defense industries in Latin America, the main findings of the analysis to this point are:

1. It is possible to profile defense and non-defense producers in Latin America exclusively by economic variables, with access to foreign exchange being the most important discriminating factor;
2. In an environment of relatively abundant foreign exchange, increased military expenditures relying in part on domestically produced equipment seem to have a positive effect on overall economic growth;
3. Increased military expenditures in countries constrained by lack of foreign exchange and possessing no domestic state enterprises in the defense area experience negative impacts on overall growth with increased defense expenditures;
4. Defense expenditures are linked largely to increased government consumption expenditures in the arms-producing countries, while simple size (GDP and the size of the armed forces) explains military expenditures in the non-producing countries;
5. Public consumption is facilitated by the willingness and ability to run deficits in the defense-producing countries, while the non-producing countries finance public expenditures largely out of tax revenues;
6. The producing countries have the ability and the willingness to use defense expenditures as a stabilization tool, while the nonproducers are burdened with an environment that precludes this type of activity.

From this economists can conclude that indigenous defense production in Latin America takes place in a certain economic environment characterized by relative availability of foreign exchange. Once established, these defense industries permit military expenditures to contribute to overall growth, while the defense producers control their expenditures on domestic arms largely by controlling the government deficit. Fiscal policy is, therefore, linked to defense expenditures to maintain stability in aggregate demand.

The finding in chapter 3 that defense expenditures improve overall economic performance in the arms-producing countries, while explained in part by the preceding budgetary analysis, may still appear counterintuitive and perhaps only a spurious correlation.

Chapter 5 provides a further step in tracing the specific linkages between military expenditure, arms production, growth, and the overall political economy of Latin American military expenditures. More precisely, the budgetary trade-offs associated with increased military expenditures in both the arms producing and non-arms-producing Latin American countries are examined in some detail to determine if specific biases occur by country type.

Clearly, if there are systematic biases toward economic expenditures (presumably growth-inducing ones) on the part of the producers, the validity of the analysis presented to date would be further confirmed.

Notes

1. R. Burt, *Defense Budgeting: The British and American Cases*, Adelphi Paper No. 112 (London: International Institute for Strategic Studies, 1974), p. 1.

2. David K. Whynes, *The Economics of Third World Military Expenditure* (London: Macmillan, 1979), p. 25.

3. For an expanded treatment of this issue, see Richard Goode, *Government Finance in Developing Countries* (Washington, D.C.: Brookings Institution, 1984), chap. 11.

4. Goode, *op. cit.*, pp. 262–63.

5
Patterns of Defense and Socioeconomic Budgetary Trade-offs in Latin America

As debt service costs have risen and revenue has levelled off or declined, Latin American governments have been forced to reevaluate programs in an effort to curtail government spending. The net result of these developments has been a number of sectoral adjustments in the area of government expenditures.

The purpose of this chapter is to empirically examine the extent, direction, and form of budgetary trade-offs between defense and socioeconomic programs in several of the major Latin American countries. An attempt will be made to answer four specific questions:

1. Is there a significant relationship between defense and socioeconomic expenditures over time?
2. Does defense spending systematically cut spending in socioeconomic programs in the major Latin American countries?
3. Are there any common elements among countries with similar defense and non–defense budget allocations?
4. Are there any systematic biases between defense and nondefense expenditures unique to arms producers (or nonproducers) as a group and, if so, what are these biases?

Trade-off Literature

To date, analyses of budgetary trade-offs have concentrated almost exclusively on the developed countries, proceeded from a variety of theoretical perspectives, and produced conflicting, mixed results. Kathleen Peroff and Margaret Podolak-Warren concluded that the "number of studies which indicates the existence of a tradeoff approximates the number that shows that none exists."[1]

While the bulk of the research on budgetary trade-offs between defense and social program expenditures has focused on the industrial countries of North America and Western Europe, Margaret Hayes has suggested that the problem of trade-offs between defense spending and social investments "is perhaps even more serious in the developing countries."[2] In a major United Nations report, the secretary general argued that when the needs of economic development are so pressing in developing countries, it is "a disturbing thought that these countries have found it necessary to increase military spending so speedily, particularly when their per capita income is so low." The report concluded that military expenditures undoubtedly absorb resources that are "substantial enough to make a considerable difference both in the level of investment for civil purposes and in the volume of resources which can be devoted to improving man's lot through social and other services."[3] The clear implication of the UN report for the developing countries is that increased defense spending may have negative consequences for socioeconomic development programs such as health, education, social security, and economic services.

In a study of the costs of defense in the United States between 1938 and 1969, B.M. Russett concluded that each dollar increase in defense spending resulted in a subtraction of "forty-two cents from personal consumption spending, twenty-nine cents from fixed capital formation, ten cents from exports, five cents from federal government civilian programs and thirteen cents from state and local government activities."[4]

Unfortunately, Russett's analysis is distorted by the data of the World War II years, in which percentage allocations to defense were two to three times larger than in other years. In a reanalysis of the data, J. Hollenhorst and G. Ault divided the 1939–68 series into three wartimes plus peacetime. They found that the majority of the significant trade-off relationships occurred in the World War II period. Other significant trade-offs varied across the four periods; in several instances negative relationships became positives.[5] The authors concluded regarding Russett's question "who pays for defense?" that:

[I]n an "intense" war period (World War II) probably everyone pays. In peacetime, however, and in the "lesser" wars of the recent past (Korea, Vietnam) the consumer pays nearly the entire bill, while the proportion of GNP consisting of state-local government expenditures and some types of fixed investment expenditures have, at times, increased along with increases in defense spending.[6]

Russett, himself, in a more detailed analysis which omitted the World War II period, found a substantial reduction in the number of significant substitution relationships.

For a variety of reasons, the United States is relatively atypical in both the pattern and content of its defense spending. While this in no way reduces the importance of the concern over possible negative trade-offs with other program expenditures, it does make the U.S. case inappropriate as a model for cross-national hypothesis testing.[7]

Smith found from his analysis of a set of OECD time series that there was a negative association between military expenditures and investment and that this result was robust whether the data were treated as time series, cross-section, or pooled, and for a variety of assumptions about stochastic structure.[8] Frederick Pryor performed an analysis similar to the Russett research using data from twelve countries in Eastern and Western Europe, plus the United States and Canada. In cross-section analysis of the fourteen countries in two different years, he found no statistically significant substitution relationships (negative regression coefficients) in either year.[9] Using time series data for 1950–62, he found "defense expenditures do not have a statistically significant relationship with non-military budgetary expenditures in any country."[10] Breaking down the nonmilitary component into GNP aggregates (private consumption, domestic investment, domestic plus foreign investment, and current civilian government expenditures), he found extremely mixed relationships. Only in those countries with relatively high defense budget components were substitution relationships found, and only with current government civilian expenditures, excluding transfers. When transfers were included, no substitution relationships were found for the same nations.

Eighty percent of world military expenditures were accounted for by six nations, five of which were included in the Pryor sample. The finding that substitution relationships occur only in those countries with high defense budgets is therefore striking. With one exception, none of the countries studied by Pryor would be classified as developing, but the United Nations notes that the military budgets of developing countries are increasing almost twice as fast as those of the developed countries.[11] Is this pattern of trade-offs in the Third World similar to that of developed countries? Benoit's major study of the impact of defense on economic growth in a sample of forty-four developing countries concluded, much to the author's surprise, that "the evidence simply did not allow one to conclude that any . . . adverse net effect on economic growth had occurred as a result of defense activities."[12] While Benoit's aggregate measure of economic growth obscures some of the more critical issues of distribution of economic resources, the conclusion he draws suggests that one must question the assumptions with which one approaches the problems of trade-offs imposed by military allocations.[13]

Most scholars studying the developing states have approached the guns-versus-butter question from a slightly different point of view—the comparison of policy outputs of military and civilian regimes and the consequence of militarism for modernization. Along these lines, political scientists have employed various methodologies and examined a wide range of variables for the purpose of evaluating the performance of military and civilian governments in Latin America.[14] Of the many hypotheses advanced and tested, one of the more interesting has been the respective roles of military and civilian regimes in the arms race versus their promotion of socioeconomic well-being. Although approaches for examining a defense-social welfare trade-off or a prodefense versus proeconomic development stance among regime types have varied, political scientists during the past several decades have generally treated regime type as the independent variable and various macro-public policy indicators as dependent variables. Similar methodologies have been employed by historians. Sociologists, in what is becoming a rapidly growing body of literature, have addressed various issues pertaining to the sociology of the military in developing countries, although most of their attention has been confined to regions outside of Latin America.[15]

Eric Nordlinger summarized the "prevailing interpretation":

> The likely consequences of military rule are economic growth, the modernization of economic and social structures and a more equitable distribution of scarce economic values and opportunities. As sponsors of these types of change, soldiers in mufti are depicted as progressive forces, whose politicization is to be commended if not recommended, rather than being condemned as usurpation of civil authority.[16]

Nordlinger, himself, disagreed with this interpretation, arguing that "except under certain conditions (for example, particularly low levels of economic development and political mobilization) soldiers in mufti are not agents of modernization" but rather act in pursuance of their military corporate interests and protect "a particular type of political stability" and middle class interests and identities.[17]

Philippe Schmitter found conflicting hypotheses in the literature on the impact of military intervention: (1) the military is dedicated to the preservation of order and maintenance of the social status quo; (2) the military is dedicated to national development goals including "important increments in the role of public authority in areas such as investment, health and education, income redistribution and industrial management;" and (3) the military is only one of several groups competing for hegemony over the political system "and the substance of policy-making is relatively indifferent to military or civilian hegemony."[18] Using both cross-sectional and longitudinal data on a variety of political and economic indicators for twenty Latin American countries, Schmitter concluded that:

> Indicators of overall system performance (outcomes) are much less predictably affected by regime-type or changes in regime-type than are indicators of direct governmental allocations (outputs) ... but no regime type seems to exclusively responsible for developmental success in Latin America. ... The military in power definitely tend to spend more on themselves—above all when they are on-again, off-again regimes. ... Civilian regimes definitely spend less on defense (when they are not plagued by frequent interruptions and threats) and more on welfare.[19]

Both types of regimes have erratic records on public investment, a fact which Schmitter acknowledged is "probably due to vagaries in resource availability more than to internal dynamics."[20]

On the other hand, in a major study Joseph Pluta concluded that little apparent relationship existed between regime type and either level of defense spending or size of armed forces. Pluta found that civilian governments, however, did tend to import a higher real dollar value of arms. Four of the five social measures used by Pluta indicated that civilian governments have taken a more active interest in social programs than their military counterparts have. Civilian governments spend more for education and health, while reductions in infant mortality are more substantial under these regimes. They also have greater newsprint consumption; hence, the demand for reading materials and the flow of (written) information is larger, indicating a greater interest in education on the part of civilian rulers.

Pluta noted that the finding regarding regime type and the level of military spending is not surprising and is supportive of similar conclusions advanced in earlier studies. The ambiguous relationship between regime type and size of armed forces may simply be a reflection of the regime type–defense budget ambiguity. However, the relatively high level of civilian government arms purchases may suggest a number of factors including, perhaps, less knowledge of technologically sophisticated weaponry, military budgets, and/or real defense needs, as well as a desire to placate the military, in effect, to reduce the likelihood of armed revolt and/or opposition to civilian-initiated reform programs.[21]

In another study of civilian and military regimes in Latin America, Dickson found that: (1) military regimes appear to have been more fiscally conservative than civilian ones and (2) civilian regimes appear to have been more developmentally oriented than military ones.[22] Military regimes were inclined to spend less and run lower deficits, even though they spent more on the military. They showed a lower rate of increase in the cost of living and maintained a stronger international liquidity position for the central bank. Civilian regimes, for their part, spent more, did more for education, and effected higher savings and investment rates, although the military had an edge in electrical production.[23]

In contrast, in her analysis of budgetary allocations to defense and a variety of socioeconomic programs in Brazil between 1950 and 1967, Hayes concluded that military spending did not necessarily yield negative consequences for social and economic investments.[24] She found that "substitutions between military allocations and allocations to other sectors do occur frequently, but that the burden of these substitutions is distributed across all categories at one time or another." Further, she judged that "substitutions are not severe." Overall defense spending "accompanied substantial increases in spending for infrastructure development and aspects of this associated with greater Central Government activity." She did find, on the other hand, that increased defense spending had some negative effects on social spending, but that this "was mild because social investment was not a major priority of any of the regimes examined." Nevertheless, Hayes reported a correlation of -0.23 between defense and social development (education, health, and welfare) expenditures, measured as percentages of the total public budget. In addition, a -0.23 correlation was registered between spending on military personnel and social development expenditures. Although "theoretical generalizations cannot be made and hypotheses cannot be accepted or rejected on the basis of evidence from a single case," Hayes's research seems to indicate a mildly negative trade-off between defense and education expenditures.[25]

In yet another study, Barry Ames and Ed Goff using a pooled cross-state time series data set (eighteen countries, 1948-68) concluded that "education and defense spending both rise and fall at the same time."[26] Correlating defense and education spending in absolute terms, as percentage changes from year to year, and relative to total budget and gross domestic product for individual countries and regimes, Ames and Goff reported rather high positive correlations in the range of +0.29 to +0.96. They reported two slightly negative correlations between defense and education expenditures measured relative to total budget, -0.08 and -0.03 for the pooled analysis and for the individual regimes, respectively. Mindful of serious autocorrelation problems in their analysis, Ames and Goff concluded that, although other unspecifiable policy areas may lose out in the budgetary process, clearly neither education nor defense "gain at the expense of the other."[27]

The evidence of the negative impact of military allocations in either developed or developing states is far less conclusive than Bruce Russett's emphatic, "I assume that defense spending has to come at the expense of something else."[28] To the extent that this generalization is sometimes correct, the evidence is inconclusive as to whether the burden varies from country to country or whether political factors (regime differences) or economic factors (levels and rates of development) have some influence on the frequency, the locus (who pays), and the weight (degree of substitution) of the trade-off burden.

In the following analysis, an attempt is made to build upon previous research reported to date and to specify more precisely the extent, direction, and form of defense-economic social spending trade-offs in the Latin American countries in the 1970s and early 1980s.

Clearly, in the context of this book the objective of this analysis is not to enter the controversy about whether the military is a modernizing agency of change, a nation-builder, or an active participant in the construction of economic and social overhead capital. Nor, alternatively, does it debate whether the military is an impediment to development—a consumer of large amounts of public money for nonproductive goods and services. The results of previous analysis of military goods producers in Latin America indicated that there were positive impacts of increased military expenditures on growth, while the nonproducers experienced negative impacts on growth.[29] Several reasons for this finding were given including the positive spin-off benefits associated with indigenous military production and the role of budgetary stabilization in producing countries. The work below attempts to extend this analysis by asking: Have the producing countries systematically different budgetary trade-offs than the non-producing countries and, if so, what are the implications for predicting likely defense expenditures in the future.

More specifically, when public policy demands exceed the available public resources, budgetary trade-offs are bound to occur between and among different policy areas; one policy area may gain at the expense of other policy areas in the allocation of scarce resources. Budgetary trade-off patterns range on a continuum between two extremes. It may be that increases in defense spending come at the expense of, say, health spending or education spending; that is, as defense spending increases, spending on education or health may actually decrease producing a negative trade-off. This result is sometimes referred to as a substitution effect. Positive trade-off occurs if defense spending increases are matched by real increases in health or education spending. For any particular Latin American country, the actual trade-off will certainly fall somewhere between these two extremes. Of course, it is always possible that defense spending bears no relationship, negative or positive, to education spending, producing a pattern in the middle of the trade-off—no trade-off continuum.

Methodology

Two basic methodological concerns relating to trade-off analysis have been discussed at some length in previous studies. The first relates to the type of data format or design that is most appropriate to a proper assessment of trade-off hypothesis. Which design should be used—a cross-sectional or time series design? The second concern refers to the definition and measurement of the expenditure variables. The present analysis rests upon a time series design wherein expenditure terms are based on ratios (defense and other budgetary expenditures as percentages of total public expenditures).

Several of the trade-off studies just summarized utilized a longitudinal or time series design but without accounting for some of the statistical problems encountered in this type of design. Others have used cross-sectional designs; these analyses have produced mixed findings, often showing no negative or substitution effects. Peroff and Podolak-Warren have argued that cross-sectional analysis is an inadequate approach to this problem in this type of analysis since it only indicates "whether different countries exhibit different priorities at a single point in time."[30] In order to determine the nature of budgetary trade-offs in a particular country, budgetary patterns over time must be examined. In the present case, analysis is based on thirteen annual time series data sets for the 1972–83 time period. The length of the time series varies slightly from country to country. The data are all taken from the International Monetary Fund's *Government Finance Statistics Yearbook* and the Stockholm International Peace Research Institute's *World Armaments and Disarmament:*

SIPRI Yearbook. The advantage of these sources is that similar conventions for categorizing data by expenditure type are constant across all of the countries.

Similar to several other trade-off studies, reliance is made on regression analysis to examine each separate time series.[31] In a regression analysis with nonmilitary spending by type as the dependent variable, defense spending as the independent variable, and various measures of government expenditures or income as the control variable, the unstandardized regression coefficient for the defense spending term indicates the direction and magnitude of the trade-off between defense and other types of government expenditures.

The general hypothesis proposed here is that trade-offs between military and other types of expenditures over time may be a more valid indicator of government priorities than examining the levels of military expenditure between, for example, military and nonmilitary regimes. The identification of a regime as military or civilian is often tenuous. (For instance, how much influence does the military still exert over the nominally civilian government of Argentina today?)[32] In addition, studies claiming that military regimes reduced social expenditures may have been based on spurious correlations. Since historically, military coups in Latin America have often been spurred by economic crises, social service reductions may have been as much a response to the dictates of austerity as an ideological choice.

A review of the trade-off literature indicates that there has been some controversy over how the expenditure variables should be measured in order to test properly for budgetary trade-offs. Peroff and Podolak-Warren point out that the "choice of measure clearly affects the results of the analysis—depending on whether the budget is expanding, stable or contracting."[33] They argue that a negative trade-off may not be detected between absolute or per capita measures of defense and nondefense expenditures, if the budgetary process is, in fact, an expanding sum game represented by a growing public sector. Therefore, the current examination measures defense and nondefense expenditures in terms of their percentages of the total public budget in order to assess policy commitments and relative policy priorities in each of the countries included in the analysis. It is expected that as defense spending increases, nondefense expenditures will decrease; that is, a substitution effect or negative trade-off is hypothesized.

In order to improve the specifications of the regression models and to obtain less biased estimates of the budgetary trade-offs, government expenditures as a percentage of gross domestic product was included as a variable.

The public finance literature indicates the importance of real per capita income as a variable in the rise of public spending and as a significant factor in budgetary trade-offs. Moreover, real per capita income is a measure of the level of economic development and the resources available to the public sector. As a result, this variable was also tested in the regression equations.

Clearly, however, real per capita income may not be the appropriate control variable for all expenditure items and for all countries. Several other logical control variables were (1) government expenditure as a share of gross domestic product, (2) total real government expenditure, (3) real government expenditure per capita, and (4) real gross domestic product.

The regression equation with the highest overall r-square was selected for each defense–government expenditure potential trade-off.

The following linear trade-off equation was estimated for each of the thirteen country time series.[34] The signs of the coefficients represent the expected direction of the relationships:

$$Y_i = A - b_1 X_1 + b_2 X_i + U$$

where Y_i = nondefense spending/total central government spending; i = (1) public services, (2) health, (3) education, (4) social security and welfare, (5) housing, (6) other community services, (7) economic services, and (8) other purposes; X_1 = defense spending/total central government spending; X_i = control variable where i = (1) total central government expenditures/gross domestic product; (2) real central government expenditures (total central government expenditures deflated by the constant price index for 1980=100.00); (3) real gross domestic product (1980=100.00); (4) real central government total expenditures per capita; and (5) real gross domestic product per capita.

Empirical Results

In general, the results for the thirteen countries were quite good in terms of the correlation coefficients obtained, while a number of statistically significant relationships were found between defense expenditures and other government expenditures. On a country-by-country basis, the statistically significant relationships found were:

Venezuela (see table 5-1)
  Negative trade-offs between defense and other government expenditures:
    1. public services,
    2. social security and welfare,

3. housing, and
   4. other purposes.

Positive trade-offs between defense and other government expenditures:
   1. economic services.

Brazil (see table 5-2)

Negative trade-offs between defense and other government expenditures:
   1. housing, and
   2. other community services.

Positive trade-offs between defense and other government expenditures:
   none.

Argentina (see table 5-3)

Negative trade-offs between defense and other government expenditures:
   1. public services, and
   2. education.

Positive trade-offs between defense and other government expenditures:
   1. other purposes.

Chile (see table 5-4)

Negative trade-offs between defense and other government expenditures:
   1. public services,
   2. education,
   3. social security, and
   4. other purposes.

Positive trade-offs between defense and other government expenditures:
   1. health,
   2. housing, and
   3. economic services.

Ecuador (see table 5-5)

Negative trade-offs between defense and other government expenditures:
   1. social security,
   2. economic services, and
   3. health.

Positive trade-offs between defense and other government expenditures:
   none.

Dominican Republic (see table 5-6)
Negative trade-offs between defense and other government expenditures:
   1. public services, and
   2. other purposes.

Positive trade-offs between defense and other government expenditures:
   none.

Mexico (see table 5-7)
Negative trade-offs between defense and other government expenditures:
   1. education.

Positive trade-offs between defense and other government expenditures:
   economic services.

Peru (see table 5-8)
Negative trade-offs between defense and other government expenditures:
   none.

Positive trade-offs between defense and other government expenditures:
   none.

Bolivia (see table 5-9)
Negative trade-offs between defense and other government expenditures:
   1. economic services, and
   3. other purposes.

Positive trade-offs between defense and other government expenditures:
   1. public services,
   2. education,
   3. health, and
   4. other community services.

Paraguay (see table 5-10)
Negative trade-offs between defense and other government expenditures:
   1. economic services.

Positive trade-offs between defense and other government expenditures:
   1. public services,
   2. health, and
   3. social security.

Costa Rica (see table 5-11)
Negative trade-offs between defense and other government expenditures:
1. health.

Positive trade-offs between defense and other government expenditures:
1. other government services.

Uruguay (see table 5-12)
Negative trade-offs between defense and other government expenditures:
none.

Positive trade-offs between defense and other government expenditures:
1. health,
2. social security, and
3. other community services.

El Salvador (see table 5-13)
Negative trade-offs between defense and other government expenditures:
1. public services,
2. education,
3. health,
4. social security,
5. housing, and
6. other community services.

Positive trade-offs between defense and other government expenditures:
1. other purposes.

Several patterns emerge:

1. In general, those countries with negative trade-offs appear to have them for all of the social expenditures—public services, education, health, and social security and welfare. Thus, with the exception of a positive trade-off in Chile between defense and health, all the statistically significant trade-offs for Venezuela, Brazil, Argentina, Chile, Ecuador, Dominican Republic, Mexico, Peru, and El Salvador were negative between this category of government expenditures and defense.

2. With the exception of a negative trade-off for Costa Rica between defense and health, Bolivia, Paraguay, Uruguay, and Costa Rica all had positive trade-offs between defense and public services, education, health, and social security and welfare.

Table 5-1
Venezuela: Defense Expenditures-Budgetary Trade-offs, 1972-83

	Budget Categories								Control Variables				Statistics		
Equation	Public Services	Education	Health	Social Security, Welfare	Housing	Other Community Services	Economic Services	Other Purposes	Government Expenditures per GDP	Government expenditures	Government Expenditures per Capita	RHO	r^2	F	DW
(1)	-1.28 (-3.36)								-0.07 (-3.47)			-0.36 (-1.31)	0.613	6.33	1.74
(2)		-0.78 (-1.43)							-0.05 (-2.14)			0.05 (0.19)	0.375	2.40	1.79
(3)			-0.21 (-1.62)							-0.09 (-5.23)		-0.34 (-1.81)	0.956	88.30	1.22
(4)				-0.60 (-2.33)							-0.01 (-2.33)	-0.09 (-0.28)	0.497	3.96	2.85
(5)					-1.94 (-2.19)					0.03 (-2.12)		-0.07 (0.22)	0.378	2.43	1.93
(6)						0.10 (0.83)			0.03 (0.66)			0.93 (8.51)	0.086	0.37	1.11
(7)							4.91 (2.56)				0.01 (2.44)	-0.30 (-1.03)	0.458	3.39	2.25
(8)								-1.78 (-2.04)	-0.03 (-1.01)			-0.22 (-0.76)	0.423	2.94	2.22

Sources: Data came from International Monetary Fund, *Government Finance Statistics Yearbook*, various issues; International Monetary Fund, *International Financial Statistics Yearbook, 1984*.

Notes: Estimates are made using Cochrane-Orcutt two-stage iteration process for serial correlation.
( ) = t statistic.
F = F statistic.
DW = Durbin-Watson statistic.

Table 5-2
Brazil: Defense Expenditure-Budgetary Trade-offs, 1972-82

	Budget Categories								Control Variables				Statistics		
Equation	Public Services	Education	Health	Social Security, Welfare	Housing	Other Community Services	Economic Services	Other Purposes	Government Expenditures per GDP	Government expenditures	Government Expenditures per Capita	RHO	r^2	F	DW
(1)	-0.03 (-0.78)								0.09 (0.06)			0.08 (0.25)	0.205	0.77	1.55
(2)		-0.04 (-0.08)							-0.04 (-1.90)			-0.14 (-0.04)	0.930	40.16	1.94
(3)			-0.05 (-0.37)								-0.08 (-0.24)	-0.43 (-1.53)	0.377	1.81	2.14
(4)				-0.03 (-0.26)						-0.03 (-0.50)		-0.27 (-0.87)	0.338	1.53	2.25
(5)					-0.07 (-2.00)				-0.10 (-2.02)			0.09 (0.30)	0.395	1.96	2.30
(6)						-0.05 (-2.32)					-0.02 (-3.42)	-0.05 (-0.14)	0.721	7.78	1.93
(7)							-0.02 (-1.64)		-1.09 (-1.45)			0.78 (4.00)	0.337	1.53	1.46
(8)								-0.09 (-1.32)			-0.03 (-0.14)	-0.07 (-0.24)	0.639	5.31	1.72

Sources: Military data came from Stockholm International Peace Research Institute, *World Armaments and Disarmament: SIPRI Yearbook, 1984*; other data are from International Monetary Fund, *Government Finance Statistics Yearbook*, various issues; International Monetary Fund, *International Financial Statistics Yearbook, 1984*.

Notes: Estimates are made using Cochrane-Orcutt two-stage iteration procedure for serial correlation correction.

( ) = t statistic.
F = F statistic.
DW = Durbin-Watson statistic.

Table 5-3
Argentina: Defense Expenditures–Budgetary Trade-offs, 1972-82

	Budget Categories								Control Variables			Statistics		
Equation	Public Services	Education	Health	Social Security, Welfare	Housing	Other Community Services	Economic Services	Other Purposes	Government Expenditures per GDP	GDP	RHO	r^2	F	DW
(1)	-0.03 (-2.27)								-0.04 (-3.19)		0.51 (1.77)	0.720	7.73	2.32
(2)		0.08 (-4.35)							-0.03 (-1.47)		0.08 (0.24)	0.766	9.86	1.80
(3)			0.01 (-1.94)							0.03 (-1.44)	0.22 (0.75)	0.429	2.25	1.96
(4)				-0.01 (-1.46)					-0.03 (-0.51)		0.85 (4.91)	0.265	1.08	1.37
(5)					-0.08 (-1.05)					-0.08 (-2.00)	0.49 (1.80)	0.375	1.80	1.84
(6)						0.018 (1.39)			-0.04 (-0.31)		0.37 (1.22)	0.264	1.07	1.63
(7)							-0.03 (-0.35)		-0.07 (-0.75)		0.38 (1.25)	0.087	0.28	1.54
(8)								0.14 (4.08)	-0.03 (-0.60)		-0.58 (-2.26)	0.809	12.71	2.49

Sources: Military data are from Stockholm International Peace Research Institute, *World Armaments and Disarmament: SIPRI Yearbook, 1984*; other data came from International Monetary Fund, *Government Finance Statistics Yearbook*, various issues; International Monetary Fund, *International Financial Statistics Yearbook, 1984*.

Notes: Estimates are made using Cochrane-Orcutt two-stage iteration procedure for serial correlation correction.
( ) = t statistic.
F = F statistic.
DW = Durbin-Watson statistic.

Table 5-4
Chile: Defense Expenditures-Budgetary Trade-offs, 1973-82

	Budget Categories								Control Variables				Statistics		
Equation	Public Services	Education	Health	Social Security, Welfare	Housing	Other Community Services	Economic Services	Other Purposes	Government Expenditures	Per Capita GDP	Government Expenditures per Capita	RHO	r²	F	DW
(1)	-0.58 (-2.27)								-0.02 (-5.23)			-0.25 (-0.80)	0.867	19.55	2.06
(2)		-0.95 (-5.25)									-0.01 (-2.11)	-0.21 (-0.66)	0.899	26.72	1.14
(3)			0.28 (2.40)								-0.08 (-0.17)	-0.09 (-0.30)	0.517	3.21	3.14
(4)				-4.37 (-3.28)					-0.06 (-2.18)			0.02 (0.06)	0.902	27.72	1.26
(5)					0.84 (3.36)				0.03 (0.44)			0.36 (1.19)	0.678	6.32	3.01
(6)						-0.02 (-0.21)			0.02 (0.89)			0.23 (0.71)	0.201	0.78	1.66
(7)							5.09 (8.17)		0.03 (2.60)			0.09 (0.28)	0.932	41.11	1.37
(8)								-1.56 (-2.70)	-0.08 (-5.82)			0.24 (0.76)	0.850	17.12	2.38

Sources: Data came from International Monetary Fund, *Government Finance Statistics Yearbook*, various issues; International Monetary Fund, *International Financial Statistics Yearbook, 1984*.

Notes: Estimates are made using Cochrane-Orcutt two-stage iteration process for serial correlation.
( ) = t statistic.
F = F statistic.
DW = Durbin-Watson statistic.

Table 5-5
Ecuador: Defense Expenditures–Budgetary Trade-offs, 1973-82

	Budget Categories						Control Variables				Statistics		
Equation	Public Services	Education	Social Security, Welfare	Economic Services	Other Purposes	Health	Government Expenditures per Capita	Government Expenditures per GDP	GDP	RHO	r^2	F	DW
(1)	-0.12 (-0.50)						-0.02 (-1.62)			0.05 (0.14)	0.404	2.03	2.25
(2)		-0.004 (-0.09)								0.06 (0.19)	0.245	0.97	1.53
(3)			-0.06 (-3.26)						-0.07 (-1.94)	0.55 (1.98)	0.640	5.34	1.82
(4)				-0.24 (-3.79)					-0.01 (-19.20)	-0.35 (-1.14)	0.986	226.96	2.58
(5)					-1.05 (-1.88)				-0.09 (-0.70)	0.32 (1.03)	0.398	1.98	1.09
(6)						-0.11 (-2.81)		-0.03 (-3.00)		0.26 (0.82)	0.634	5.20	2.05

Sources: Data came from International Monetary Fund, *Government Finance Statistics Yearbook*, various issues; International Monetary Fund, *International Financial Statistics Yearbook, 1984*.

Notes: Estimates are made using Cochrane-Orcutt two-stage iteration procedure for serial correlation correction.
( ) = t statistic.
F = F statistic.
DW = Durbin-Watson statistic.

Table 5-6
Dominican Republic: Defense Expenditures–Budgetary Trade-offs, 1973-82

	Budget Categories							Control Variables				Statistics		
Equation	Public Services	Education	Health	Social Security, Welfare	Housing	Other Community Services	Economic Services	Other Purposes	Government Expenditures per Capita	Per Capita GDP	Gross Domestic Product	RHO	r^2	F	DW
(1)	-0.57 (-2.79)									-0.03 (-0.38)		-0.60 (-2.24)	0.588	4.28	2.37
(2)		0.33 (0.64)							-0.04 (-1.61)			0.55 (2.01)	0.387	1.90	1.21
(3)			-0.09 (-0.19)						-0.02 (-0.78)			0.09 (0.28)	0.101	0.33	2.35
(4)				0.12 (0.42)					-0.01 (-0.06)			-0.70 (-3.02)	0.171	0.62	2.35
(5)					0.51 (0.62)					-0.07 (-1.67)		0.31 (1.00)	0.384	1.87	2.06
(6)						-0.025 (-1.77)				0.06 (1.13)		-0.35 (-1.12)	0.506	3.07	2.06
(7)							-1.49 (-1.16)			-0.01 (-2.26)		0.06 (-0.19)	0.527	3.34	2.77
(8)								-0.98 (-2.32)			0.02 (2.37)	0.13 (0.40)	0.633	5.19	2.30

Sources: Military data are from Stockholm International Peace Research Institute, *World Armaments and Disarmament: SIPRI Yearbook, 1984*; other data are from International Monetary Fund, *Government Finance Statistics Yearbook*, various issues; International Monetary Fund, *International Financial Statistics Yearbook, 1984*.

Notes: Estimates are made using Cochrane-Orcutt two-stage iteration procedure for serial correlation correction.
( ) = t statistic.
F = F statistic.
DW = Durbin-Watson statistic.

Table 5-7
Mexico: Defense Expenditures–Budgetary Trade-offs, 1973-82

	Budget Categories						Control Variables				Statistics		
Equation	Public Services	Education	Health	Social Security, Welfare	Economic Services	Other Purposes	GDP per Capita	Government Expenditures	Government Expenditures per Capita	GDP	RHO	r^2	F	DW
(1)	-0.014 (-1.46)							-0.03 (-1.29)			0.25 (0.80)	0.263	1.07	1.98
(2)		-0.041 (-4.56)							0.01 (5.44)		-0.41 (-1.37)	0.834	15.16	1.59
(3)			0.014 (1.93)						-0.05 (-0.500)		0.47 (1.61)	0.754	9.22	2.05
(4)				-0.011 (-0.60)						-0.09 (-4.11)	-0.64 (-2.68)	0.977	130.74	2.07
(5)					0.011 (2.04)		0.09 (1.40)				0.09 (0.29)	0.466	2.62	1.53
(6)						-0.024 (-1.66)	-0.07 (-0.96)				-0.12 (-0.37)	0.491	2.89	2.26

Sources: Military data came from Stockholm International Peace Research Institute, *World Armaments and Disarmament: SIPRI Yearbook, 1984*; other data are from International Monetary Fund, *Government Finance Statistics Yearbook*, various issues; International Monetary Fund, *International Financial Statistics Yearbook, 1984*.

Notes: Estimates are made using Cochrane-Orcutt two-stage iteration procedure for serial correlation correction.
( ) = t statistic.
F = F statistic.
DW = Durbin-Watson statistic.

Table 5-8
Peru: Defense Expenditures-Budgetary Trade-offs, 1973-81

	Budget Categories						Control Variables				Statistics		
Equation	Public Serv- ices	Educa- tion	Health	Social Secu- rity	Housing	Other Pur- poses	Govern- ment Expend- itures per Capita	GDP	GDP per Capita	RHO	r^2	F	DW
(1)	-0.04 (-0.61)						-0.08 (-1.15)			-0.27 (-0.85)	0.267	0.72	1.97
(2)		-0.03 (-0.15)						-0.02 (-2.87)		0.19 (0.56)	0.640	3.65	1.23
(3)			0.02 (0.51)						0.08 (0.36)	-0.23 (-0.69)	0.05	0.11	1.99
(4)				-0.02 (-1.55)				-0.15 (-3.61)		0.06 (0.18)	0.815	8.82	0.86
(5)					0.09 (0.73)			-0.04 (-12.37)		-0.54 (-1.84)	0.975	80.05	1.58
(6)						-0.02 (-1.05)			-0.06 (-6.76)	0.04 (0.10)	0.908	19.80	2.65

Sources: Military data came from Stockholm International Peace Research Institute, *World Armaments and Disarmament: SIPRI Yearbook, 1984*; other data are from International Monetary Fund, *Government Finance Statistics Yearbook*, various issues; International Monetary Fund, *International Financial Statistics Yearbook, 1984*.

Notes: Estimates are made using Cochrane-Orcutt two-stage iteration procedure for serial correlation correction.
( ) = t statistic.
F = F statistic.
DW = Durbin-Watson statistic.

Table 5-9
Bolivia: Defense Expenditures–Budgetary Trade-offs, 1972-82

	Budget Categories								Control Variables			Statistics		
Equation	Public Services	Education	Health	Social Security, Welfare	Housing	Other Community Services	Economic Services	Other Purposes	Government Expenditures per Capita	Government Expenses	RHO	r^2	F	DW
(1)	0.44 (6.33)								0.05 (0.67)		0.72 (3.13)	0.874	20.94	2.44
(2)		0.62 (3.00)							0.03 (2.57)		0.25 (0.78)	0.752	9.10	1.60
(3)			0.62 (3.38)						0.01 (2.13)		-0.53 (-1.88)	0.209	7.33	2.44
(4)				0.65 (0.48)					0.01 (2.70)		0.19 (0.60)	0.484	2.82	2.16
(5)					0.08 (1.56)				0.03 (1.15)		0.02 (0.06)	0.418	2.07	2.18
(6)						0.06 (2.23)				0.04 (1.62)	0.29 (0.91)	0.476	2.72	1.80
(7)							-1.01 (-2.23)			-0.02 (-3.90)	0.51 (1.82)	0.771	10.14	2.38
(8)								-3.30 (-12.81)	-0.01 (-15.66)		-0.33 (-1.06)	0.985	201.25	2.62

Sources: Data came from International Monetary Fund, *Government Finance Statistics Yearbook*, various issues; International Monetary Fund, *International Financial Statistics Yearbook, 1984*.

Notes: Estimates are made using Cochrane-Orcutt two-stage iteration procedure for serial correlation correction.
( ) = t statistic.
F = F statistic.
DW = Durbin-Watson statistic.

Table 5-10
Paraguay: Defense Expenditures–Budgetary Trade-offs, 1972–82

	Budget Categories								Control Variables			Statistics		
Equation	Public Services	Education	Health	Social Security, Welfare	Housing	Other Community Services	Economic Services	Other Purposes	GDP per Capita	Government Expenditures per GDP	Government Expenditures	RHO	r^2	F	DW
(1)	1.83 (2.75)								0.08 (2.68)			-0.35 (-1.20)	0.536	3.47	2.25
(2)		0.35 (1.45)								-0.03 (-0.76)		0.12 (0.38)	0.353	1.63	1.65
(3)			0.37 (2.44)						0.03 (4.49)			-0.04 (-0.12)	0.766	9.86	2.51
(4)				2.71 (2.51)							0.03 (3.27)	-0.80 (-4.35)	0.615	4.79	2.52
(5)					0.18 (1.00)				0.03 (3.97)			-0.06 (-0.20)	0.796	11.75	1.91
(6)						0.05 (1.92)			0.40 (3.90)			-0.40 (-1.40)	0.749	8.97	2.20
(7)							-4.74 (-4.98)		-0.02 (-3.76)			-0.71 (-3.24)	0.725	11.07	2.33
(8)								-1.36 (-1.66)			-0.03 (-4.20)	-0.4 (-0.37)	0.798	11.87	2.03

Sources: Military data came from Stockholm International Peace Research Institute, *World Armaments and Disarmament: SIPRI Yearbook, 1984*; other data are from International Monetary Fund, *Government Finance Statistics Yearbook*, various issues; International Monetary Fund, *International Financial Statistics Yearbook, 1984*.

Notes: Estimates are made using Cochrane-Orcutt two-stage iteration process for serial correlation correction.

( ) = t statistic.
F = F statistic.
DW = Durbin-Watson statistic.

Table 5-11
Costa Rica: Defense Expenditures–Budgetary Trade-offs, 1972–82

	Budget Categories								Control Variables			Statistics		
Equation	Public Services	Education	Health	Social Security, Welfare	Housing	Other Community Services	Economic Services	Other Purposes	Government Expenditures per Capita	GDP per Capita	RHO	r^2	F	DW
(1)	-17.59 (-0.89)								-0.01 (-1.56)		-0.38 (-0.66)	0.12	0.56	0.86
(2)		1.24 (1.41)								0.01 (0.26)	0.92 (9.81)	0.872	27.43	1.02
(3)			-12.13 (-3.18)						0.02 (0.49)		0.94 (12.83)	0.561	5.11	0.84
(4)				7.60 (2.48)						-0.02 (-1.50)	0.80 (4.23)	0.667	8.03	1.23
(5)					-1.37 (-1.85)				0.05 (-1.87)		-0.39 (-1.23)	0.464	3.47	2.00
(6)						0.55 (4.14)			0.02 (3.68)		-0.72 (-2.46)	0.941	63.94	1.21
(7)							1.56 (0.69)		-0.02 (-1.83)		-0.04 (-0.11)	0.357	2.22	1.72
(8)								-20.50 (-0.96)	-0.01 (-1.65)		-0.39 (-0.68)	0.147	0.69	0.86

Sources: Data came from International Monetary Fund, *Government Finance Statistics Yearbook*, various issues; International Monetary Fund, *International Financial Statistics Yearbook, 1984*.

Notes: Estimates are made using Cochrane-Orcutt two-stage iteration procedure for serial correlation correction.
( ) = t statistic.
F = F statistic.
DW = Durbin-Watson statistic.
L = variable lagged one year.

Table 5-12
Uruguay: Defense Expenditures–Budgetary Trade-offs, 1973-83

	Budget Categories								Control Variables				Statistics		
Equation	Public Services	Education	Health	Social Security, Welfare	Housing	Other Community Services	Economic Services	Other Purposes	Government Expenditures per Capita	GDP	GDP per Capita	RHO	r^2	F	DW
(1)	0.10 (0.33)								-0.03 (-2.78)			0.68 (2.91)	0.546	3.61	2.74
(2)		0.05 (0.23)							0.05 (0.07)			0.85 (5.27)	0.01	0.03	2.65
(3)			0.62 (3.26)							-0.05 (-1.21)		-0.65 (-2.75)	0.617	4.83	1.85
(4)				1.55 (2.48)							-0.01 (-2.34)	-0.43 (-1.51)	0.541	3.53	1.88
(5)					0.01 (0.24)						0.06 (0.20)	0.45 (1.61)	0.023	0.06	2.17
(6)						0.16 (2.61)					0.02 (4.05)	-0.14 (-0.47)	0.840	15.80	2.10
(7)							0.60 (1.37)					0.55 (2.07)	0.216	0.827	2.14
(8)								-1.27 (-1.91)			-0.05 (-0.96)	-0.28 (-0.94)	0.508	3.10	2.13

Sources: Military data came from Stockholm International Peace Research Institute, *World Armaments and Disarmament: SIPRI Yearbook, 1984*; other data are from International Monetary Fund, *Government Finance Statistics Yearbook*, various issues; International Monetary Fund, *International Financial Statistics Yearbook, 1984*.

Notes: Estimates are made using Cochrane-Orcutt two-stage iteration procedure for serial correlation correction.
( ) = t statistic.
F = F statistic.
DW = Durbin-Watson statistic.

Table 5-13
El Salvador: Defense Expenditures–Budgetary Trade-offs, 1973–83

	Budget Categories							Control Variables				Statistics		
Equation	Public Services	Education	Health	Social Security, Welfare	Housing	Other Community Services	Economic Services	Other Purposes	Government Expenditures per GDP	GDP per Capita	Government Expenditures	RHO	r^2	F	DW
(1)	−0.46 (−6.02)								−0.03 (−3.23)			−0.31 (−1.06)	0.841	15.86	1.96
(2)		−0.90 (−7.46)							−0.05 (−4.18)			−0.20 (0.42)	0.890	24.39	1.94
(3)			−0.14 (−2.00)						−0.07 (−0.31)			−0.17 (−0.54)	0.456	2.51	2.38
(4)				0.15 (1.61)						0.02 (1.62)		0.36 (1.22)	0.283	1.18	1.93
(5)					−0.13 (−4.69)						0.02 (1.81)	0.41 (1.43)	0.593	4.38	1.42
(6)						−0.40 (−4.69)			0.02 (−3.88)			0.78 (3.96)	0.765	9.80	2.72
(7)							−0.28 (−4.69)				0.05 (0.91)	0.04 (0.12)	0.223	0.86	2.31
(8)								0.59 (6.51)	−0.08 (−0.81)			−0.54 (−2.03)	0.919	34.47	2.41

Sources: Military data came from Stockholm International Peace Research Institute, *World Armaments and Disarmament: SIPRI Yearbook, 1984;* other data are from International Monetary Fund, *Government Finance Statistics Yearbook,* various issues; International Monetary Fund, *International Financial Statistics Yearbook, 1984.*

Notes: Estimates are made using Cochrane-Orcutt two-stage iteration process for serial correlation correction.
( ) = t statistic.
F = F statistic.
DW = Durbin-Watson statistic.

3. Countries that tended to have negative trade-offs between defense and social services (public services, education, health, and social security and welfare) tended (with the exception of Chile) to have a positive trade-off with economic services.
4. Countries with a positive trade-off between defense and social services tended to have a negative trade-off with economic services.
5. With the exception of El Salvador and Argentina, all countries that had a statistically significant relationship between defense and other purposes had a negative trade-off between defense and other purposes.

Conclusions

In general, if one rules out El Salvador as a somewhat special case due to its long-running civil war, what do the two groups of countries: (1) Venezuela, Brazil, Argentina, Chile, Ecuador, Dominican Republic, Mexico, and Peru; and (2) Bolivia, Paraguay, Uruguay, and Costa Rica have in common? Are there underlying factors that account for their being grouped together on the basis of their trade-off patterns? Or are these trade-offs due to variables unique to each country's budgetary process?

One can observe at this point that each group includes countries that vary considerably in terms of political development, economic system, territory and population size, demography, location, level of socioeconomic development, resource availability, literacy, relative military size, defense expenditures, and level of military involvement in the political system. (See tables 5–14 and 5–15.) Both groups of countries contain democracies and military regimes that were in office throughout the entire period under review. Clearly, the popular interpretation that military regimes spend relatively less on social services, while civilian regimes spend relatively more cannot explain the pattern of negative and positive trade-offs reported here.

Schmitter has suggested that civilians, while increasing spending on social programs such as education, may feel constrained to bribe soldiers to keep them out of power.[35] Furthermore, the military budget enlarged by U.S. military assistance and often committed to heavy capital expenditures may be relatively immune to short-term political changes.[36]

It is possible, too, that defense and social programs may rise together because both are supported by relatively powerful constituencies. It may be that deals or compromises are struck between

Table 5-14
Alternative Classifications of Latin American Countries by Ideology and Level of State Economic Intervention, 1970s

	Ideology		
Conservative	Non-Ideological and Pragmatic	Nationalist	Non-Marxist but Socialist
Chile	Costa Rica	Mexico	Uruguay
El Salvador	Ecuador		Bolivia
Argentina	Dominican Republic		Peru
Brazil			
Paraguay			

Level of State Economic Intervention		
Low	Medium	High
Chile	Argentina	Bolivia
El Salvador	Brazil	Peru
Costa Rica	Paraguay	
Ecuador	Dominican Republic	
	Mexico	
	Uruguay	

Source: Based on Carl Stone, *Understanding Third World Politics and Economics* (Brown's Town, Jamaica: Earle Publishers Ltd., 1980), table 2.3.

these two firmly entrenched constituencies. Consequently, both defense and social program budgets could benefit at the expense of policy areas that lack similarly powerful spokesmen and organizational pressure.[37]

One situation the results indicate is that there is considerable variation in the types of trade-offs that occur in Latin America. The evidence seems to support the conclusion of Ames and Goff that "Latin America may not have a common allocation process; instead, different models may explain different groups of countries or time periods."[38]

A closer examination of the countries provided in table 5–16 indicates at least one common element—whether or not a country is an arms producer. Again leaving out El Salvador, the countries that generally experience negative trade-offs between defense expenditures and social welfare expenditures tend to be the arms producers, while those countries that experience positive relationships between defense and social expenditures tend to be the non–arms producers.

The military sector in countries possessing a domestic arms industry is able to draw on a number of interrelationships with the civil economy; the government might, for example, place weapons production contracts with private manufacturing firms, while soldiers might be expected to spend their wages in civilian markets.[39] The

Table 5-15
Alternative Classifications of Latin American Countries by Types of Regime, Economic Management, and Alliances to Major Power Blocs (1978)

Political Regime				Economic System		
Competitive Policy System	One Dominant Party	Military Rule	Single-Party System	Free Market Economy	State Interventionist Market Economy	State-Controlled Market Economy
Costa Rica	El Salvador	Chile	None	Costa Rica	Venezuela	Bolivia
Dominican Republic	Mexico	Ecuador		Dominican Republic	Mexico	Peru
Venezuela	Paraguay	Argentina		El Salvador	Paraguay	Uruguay
		Brazil				
		Bolivia				
		Peru				
		Uruguay				

Alliances	
Prowestern Capitalist	Neutral or Nonaligned
Chile	Mexico
Dominican Republic	Peru
Costa Rica	
El Salvador	
Venezuela	
Argentina	
Brazil	
Uruguay	
Bolivia	

Source: Based on Carl Stone, *Understanding Third World Politics and Economics* (Brown's Town, Jamaica: Earle Publishers Ltd., 1980), tables 1.7, 1.9.

Table 5-16
Latin American Arms Producers' and Non-Arms Producers' Defense Expenditures-Budgetary Trade-offs

				Budget Category				
	Public Services	Education	Health	Social Services, Welfare	Housing	Other Community Services	Economic Services	Other Purposes
Arms Producers								
Venezuela	-3.36	-1.43	-1.62	-2.33	-2.19	0.83	2.56	-2.04
Brazil	-0.78	-0.08	-0.37	-0.26	-2.00	-2.32	-1.64	-1.32
Argentina	-2.27	-4.35	-1.94	-1.46	-1.05	1.39	-0.35	-4.08
Chile	-2.27	-5.25	2.40	-3.28	3.36	-0.21	8.17	-2.70
Ecuador	-0.50	-0.09	-2.81	-3.26	—	—	-3.79	-1.88
Dominican Republic	-2.79	0.64	-0.19	0.42	0.62	-1.77	-1.16	-2.32
Mexico	-1.64	-4.56	1.93	-0.60	—	—	2.04	-1.66
Peru	-0.61	-0.15	0.51	-1.55	0.73	—	—	-1.05
Non-Arms Producers								
Bolivia	6.33	3.00	3.38	0.48	1.56	2.13	-2.23	-12.81
Paraguay	2.75	1.45	2.44	2.51	1.00	1.92	-4.98	-1.66
Uruguay	0.33	0.23	3.26	2.48	0.24	2.61	1.37	-1.91
Costa Rica	-0.89	†1.41	-3.18	2.48	-1.85	4.14	0.69	-0.96
El Salvador	-6.02	-7.46	-2.00	1.61	-2.32	-4.69	-1.00	6.51

Notes: Based on t values for budget category regressed on military expenditures presented in tables 5-1 through 5-13.
 - Represents a negative relationship between defense and budgetary items.

military sector in the producing countries is the one major area that is under the direct control of the central government. Economic expansion can therefore be affected immediately by, for example, the ordering of a new weapons system. In contrast, indirect policies such as marginal tax changes would take a much longer period to produce noticeable multiplier effects. Such control is also useful in the possible event of excessive expansion of the economy, as weapons systems can very often be immediately cancelled or contracted to help deflate the system.

Whynes notes:

> Once this regulation system has become established, several groups of people will find it economically advantageous to maintain it in existence. These groups will include senior soldiers, the owners and managers of private industries with which the government places defense contracts, and also politicians whose careers are tied to the defense sector.[40]

Clearly, if military expenditures are used in an environment where domestic production is possible, they have the potential to perform an important stabilizing role, namely, they could expand relative to other expenditures when the economy is in a recession and be reduced relative to other less discretionary expenditures during times of overheating or lack of foreign exchange. This use of military expenditure as a stabilizing element would produce the negative trade-offs observed for the arms producers in either a zero-sum environment or an expanding-sum environment (where all expenditures grow over time, but military expenditures fluctuate more vis-à-vis other types of government allocations).

The generally positive trade-off between military expenditures and economic services would tend to reinforce this conclusion. For example, it has often been claimed that many governments of less developed countries tend to regard capital expenditure as investment while seeing recurrent expenditure as consumption.[41] Economic growth is seen to depend largely on investment, so that government recurrent expenditure has to be curbed in order to generate "public savings" for investment purposes. There are also political reasons for this belief. Governments are more likely, at least in the short run, to obtain greater political benefits by having more, but less efficient, projects than by having fewer, but more efficient, ones. The former are simply more visible and more politically rewarding.

One important implication of this view is that scarce government revenue is more likely to be spent on new projects or on the expansion of existing ones than on recurrent operational and maintenance costs. There are certainly examples in less-developed countries of new schools being built and opened without there being sufficient qualified teachers to staff them, or even to staff already existing ones. If, in fact, this view is correct, one might expect economic services in general to be positively correlated—or at least not statistically significant—when regressed on defense expenditures.

One comes back to the fact that a fairly close link exists between the surplus or deficit in the government budget, public consumption, and military expenditures in the arms-producing countries. These countries show defense expenditures linked to budgetary deficits, that is, defense expenditures rise with government deficits. Other expenditures may be cut back during periods of high deficits. With surpluses, defense expenditures, everything else being equal, tend to decline in percent terms.

These patterns are not found in the nonproducing countries. Apparently because these countries depend more on tax revenues, all expenditures are increased as revenues rise, while they are decreased when revenues decline. The non-arms producing countries would not be able to attach any special stabilizing role to military expenditures that could not be performed as well by other types of expenditure.

Notes

1. Kathleen Peroff and Margaret Podolak-Warren, "Does Spending on Defense Cut Spending on Health? A Time Series Analysis of the U.S. Economy, 1929-74," *British Journal of Political Science* (January 1979), p. 22.

2. Margaret Hayes, "Policy Consequences of Military Participation in Politics: An Analysis of Tradeoffs in Brazilian Federal Expenditures" in Craig Liske, ed., *Comparative Public Policy* (New York: Wiley, 1976), p. 23.

3. United Nations Secretary General, *Economic and Social Consequences of the Arms Race and Military Expenditure* (United Nations document no. A/8469/Rev. 1, 1971), pp. 19, 29.

4. B.M. Russett, *What Price Vigilance?* (New Haven: Yale University Press, 1970), p. 141.

5. J. Hollenhorst and G. Ault, "An Alternative Answer to: Who Pays for Defense?" *American Political Science Review* (September 1971), pp. 760-63.

6. *Ibid.*, pp. 762-63.

7. Hayes, *op. cit.*, p. 24.

8. Ronald P. Smith, "Military Expenditure and Investment in OECD Countries, 1954-1973," *Journal of Comparative Economics* (March 1980), pp. 19-32.

9. F.L. Pryor, *Public Expenditures in Communist and Capitalist Nations* (Homewood, Ill.: Richard D. Irwin, 1968).

10. *Ibid.*, p. 122.

11. United Nations Secretary General, *op. cit.*, p. 19.

12. Emile Benoit, *Defense and Economic Growth in Developing Countries* (Lexington, Mass.: Lexington Books, 1973), p. xix.

13. Hayes, *op. cit.*, p. 24.

14. See, for example, Eric Nordlinger, "Soldiers in Mufti: The Impact of Military Rule upon Economic and Social Change in the Non-Western States," *American Political Science Review* (December 1970), pp. 1131-48; P. Schmitter, "Military Intervention, Political Competitiveness and Public Policy in Latin America, 1950-67" in M. Janowitz and J. Van Doorn, eds., *On Military Intervention* (Rotterdam: Rotterdam University Press, 1971), pp. 425-506; Jerry Weaver, "Assessing the Impact of Military Rule: Alternative Approaches" in P. Schmitter, ed., *Military Rule in Latin America: Function, Consequences and Perspectives* (Beverly Hills, Calif.: Sage, 1973), pp. 58-116.

15. Joseph Pluta, "The Performance of South American Civilian and Military Governments from a Socio-Economic Perspective," *Development and Change* (July 1979), p. 461.

16. E. Nordlinger, *op. cit.*, pp. 1131-32.

17. *Ibid.*, p. 1134.

18. Schmitter, *op. cit.*, pp. 430-32.

19. *Ibid.*, pp. 492-93.

20. *Ibid.*, p. 493.

21. Pluta, *op. cit.*, pp. 476-78.

22. Thomas Dickson, "An Economic Output and Impact Analysis of Civilian and Military Regimes in Latin South America," *Development and Change* (July 1977), pp. 325-46.

23. *Ibid.*, p. 341.

24. Hayes, *op. cit.*, p. 25.

25. *Ibid.*, pp. 35, 48-50.

26. Barry Ames and Ed Goff, "Education and Defense Expenditures in Latin America: 1948-1968" in C. Liske, ed., *op. cit.*, pp. 175-98.

27. *Ibid.*, pp. 179-80.

28. Russett, *op. cit.*, p. 133.

29. R.E. Looney and P.C. Frederiksen, "The Impact of Public Enterprises on Economic Growth in Latin America: The Case of Defense Industries," paper presented at the North American Economics and Finance Association Third International Meeting, Mexico City, June 26-27, 1985.

30. Peroff and Podolak-Warren, *op. cit.*, p. 24.

31. Regressions were performed using defense expenditures from both the IMF and Stockholm International Peace Research Institute. The results were similar for the two sets of data. Only the best set of results is presented in tables 5-1 through 5-13.

32. See Robert Cox, "Argentina: Souring on the Democratic Dream," *Harper's* (May 1985), pp. 49-58.

33. Peroff and Podolak-Warren, *op. cit.,* pp. 24-25.

34. A similar formulation was used by J. Viner in his analysis of budgetary trade-offs for education. See his "Budgetary Tradeoffs between Education and Defense in Latin America: A Research Note," *Journal of Developing Areas* (October 1983), pp. 77-92.

35. P.C. Schmitter, "Military Intervention, Political Competitiveness and Public Policy in Latin America, 1950-67" in Janowitz and Van Doorn, eds., *op.cit.,* pp. 425-506.

36. *Ibid.,* p. 492-93.

37. Viner, *op. cit.,* p. 87.

38. Ames and Goff, *op. cit.,* p. 194.

39. R.E. Looney and P.C. Frederiksen, "The Impact of Public Enterprises on Growth in Latin America: The Case of Defense Industries," *op cit.*

40. David Whynes, *The Economics of Third World Military Expenditure* (Austin: University of Texas Press, 1979), p. 27.

41. Cf. David Lim, "Government Recurrent Expenditure and Economic Growth in Less Developed Countries," *World Development* (April 1983), pp. 377-80.

Part II
Venezuela

With the exception of chapter 5, the budgetary mechanisms inferred from the empirical analysis of arms and non-arms producers have been based on cross-section analysis. While a number of useful insights into the political economy of Latin America can be obtained from this approach, it has clearly reached a state of diminishing returns.

Furthermore, even assuming the analysis in part I to be accurate and widely applicable, the number of observations in the sample and the time period selected (1981–82) are clearly crucial. A cross-section of the LDCs today, for example, would most likely yield somewhat different results owing to such factors as the post-1982 debt crisis and the impact of declining oil prices on oil exporters' military expenditures.

Finally, although attempts have been made by other researchers to introduce political variables into cross-section analysis, their results are largely unsatisfactory. In addition to the conceptual problems of comparing regime types across countries, the impact of political change is likely to be distributed over time and not simply captured at one point in time.

Parts II and III of the book attempt to overcome these limitations through examining Latin American defense allocations and budgetary processes over time. Overlaying political variables on the budgetary patterns identified in part I allows the explicit identification of the consequences of regime change on the size of the defense burden and the trade-offs with socioeconomic expenditure acceptable to alternative regimes.

Logically, one arms-producing country and one non–producing country might have been selected for analysis. Instead, a minor military force and relatively small producer, Venezuela, was selected for part II, along with a major military force and arms producer, Argentina, for part III.

To some degree two producers were selected because the budgetary patterns for this group of countries appear more striking (and controversial). More importantly, given space limitations, it seemed more appropriate to document rather convincingly one way or the other the applicability of the mechanisms identified in part I for a group of countries.

The differences between the countries are striking. Venezuela, a long-standing stable democracy and oil producer, has on the surface few similarities other than arms production with politically unstable and economically industrialized Argentina. Clearly, if the countries exhibit similar budgetary patterns, considerable credence can be given to the tentative results produced in part I.

6
Austerity and Military Expenditures in Venezuela

Venezuela's years of economic boom and easy money are over. Income from petroleum exports, which make up around 95 percent of Venezuela's total exports and are the barometer of the nation's economic activity, declined significantly in 1983 and 1984, causing serious strains on government finances and the economy as a whole.

Assuming that the world petroleum market remains stable over the short and medium term, prospects are for very little real price growth until the late 1980s. On the other hand, it is likely that Venezuela will continue to depend on oil as its chief source of income until the end of the century and it is not likely that nontraditional exports will play a major role in the country's balance of payments for at least a decade.

Venezuela is currently experiencing its highest unemployment levels in recent years, general dissatisfaction with the government, reduced government revenues, serious problems in the private sector, and gloomy short- and medium-term prospects. In brief, the country today faces a combination of economic, financial, and social problems greater than any seen since the tumultuous days of the early 1960s. Furthermore, because of the recent softness of the world oil market, Venezuela cannot count on obtaining substantial sums of hard currency in return for its exports of crude and refined products.

Patterns of Austerity

In times of economic austerity such as Venezuela is currently experiencing, the government, faced with declining revenues and political restraints on increasing taxes, must resort to major budgetary cutbacks. However, relatively little is known about how governments make expenditure decisions or, perhaps more importantly, how they trade off between consumption and investment or between sectors and categories of expenditures. Anecdotal evidence suggests that officials follow rather ad hoc rules for making large contractions in a short period of time—cutting new rather than ongoing projects, new rather than present employment, and materials and travel expenses rather than personnel, while favoring ministries that are politically powerful or reducing those that had expanded most rapidly in the past.[1]

In general, the programs, once enlarged, seem difficult to reduce, particularly if they generate large employment benefits.[2] Likewise, governments seem unwilling to reduce areas that are supported by foreign assistance, both because they fear antagonizing aid donors and for the more practical reason that savings from such expenditure cuts are significantly less, since aid is also reduced by a proportionate amount.

As to the choice of which sectors to cut back, it is often felt that some sectors are more vulnerable than others to reductions. The defense sector in particular is usually considered difficult to reduce, while other sectors (particularly the social sectors such as health, education, and rural development) are considered vulnerable. The alleged vulnerability of the social sectors is clearly evident in writings coming from the World Bank:

> In the difficult past few years, budgetary crises have often meant that social services were cut back, in the process unravelling carefully designed programs.[3]

> Since many human development programs are publicly funded, they are especially vulnerable when growth is threatened and budgets are under pressure. ... The recurrent costs of social programs, especially salary costs, tended to make them a permanent and, therefore, vulnerable part of government budgets.[4]

> Quick-fix relief through disproportionate cutbacks—in, for example, education or rural development—may well have negative consequences for the entire economy.[5]

> Many member countries have had to reduce and reorient investment programs to curtail recurrent expenditures and to delay the completion of high priority development projects. Programs in health, education and other social sectors have been particularly vulnerable.[6]

> In the crisis situations confronting African governments, education, training and health programs are continuously in danger of

becoming the residual legatees of both resources and attention by policymakers.[7]

Despite these rather strongly held views and circumstantial evidence, little empirical investigation has been made on the vulnerability of different sectors to reductions in public expenditures. In a recent study of thirty-seven cases of budgetary reductions (in countries where real expenditures declined in one or more years), the vulnerability of different sectors to budgetary reduction was examined.[8] Here, vulnerability was loosely defined:

1. A sector was well protected if expenditures on it were reduced by less than the percentage of reduction in total expenditures.
2. A sector was vulnerable if its percentage of reduction exceeded the average.

In brief, a simple ratio of percentage changes in sectoral expenditures to those in total spending served as the measure of vulnerability. Where the ratio had a greater value than one, it indicated that the sector was highly vulnerable, while a value between zero and one indicated low vulnerability, with less than proportional reductions in the relevant sector. A negative value indicated that despite overall expenditure reductions, the sector was allowed to expand.

The result (see table 6-1) based on a aggregation of the results from 37 observations, showed an average decline of 10.6 percent in real government expenditures, while the decline for the social sectors was only 5 percent, producing a vulnerability index of 0.4. By contrast, the index is 0.6 for administrative and defense sectors and over 1 for production and infrastructure. In short, social sectors were less vulnerable to cuts than defense and administration, which in turn were considerably less vulnerable than production and infrastructure—contrary to the generally accepted view. The fact that social sectors and defense were both relatively protected suggests that there were high political costs associated with reducing them. On the other hand, countries appeared to have been more willing to cut spending on infrastructure and production which had adverse implications for longer-term growth prospects but fewer early, direct, and immediate political costs.

These conclusions were not very different for countries belonging to different income groups. The low-income countries in table 6-1 appear to have afforded slightly more protection to the social sectors and production and slightly less to administration and defense, but the difference is marginal. The middle-income countries, such as

Table 6-1
Impact of Reduction in Government Expenditures

			Expenditures		
	Social	Defense and Administration	Production	Infrastructure	Miscellaneous
Average percent change in real expenditures	−5	−8	−11	−22	−7
Index of vulnerability					
Low income (17 observations)	0.4	0.6	1.2	1.7	0.8
Middle income (20 observations)	0.2	0.9	0.6	1.2	0.5
	0.5	0.4	1.7	1.9	1.1

Source: Norman Hicks and Anne Kubisch, "Cutting Government Expenditures in LDCs," *Finance and Development* (September 1984), p. 38.

Note: Statistics cover capital and recurring expenditures for 32 developing countries for various periods, 1972–80.

Venezuela and Argentina, by contrast, gave more protection to administration and defense, but the difference is marginal. The middle-income countries, such as Venezuela and Argentina, by contrast, gave more protection to administration and defense and less to the productive and infrastructural sectors.

The apparent bias toward maintaining expenditures in social services and defense may reflect the government's preference for present consumption over investment and future consumption, since social sectors and defense typically have a heavy bias toward recurrent expenditures and within these there is a sizable employment component. Politicians in Venezuela, particularly in election years, may find it more acceptable to reduce investment, growth, and future consumption, especially if these reductions are uncertain and far off, than to make politically difficult cost cuts in present consumption. Since the social sectors and defense/administration are relatively labor intensive with high recurrent costs, reducing expenditures on them not only cuts back services highly valued by the public, but also causes relatively high unemployment per unit of reduction.

The Venezuelan Case

These general observations on the manner in which governments deal with austerity seem to hold fairly well historically for Venezuela. Since 1950, there have been six years (not including 1984, for which exact official data is still pending) of overall real cuts in government expenditure: 1959, 1960, 1962, 1979, 1982, and 1983. In the earlier period, 1959-60, military expenditures were reduced in line with overall expenditures in 1959, and slightly more in 1960. As for the later years, however, military expenditures were reduced 4.0 percent compared to overall government expenditure reductions of 12 percent in 1962, 0.4 percent in contrast to overall government reductions of 15.3 percent in 1979, and 3.9 percent compared to an overall expenditure cut of 8.6 percent in 1982. The reduction of military expenditure by 0.8 percent in 1983 was certinly less than the actual overall reduction in real government expenditures for that year.

In examining longer-term patterns in national priorities, various indices of Venezuela's military expenditures are available:

1. The nation's military expenditures as a percentage of GNP;
2. Per capita military expenditures—military expenditure divided by the nation's population;

Table 6-2
Patterns of Venezuelan Military Expenditures, 1950-83
(millions of bolivares)

	Nominal Military Expenditures	Real Military Expenditures	Growth in Real Military Expenditures	Growth in Real Government Expenditures	Growth in Real Government Revenues	Real Military Expenditures as a Percentage of			
						Real GDP	Real Government Consumption	Real Government Expenditures	Real Government Revenues
1950	182.0	505.5	—	—	—				
1951	201.0	555.2	9.8	10.0	17.5	1.54	11.38	8.77	9.49
1952	212.0	577.7	4.1	1.6	4.8	1.54	11.55	8.76	8.87
1953	210.0	581.7	0.5	4.8	7.0	1.52	11.58	8.97	8.80
1954	270.0	745.9	28.2	6.2	3.6	1.42	10.94	8.62	8.29
1955	338.0	936.3	25.6	15.4	13.2	1.65	12.74	10.41	10.25
1956	381.0	1046.7	11.8	11.3	45.9	1.89	15.09	11.33	11.38
1957	496.0	1393.3	33.2	33.7	26.4	1.87	16.71	11.38	8.71
1958	601.0	1606.9	15.4	35.6	-17.1	2.08	19.38	11.33	9.71
1959	607.0	1548.5	-3.7	-3.7	10.3	2.45	16.83	9.63	12.77
1960	540.0	1330.1	-14.1	-10.7	-11.9	2.37	19.39	9.64	11.15
1961	533.0	1349.4	1.4	6.4	-16.5	2.10	14.67	9.27	10.86
1962	509.0	1295.2	-4.0	-12.0	2.6	1.97	14.68	8.84	9.20
1963	613.0	1544.1	19.2	12.2	10.5	1.72	14.34	9.64	8.61
1964	650.0	1600.0	3.7	5.3	5.7	1.90	14.84	10.24	9.29
1965	742.0	1796.6	12.2	8.6	0.1	1.82	15.37	10.09	9.11
1966	782.0	1681.9	3.6	5.8	4.9	1.96	15.85	10.42	10.21
1967	885.0	2107.1	13.2	10.7	10.2	1.97	15.27	10.21	10.08
1968	894.0	2103.5	-0.1	5.0	1.6	2.12	16.29	10.43	10.36

Year							
1969	867.0	1988.5	-5.5	4.2	3.9	1.99	16.08	9.91	10.19
1970	891.0	1993.3	0.2	1.5	14.2	1.87	14.72	8.99	10.01
1971	1113.0	2414.3	21.1	7.5	18.8	1.70	12.93	8.88	8.78
1972	1294.0	2729.9	13.1	11.2	2.5	1.94	14.34	10.00	8.96
1973	1400.0	2834.0	3.8	7.6	24.5	2.10	15.22	10.17	9.88
1974	2022.0	3779.4	33.3	47.7	141.1	1.91	14.59	9.81	8.24
1975	2520.0	4278.4	13.2	9.6	-13.1	1.80	15.83	8.85	4.56
1976	1997.0	3149.8	-26.4	10.1	-12.7	2.10	15.81	9.15	5.94
1977	2472.0	3614.0	14.8	19.9	7.6	1.47	10.10	6.11	5.01
1978	2673.0	3651.6	1.0	2.5	-0.3	1.58	10.77	5.85	5.76
1979	2993.0	3635.7	-0.4	-15.3	19.1	1.58	11.11	5.76	6.25
1980	3893.0	3893.0	7.1	4.1	30.5	1.44	10.78	6.79	5.88
1981	4550.0	3922.4	0.7	30.4	46.7	1.53	11.08	6.98	5.86
1982	4800.0	3770.6	-3.9	-8.6	-14.1	1.59	10.67	5.39	4.66
1983	5060.0	3739.8	-0.8	n.a.	n.a.	1.77	12.27	n.a.	n.a.

Sources: Nominal military expenditures are taken from Stockholm International Peace Research Institute, *World Armaments and Disarmament: SIPRI Yearbook*, various issues. Real military expenditures are derived by deflating with the International Monetary Fund consumer price index for Venezuela (1980 = 1.00). Government revenues and expenditures data come from International Monetary Fund, *International Financial Statistics Yearbook*, various issues.

Note: n.a. = not available.

3. The number of personnel in the nation's armed forces per se;
4. The number of military personnel divided by population;
5. Military expenditures divided by the number of military personnel;
6. Military expenditures per se;
7. Military expenditures as a percentage of the federal budget;
8. Military expenditures as a percentage of government consumption;
9. Military expenditures as a percentage of government revenues.

Of these, the most widely used index is the first, military expenditures as a percentage of GNP. Clearly, however, there are some major problems with this particular measure. For example, the largest proportion of GNP is unavailable for direct allocation by national leaders and policymakers and, thus, the percent-of-GNP measure cannot demonstrate the priorities of such policymakers. In addition, since Venezuela's GNP is relatively large by Third World standards, it takes large changes in military expenditures to appear as anything more than a change of a few tenths of 1 percent in such an index.

As with the examination of austerity measures above, real military expenditures as a percentage of the nation's federal budget is probably the most useful measure of longer-run movements in national priorities. It focuses precisely on the priorities of the nation's policymakers. By this measure, it is clear that there have been at least six major cycles in Venezuela's pattern of defense expenditures (as shown in table 6–2):

1. The 1951–54 period found Venezuelan military expenditures averaging 8.78 percent of government expenditures.
2. In a 1955–58 upswing, defense spending averaged 11.11 percent of total central government expenditures.
3. The 1959–63 period showed a downturn in defense expenditures, which averaged 9.4 percent of federal spending.
4. A slight upturn occurred between 1964 and 1968, with defense expenditures averaging 10.3 percent of the federal government's budgets.
5. Two downturns have occurred since 1968, The first was from 1969 to 1976, when defense spending averaged 9.47 percent of the federal budget. During 1977–82, defense expenditures averaged 6.15 percent of the federal budget.

Despite several cyclical patterns, military expenditures in Venezuela generally seem to enjoy a particular stability and are not all that vulnerable to financial-austerity-induced cutbacks. In table 6-2, the stability in military expenditures is also apparent in longer-term trends in the ratios of military expenditures to other major macroeconomic aggregates. In terms of real gross domestic product, military expenditures have averaged between 1.5 and 2 percent over the 1950–83 period.

In terms of the shares of real government consumption or real government revenues, however, military expenditures seem to be somewhat more volatile. Several cyclical patterns emerge:

1. In terms of real government revenues, a more stable pattern appears, with less fluctuation over time and fewer major cycles in military expenditures.
2. Military expenditures show most stability in terms of the government's real level of consumption.
3. The link between all measures of economic activity—real GDP, real government expenditures, real government revenues, real government consumption, and real defense expenditures—seems to be weakening. That is, there does not appear to be the degree of stability in the 1970s and 1980s that characterized the 1950s and 1960s.
4. The historical stability in defense expenditures would seem to indicate that the government's current austerity measures will not result in major cutbacks in military-related activities.

Conclusions

On one hand, the results presented here suggest that a high level of stability exists in Venezuelan defense expenditures but that this stability may not hold up during the country's current period of austerity. On the other hand, the results suggest that cutbacks in defense expenditures are likely to be much lower than in other functional areas.

Notes

1. Cf. Naomi Caiden and Aaron Wildavsky, *Planning and Budgeting in Poor Countries* (New York: John Wiley, 1974).

2. A thorough analysis of these conditions is given in Richard Goode, *Government Finance in Developing Countries* (Washington, D.C.: Brookings Institution, 1984).

3. World Bank, *IDA in Retrospect* (Washington, D.C.: World Bank, 1983), p. 52.

4. World Bank, *World Development Report 1981* (New York: Oxford University Press, 1981), pp. 97–98.

5. World Bank, *Focus on Poverty 1983* (Washington, D.C.: World Bank, 1983).

6. World Bank, *World Bank Program on Special Assistance to Member Countries* (Washington, D.C.: World Bank, 1984), p. 1.

7. World Bank, *Sub-Saharan Africa: Progress Report on Development Prospects and Programs* (Washington, D.C.: World Bank, 1983), p. 30.

8. Norman Hicks and Anne Kubisch, "Cutting Government Expenditures in LDCs," *Finance and Development* (September 1984), pp. 37–39.

7
Factors Underlying Venezuelan Defense Expenditures, 1950-83

The U.S. Arms Control and Disarmament Agency points out that "a country's military expenditures are not necessarily representative of military capability." They do not define a country's efficiency and allocation of expenditures or "whether the quantity and quality of force supported by them serves national purposes."[1]

The raw data do enable the measuring of the economic burden, the impact on the average person in the country, and the degree to which a country values military spending over other forms of government outlay. Inevitably, the questions that arise from study of the data on military expenditures are the reasons for the expenditure and, particularly, the trend of military expenditures. Specifically, is there a threat to the security of the particular country; is destabilization by outside forces forcing the expansion of military outlay? Otherwise, why is the burden being assumed?[2] Has the trend of military expenditures simply been affected by the easy income of windfall export earnings such as that experienced by OPEC countries in the 1970s?

In a 1973 study of defense expenditures and military rule in Latin America, Schmitter concluded that the single best explanatory factor for the rise or fall of military budgets in individual countries was the performance of GNP.[3] That finding has been verified by other studies of defense expenditures in Latin America.

Gertrude Heare found in a 1971 study of the six leading military spenders in Latin America (Argentina, Brazil, Chile, Colombia, Peru, and Venezuela) that between 1940 and 1970, their outlays fluctuated in the aggregate between 2.5 percent and 3.0 percent of GNP. Moreover, absolute expenditures in constant prices tended to rise over these three decades as national economies grew. In brief reviews of the history of military spending in each country, Heare could find no uniform pattern over time. She did point out that expenditures jumped notably with internal conflicts (or with the threat thereof), with periods of economic prosperity, or with specific attempts to catch up with lags in construction, pay scales, or equipment replacement. She also noted that military budgets declined in times of economic depression or hardship.[4]

The general purpose of this chapter is to examine in much more detail than Heare or Schmitter the pattern of military expenditures in a country, Venezuela, having little apparent need to increase allocations for defense over time.[5] The specific purpose of this chapter is, given the fact that Venezuela did increase its military expenditures throughout this period, to determine the main factors underlying this expansion.

Analysis of Trends in Venezuelan Defense Expenditures

The general observation concerning the stability in Venezuelan military expenditures is borne out by the lack of any particular trend in Venezuelan defense expenditures. In particular, table 7-1's econometric analysis of the various ratios confirms the overall pattern of stability in Venezuela's defense allocations:

1. Military expenditures as a percent of GDP;
2. Military expenditures as a percent of government consumption;
3. Military expenditures as a percent of government expenditure; and
4. Military expenditure as a percent of government revenue.

The following dummy variables were included in the regression equation on a one-by-one basis to test for structural changes associated with the post-1973 oil price increases.[6] Since it is not apparent whether the 1973-74 oil price increases acted immediately or with a lag, or whether the 1978-79 price increases produced a structural shift similar to the 1973-74 period, several dummy specifications were tested:

$DUMA$ (0) 1950-73
            (1) 1974-83

$DUMB$ (0) 1950-72
            (1) 1973-83

$DUMC$ (0) 1950-73
            (1) 1974-78
            (2) 1979-83

DUMD (0) 1950–73
      (1) 1974–79
      (2) 1980–83

In addition, a dummy variable was included in the regressions to test for possible structural shifts associated with different Venezuelan governments:

DUMP (0) 1950–57: the dictatorship
      (1) 1958–68: Democratic Action party (AD)
      (2) 1969–73: Social Christian party (COPEI)
      (3) 1974–78: Democratic Action party (AD)
      (4) 1979–83: Social Christian party (COPEI)

With regard to changes of regime in Venezuela, the two major political parties, the AD and COPEI, are both moderately left of center.[7] The two parties began Venezuela's democratic period as partners in a coalition government in 1958. However, by the mid-1980s, their platforms differed, but more in implementation than in substance.

The AD is the oldest and largest party in Venezuela. Substantively, it can be characterized as socialist-populist, similar in general orientation to the Iranian and German Social Democratic parties and the British Labor Party. It is pragmatic in outlook; it argues in favor of a mixed economic system and dedicates itself to the policy of "sowing the oil" to diversify the economy and develop the nation's infrastructure. It has strong commitments to education and agrarian reform, conducts an active foreign policy, and devotes itself to the concept of a representative democracy. The AD enjoys a broad base of support; the peasant *(campesino)* movement and organized labor, however, stand out among the staunchest components of its constituency.

The COPEI has held a strong second place to the AD since the mid-1960s, when it copied the AD's organization structure. The COPEI characterizes itself as the "loyal opposition" to the AD majority and commits itself to the translation of Christian social doctrine into political principals and programs. Specifically, it espouses such causes as agrarian reform, education, social welfare, and economic nationalism. Its constituency, which shares many AD interests, is generally more conservative and includes a less significant labor element. If anything, therefore (ceteris paribus), one might expect a structural shift toward proportionately (ceterin paribus) greater amounts of public expenditures allocated to defense during COPEI administrations.

Table 7-1
Venezuela: Time Series Analysis of Defense Expenditures as a Percentage of Government Revenues, 1950-82

Equation	Independent Variables								Statistics		
	DUMA	DUMB	DUMC	DUMD	DUMP	Time	RHO		r^2	F	DW
(1) Military expenditures as a percentage of revenues =											
	-4.15 (-8.44)						0.25 (1.51)		0.704	71.36	1.87
(2)		3.93 (-8.59)					0.120 (0.69)		0.711	73.92	1.94
(3)			-2.34 (-5.16)				0.46 (2.95)		0.471	26.67	1.85
(4)				-2.47 (-5.30)			0.42 (2.69)		0.484	28.09	1.93
(5)					1.68 (2.64)		0.91 (13.12)		0.188	6.98	2.19
(6)	-3.95 (-5.12)					-0.01 (-0.32)	0.25 (1.50)		0.705	33.52	1.87
(7)		-3.71 (-4.75)				-0.01 (-0.34)	0.13 (0.78)		0.704	33.44	1.94
(8)			-1.95 (-2.95)			-0.05 (-0.81)	0.43 (2.76)		0.501	14.09	1.85
(9)				-2.00 (-2.97)		-0.05 (-0.96)	0.40 (2.51)		0.515	14.89	1.92

(10)		1.95 (3.35)	−0.29 (−5.45)	0.49 (3.18)	0.507	14.42	1.92
(11)			0.14 (1.05)	0.95 (17.45)	0.034	1.11	2.25

Notes: Estimations were made using Cochrane-Orcutt two-stage iteration process for serial correlation.
See text for definition of variables.
( ) = t statistic.
F = F statistic.
r^2 = correlation coefficient.
DW = Durbin-Watson statistic.

The regression results for the ratio of military expenditures to gross domestic product and government consumption were not statistically significant for the time trend or any of the dummy variables. This means there is statistical verification of any secular increase or decrease in either the percentage of gross domestic product or government consumption allocated to defense expenditures. Furthermore, the oil price shocks and change in political regimes were not statistically significant in causing structural shifts in the ratio of military expenditures to either gross domestic product or government consumption.

The regression results for military expenditures as a proportion of government revenues and government expenditures also produced no statistically significant time trend. (See tables 7-1 and 7-2.) However, both ratios were strongly affected by the oil price dummies, with the political variable also statistically significant and positive for the ratio of military expenditures to government revenues. The dummy variables for the oil price increases were highly significant for the military expenditures ratio, but had consistently lower t ratios and r^2 for the ratio of military expenditures to government expenditures. The negative sign on the oil dummies indicates that the government may have decided to allocate the bulk of the oil windfalls to nondefense activities, while the positive sign on the political variable suggests that COPEI administrations may be more responsive than AD administrations in allocating funds for the military.

The effect of the oil price increases is also apparent in an analysis of the time trend in real military expenditures. Total real military expenditures display a strong time trend in Venezuela with slightly over 75 percent of the fluctuations in military expenditures explained by time alone. (See table 7-3.) Several of the measures of structural shift associated with the oil price and revenue changes are also statistically significant with the highest correlation coefficient (0.938 in equation 8 in table 7-3) being associated with the trend in oil price increases beginning in 1973.

Clearly, the results imply a strong time trend and, therefore, stability in defense expenditures. The time trend pattern has, however, been broken sharply and shifted upward by the sudden affluence associated with the oil price increases experienced in the 1970s. Overlapping the structural shifts associated with the oil price phenomenon is another set of shifts associated with the difference in priorities vis-à-vis the defense sector associated with the two main political parties, with the COPEI more inclined to allocate funds for this purpose.

These patterns are more apparent when an analysis of residuals from the regression equation is made. The residuals around the time trend regression equations (the first five columns in table 7-4) show that military expenditures have experienced several cyclical patterns with abnormally low allocations occurring in the early 1950s (1952-53), then rather high allocations up to 1960, followed by a period of lower than predicted defense expenditures, (1960-70). The 1970s, in turn, were generally a period of abnormally high allocations occurring in the defense industry, with only 1970, 1973, 1976, and 1979 expenditures falling below the trend line. When dummy variables were added to the regression equation to account for the structural shift associated with the petroleum boom in the 1970s, a somewhat different picture emerged:

1. Not only is the regression equation significantly improved (from an r^2 of 0.752 for time to 9.938 for time plus *DUMB*), but several years in the 1960s are no longer seen as times of abnormally low expenditures.
2. In addition, given the correction for the 1973-74 oil price increases, several years in the 1970s and early 1980s despite rapid increases in oil revenues, are now below their historical trend (1978, 1979, 1981, 1982, and 1983 with *DUMA*).
3. A regression of real military expenditures on real government revenues plus structural shifts associated with petroleum and political developments improves the correlation coefficient to 0.961, indicating that the secular increase in petroleum revenues adjusted for structural shifts has played a more important role in explaining military expenditures than simply a gradual increase in military expenditures associated with an expanding economy.
4. The analysis of residuals on the regression of military expenditures on revenues plus structural changes (column 9, table 7-4) indicates that, contrary to the residuals around the time regression, the later 1960s were actually a period of relatively high allocations to military activities, while the 1970s, if anything, were a period of relatively low allocations. (1970, 1971, 1974, 1976, 1977, and 1978 all lie below the regression line.)

In general, therefore, the introduction of dummy variables to the trend analysis confirms the tentative conclusions obtained earlier that while the increase in oil revenues has greatly facilitated the increase in the allocations to the defense sector, during the 1970s,

Table 7-2
Venezuela: Trend Analysis of Military Expenditures as a Percentage of Government Expenditures, 1950-82

Equation	Independent Variables							Statistics			
	DUMA	DUMB	DUMC	DUMD	DUMP	Time	RHO	r^2	F	DW
(1) Military expenditures as a percentage of government expenditures	-2.57 (-4.06)						0.58 (4.08)	0.354	16.51	1.63
(2)		-1.26 (-1.51)					0.79 (7.40)	0.071	2.29	1.78
(3)			-1.57 (-3.91)				0.54 (3.71)	0.338	15.34	1.63
(4)				-1.67 (-3.93)			0.58 (4.03)	0.340	15.47	1.70
(5)					-0.24 (-0.52)		0.89 (11.56)	0.008	0.27	1.82
(6)	-1.32 (-1.53)					-0.11 (-1.86)	0.66 (4.98)	0.350	7.54	1.75
(7)		-0.44 (-0.49)				-0.16 (-2.23)	0.72 (6.03)	0.254	4.77	1.84
(8)			-0.22 (-0.35)			-0.16 (-2.18)	0.72 (5.89)	0.257	4.84	1.81
(9)				-0.71 (-1.19)		-0.12 (-1.88)	0.66 (5.03)	0.327	6.82	1.78

(10)	-0.02	-0.19	0.75	0.231	4.21	1.85
	(-0.44)	(-2.69)	(6.42)			
(11)		0.06	0.98	0.008	0.24	1.91
		(0.50)	(25.80)			

Notes: Estimations were made using Cochrane-Orcutt two-stage iteration procedure for serial correlation correction.
See text for definition of variables.
( ) = t statistic.
F = F statistic.
r^2 = correlation coefficient.
DW = Durbin-Watson statistic.

Table 7-3
Venezuelan Defense Expenditures, Trend-Structural Analysis, 1950-83

Equation	Time	Independent Variables						RHO	Statistics		
		DUMA	DUMB	DUMC	DUMD	DUMP			r^2	F	DW
(1)	114.25 (9.69)							0.56 (3.94)	0.752	94.07	1.87
(2)		978.57 (3.55)						0.91 (12.32)	0.289	12.63	2.63
(3)			91.42 (0.28)					0.94 (16.16)	0.002	0.079	2.25
(4)				−486.47 (2.34)				0.91 (12.70)	0.150	5.50	2.43
(5)					618.06 (3.15)			0.98 (12.10)	0.242	9.93	2.42
(6)						−263.32 (−1.67)		0.95 (18.01)	0.083	2.80	2.30
(7)	82.23 (7.20)	805.56 (3.73)						0.41 (2.57)	0.892	124.27	1.99
(8)	84.91 (9.08)		737.06 (3.95)					0.11 (0.64)	0.938	229.75	1.90
(9)	94.09 (5.65)			291.10 (1.62)				0.54 (3.72)	0.784	56.60	1.93
(10)	88.53 (5.13)				381.95 (2.05)			0.58 (4.15)	0.761	48.01	1.94

| (11) | | 135.02
(11.00) | | -342.03
(-2.40) | 0.44
(2.87) | 0.853 | 87.36 | 1.89 |
| (12) | 489.65
(2.07) | 108.40
(6.27) | | -226.44
(-1.54) | 0.21
(1.28) | 0.927 | 114.79 | 1.89 |

Notes: Estimations were made using Cochrane-Orcutt two-stage iteration process for serial correlation.
See text for definition of variables.
( ) = t statistic.
F = F statistic.
r^2 = correlation coefficient.
DW = Durbin-Watson statistic.

128 · Venezuela

Table 7-4
Venezuelan Real Defense Expenditures: Trend Analysis, Residuals (Actual-Estimated)

	Time	Time DUMA	Time DUMB	Time DUMP	Time DUMB DUMP	Trend Variable GEP	GEP DUMC	GRP	GRP DUMD DUMP	GDPNP	GCNP	GCNP DUMA
1951	43.2	-73.0	-59.7	34.8	-24.1	-170.0	-157.0	-133.0	-230.0	-194.0	-212.0	-200.0
1952	-12.5	-120.0	-118.0	-39.6	-97.3	-175.0	-165.0	-146.0	-221.0	-205.0	-215.0	-210.0
1953	-71.2	-173.0	-192.0	-120.0	-183.0	-195.0	-185.0	-166.0	-237.0	-241.0	-246.0	-233.0
1954	40.4	-59.6	-104.0	-32.4	-104.0	-42.1	-28.9	-2.2	-85.8	-122.0	-118.0	-87.7
1955	88.6	15.1	-7.2	10.0	-34.4	-11.9	7.2	25.1	75.5	-40.8	-26.2	-16.6
1956	42.1	-1.0	6.5	-39.4	-50.3	-57.9	-38.6	-91.0	-27.7	-82.7	-11.8	-37.0
1957	277.0	25.2	265.0	183.0	187.0	118.0	155.0	160.0	223.0	94.4	184.0	180.0
1958	246.0	27.5	365.0	509.0	467.0	-15.2	36.6	156.0	197.0	247.0	20.3	46.8
1959	17.4	80.6	207.0	127.0	228.0	-103.0	-83.6	-165.0	74.5	93.6	123.0	6.9
1960	-218.0	-163.0	-80.2	-140.0	62.7	-231.0	-222.0	-278.0	-80.0	-73.0	-255.0	-288.0
1961	-127.0	-103.0	-112.0	-97.0	-80.	-115.0	-86.8	-130.0	-185.0	-47.2	-60.8	-70.1
1962	-242.0	-213.0	-244.0	-234.0	-223.0	-95.0	-87.3	-169.0	-265.0	-177.0	-104.0	-125.0
1963	-13.3	9.0	-64.3	-35.9	-47.4	89.3	122.0	107.0	-95.1	50.8	34.0	84.3
1964	-146.0	-84.6	-111.0	-165.0	-130.0	-37.9	-10.0	-54.7	-64.9	-62.6	22.8	9.9
1965	-32.6	39.1	3.2	-69.4	-31.1	86.8	120.0	104.0	131.0	91.7	97.5	115.0
1966	-127.0	-24.2	-28.7	-166.0	-93.9	-3.6	28.9	24.4	175.0	63.5	17.6	25.0
1967	31.3	146.0	134.0	-24.9	52.9	149.0	190.0	142.0	337.0	220.0	201.0	216.0
1968	-16.0	-6.9	27.4	-213.0	-89.0	-34.8	2.0	-61.1	335.0	41.0	82.9	51.6
1969	-323.0	-169.0	-163.0	-58.8	-61.5	-149.0	-112.0	-153.0	-124.0	-37.6	-63.0	-77.5
1970	-304.0	-166.0	-221.0	-230.0	-166.0	-36.7	-2.4	-107.0	-292.0	-136.0	-154.0	-72.3
1971	63.8	204.0	125.0	114.0	170.0	331.0	376.0	279.0	-77.4	240.0	233.0	345.0
1972	93.4	299.0	318.0	167.0	308.0	258.0	313.0	268.0	229.0	342.0	279.0	345.0
1973	-29.6	226.0	-426.0	54.0	-231.0	110.0	164.0	-27.3	52.2	65.0	118.0	179.0
1974	807.0	274.0	515.0	537.0	488.0	550.0	291.0	61.5	-541.0	168.0	652.0	64.4
1975	726.0	667.0	833.7	691.0	145.0	527.0	544.0	689.0	398.0	193.0	554.0	464.0
1976	-732.0	-714.0	-427.0	-735.0	-578.0	-1060.0	-1030.0	-910.0	-219.0	-803.0	-1090.0	-1130.0
1977	314.0	163.0	87.7	160.0	48.6	106.0	185.0	439.0	186.0	22.2	22.2	211.0
1978	41.5	-37.7	-1.9	-85.1	-100.0	0.1	25.6	127.0	465.0	-98.1	-5.31	36.1
1979	-44.8	-117.0	-96.5	151.1	18.6	335.0	-134.0	-55.3	-62.7	-428.0	-167.0	-82.4
1980	170.0	97.0	86.0	186.0	144.0	253.0	196.0	189.0	248.0	-51.3	11.3	146.0
1981	5.2	-27.0	11.4	26.0	32.6	-452.0	-390.0	-251.0	-491.0	1.6	-189.0	-47.9
1982	-213.0	-239.0	-219.0	-214.0	-210.0	69.0	-26.4	182.0	117.0	37.1	56.7	20.7
1983	-209.0	-257.0	-308.0	-251.0	-293.0	—	—	—	—	229.0	219.0	132.0

r^2	0.752	0.892	0.938	0.853	0.927	0.360	0.443	0.322	0.961	0.858	0.729	0.566
F	94.07	124.27	229.7	87.36	114.79	16.87	11.15	14.24	221.86	188.50	83.48	19.54
DW	1.87	1.99	1.91	1.89	1.89	2.11	2.32	2.80	2.00	2.13	1.94	2.35

Notes: Estimations were made using Cochrane-Orcutt two-stage iteration process for serial correlation.
See text for definition of variables.
( ) = t statistic.
F = F statistic.
r^2 = correlation coefficient.
DW = Durbin-Watson statistic.

130 · *Venezuela*

that sector received relatively small allocations in light of the amount of funds suddenly placed at the disposal of the government. Again, defense expenditures in the country appear to be quite stable, neither reduced in line with other government programs during periods of austerity, nor increased dramatically during periods of affluence.

Historical Defense-Macroeconomic Patterns

The previous section identified government revenue patterns as a major element associated with movements in defense expenditures. Clearly, a large percentage of the Venezuelan government's revenues is made up of oil revenues. Futhermore, higher oil revenues permit not only greater expenditure outlays but, in addition, have exerted considerable political pressure on the country's respective ministries to increase allocations in all areas. Thus, the magnitude of oil revenues appears to be of critical importance in determining the volume of public expenditures in Venezuela.

To show the historical relationship of government revenues to military expenditures in Venezuela, regressions were performed using various macroeconomic variables and fiscal indices as regressors. The independent variables included the levels of real government expenditures (*GEP*), real gross domestic product (*GDPNP*), real government debt (*GDP*), real government consumption (*GCNP*), real government current deficit (*GDEFP*), real government revenues (*GRP*), the financial system's real credit to the government (*MSGCP*), and the public sector's real foreign borrowing (*GFBP*). In addition, the five dummy variables described above were included to test for structural shifts in the specified equations.

To test for stability in the relationships, the 1950–82 time period was arbitrarily broken down into two subperiods of more or less equal intervals, 1950–65 and 1966–82. The results in table 7–5, obtained by regressing each variable on defense expenditure, indicate (based on the correlation coefficient) that for the period as a whole (1950–82), defense expenditures were most closely related to *GNPNP*, followed by *GCNP*, *GEP*, and *GRP*. Interestingly, *MSGCP*, *GFBP*, and *GDP* had negative signs. In general, a number of dummy variables were also significant. The results for the subperiods indicate that the linkage between defense expenditures and these variables was more stable in the 1950–65 period (see table 7–6), weakening somewhat in the 1966–82 period (see table 7–7). The size of the coefficients for all of the independent variables is also considerably lower for the 1966–82 period, confirming the conclusion reached in the previous section that a weakening over time occurred between these major macroeconomic aggregates and defense spending.

Note for the period as a whole (table 7–8), the significant increase in the elasticity of defense expenditures (from 0.33 to 0.94) when a dummy variable (*DUMA*) was added to the regression equation to capture the structural shift associated with the 1973–74 oil price increase. Clearly, the negative sign on the dummy and the rise in elasticity indicate that military expenditures have not kept pace directly with the post-1973–74 increases in oil revenues.

To gain some idea of the responsiveness of defense expenditures to movements in the macrofiscal variables, regressions were performed on the variables in their logarithmic form. In this specification, the coefficients of the regression equations are interpreted as elasticities (a 1-percent change in the independent variable produces an x percent change in real defense expenditures). The results shown in tables 7–8 through 7–10 are consistent with those presented in tables 7–5 through 7–7. In general, the strength of the independent variables in affecting real defense expenditures has declined somewhat over time. For example, during the 1950–65 period (table 7–9), a 1-percent change in real government revenue was associated with a 0.99 percent change in real defense expenditures. As table 7–10 shows, by 1966–82, the same 1-percent change in government expenditures was associated with only a 0.48 percent increase in defense spending. The major exception to this pattern is government consumption. During the 1950–65 period, real government consumption was weakly related (and not statistically significant) to defense expenditure—a 1-percent increase in real consumption associated with a 0.55-percent increase in real defense expenditures. By 1966–82, not only was real government debt highly significant statistically when regressed on defense, but its elasticity increased to 0.63 (table 7–10). Taking into account the structural shift associated with the post-1973 increase in petroleum prices, however, it appears that the overall (1950–82) elasticity of military expenditures with respect to government revenues is around 1.00, the same as in the 1950–65 subperiod.

It should be noted that the negative sign on government debt (*GDP*) is as was predicted by the cross-section analysis presented in part I of this book. Specifically, Group 2 countries, one of which is Venezuela, have apparently not resorted to external public borrowing as a means of financing higher levels of military expenditure.

Table 7-5
Determinants of Venezuelan Military Expenditures, 1950-82

Equation	Independent Variables										Statistics		
	GRP	GEP	GDPNP	GCNP	DUMA	DUMB	DUMC	DUMD	DUMP	RHO	r^2	F	DW
(1) MEP =	0.018 (3.77)									0.91 (12.78)	0.321	14.24	2.80
(2)		0.04 (4.10)								0.81 (7.95)	0.360	16.87	2.11
(3)			0.02 (13.82)							0.44 (2.79)	0.854	176.49	2.17
(4)				0.10 (8.71)						0.59 (4.08)	0.716	75.84	1.98
(5)	0.037 (14.64)								389.83 (4.41)	0.17 (0.98)	0.928	181.72	2.07
(6)		0.027 (3.04)					408.82 (2.97)			0.81 (7.96)	0.443	11.15	2.32
(7)		0.021 (2.01)						455.56 (2.05)		0.84 (8.96)	0.390	8.96	2.27
(8)			0.018 (10.19)				-364.58 (-2.05)			0.25 (1.47)	0.921	163.00	1.96
(9)				0.06 (2.62)	767.56 (2.22)					0.73 (6.11)	0.576	19.05	2.34
(10)				0.06 (2.59)				428.01 (1.80)		0.75 (6.51)	0.516	14.94	2.21

(1) $MEP =$	−0.027 (−3.39)					0.95 (17.90)	0.276	11.49	2.49
(2)		−0.029 (−2.24)				0.95 (17.92)	0.143	5.03	2.19
(3)			−0.018 (−1.71)	957.67 (3.47)		0.94 (16.79)	0.325	6.76	2.73
(4)			−0.022 (−1.86)		−317.50 (−1.86)	0.96 (21.35)	0.185	3.17	2.38
(5)	−0.021 (−2.35)			390.17 (1.87)		0.92 (13.53)	0.348	7.48	2.61
(6)		−0.028 (−2.54)		939.03 (3.62)		0.93 (14.43)	0.403	9.44	2.71
(7)		−0.037 (−3.32)		713.59 (3.98)		0.92 (13.72)	0.437	10.87	2.08
(8)		−0.038 (−3.22)			−404.88 (−2.79)	0.961 (19.92)	0.328	6.89	2.35

Notes: Estimations were made using Cochrane-Orcutt two-stage process for serial correlation.
See text for definition of variables.
( ) = t statistic.
F = F statistic.
r^2 = correlation coefficient.
DW = Durbin-Watson statistic.

Table 7-6
Determinants of Venezuelan Military Expenditures, 1950-65

Equation	Independent Variables								Statistics		
	GRP	GEP	GDPNP	GCNP	GDP	MSGCP	DUMP	RHO	r^2	F	DW
(1) MEP =	0.084 (5.40)							0.43 (1.85)	0.691	29.16	1.74
(2)		0.08 (6.82)						0.75 (4.48)	0.781	46.61	1.64
(3)			0.021 (4.58)					0.68 (3.72)	0.617	21.01	1.61
(4)				0.096 (2.50)				0.83 (5.80)	0.325	6.28	1.80
(5)					0.056 (-2.31)			0.92 (9.77)	0.293	5.36	2.23
(6)						-0.11 (-5.40)	758.82 (9.56)	0.21 (0.81)	0.891	49.50	1.89
(7)	0.061 (3.38)						338.71 (3.04)	0.63 (3.20)	0.688	13.23	1.53
(8)		0.10 (7.47)					-257.54 (-2.87)	0.85 (6.46)	0.840	31.60	1.87
(9)			0.019 (3.89)				211.35 (1.91)	0.76 (4.47)	0.636	10.52	1.73

Notes: Estimations were made using Cochrane-Orcutt two-stage iteration procedure for serial correlation. See text for definition of variables.
( ) = t statistic.
F = F statistic.
r^2 = correlation coefficient.
DW = Durbin-Watson statistic.

Table 7-7
Determinants of Venezuelan Military Expenditures, 1966-82

Equation	Independent Variables						Statistics		
	GRP	GEP	GDPNP	GCNP	DUMB	RHO	r^2	F	DW
(1) MEP =	0.033 (16.06)					-0.36 (-1.57)	0.948	258.03	2.11
(2)		0.033 (3.90)				-0.44 (2.00)	0.521	15.26	1.88
(3)			0.012 (7.58)			0.13 (0.57)	0.804	57.54	1.98
(4)				0.076 (4.90)		1.32 (1.37)	0.632	24.02	1.88
(5)	0.025 (4.20)				413.41 (1.49)	-0.36 (-1.61)	0.955	130.12	2.27
(6)		0.014 (1.80)			1018.26 (3.41)	-0.17 (-0.69)	0.887	47.51	2.19
(7)			0.007 (2.41)		692.04 (1.95)	-0.17 (-0.720)	0.905	56.97	2.14
(8)				0.031 (1.82)	985.13 (3.14)	-0.21 (-0.89)	0.897	52.38	2.24

Table 7-7 continued

	Independent Variables								Statistics		
Equation	MSGCP	GFBP	GDP	GDEFP	DUMC	DUMD	DUMP	RHO	r^2	F	DW
(1) MEP =	-0.026 (-2.37)							0.83 (6.08)	0.287	5.63	2.50
(2)		-0.028 (-1.59)						0.85 (6.51)	0.154	2.55	2.28
(3)			-0.024 (1.50)				-481.08 (-2.07)	0.91 (9.27)	0.300	2.57	2.73
(4)	-0.022 (-2.85)				627.56 (4.73)			0.18 (0.75)	9.785	21.97	2.10
(5)				0.032 (1.89)			-561.55 (2.41)	0.87 (7.35)	0.356	3.32	3.09
(6)		-0.035 (-2.27)				706.86 (3.24)		0.72 (4.18)	0.502	6.06	2.08
(7)		-0.045 (-3.01)					-624.47 (-3.09)	0.87 (7.39)	0.517	6.42	3.00

Notes: Estimations were made using Cochrane-Orcutt two-stage iteration procedure for serial correlation. See text for definition of variables.
( ) = t statistic.
F = F statistic.
r^2 = correlation coefficient.
DW = Durbin-Watson statistic.

Table 7-8
Venezuelan Military Expenditure Elasticities, 1950-82

Equation	Independent Variables								Statistics		
	GRP	GEP	GDPNP	GCNP	GDP	DUMA	RHO		r^2	F	DW
(1)	0.33 (3.54)						0.89 (11.08)		0.295	12.56	2.24
(2)		0.64 (7.36)					0.78 (7.10)		0.643	54.24	1.95
(3)			0.87 (9.15)				0.69 (5.46)		0.736	83.84	2.11
(4)				0.71 (6.13)			0.76 (6.69)		0.556	37.59	2.06
(5)					−0.056 (−2.80)		0.92 (14.16)		0.208	7.88	2.23
(6)	0.94 (14.63)					−0.47 (−4.30)	0.17 (1.44)		0.944	236.24	1.92
(7)		0.59 (4.90)				0.05 (0.38)	0.80 (7.48)		0.615	22.44	1.97
(8)			0.97 (7.81)			−0.11 (−0.83)	2.62 (4.49)		0.818	63.15	2.04
(9)				0.47 (2.69)		0.19 (1.56)	0.83 (8.63)		0.404	9.51	2.06
(10)					−0.058 (−3.22)	0.30 (3.10)	0.91 (12.26)		0.394	9.11	2.50

Notes: Estimations were made using Cochrane-Orcutt two-stage iteration process for serial correlation.
See text for definition of variables.
( ) = t statistic.
F = F statistic.
r^2 = correlation coefficient.
DW = Durbin-Watson statistic.

Table 7-9
Venezuelan Military Expenditure Elasticities, 1950-65

Equation	Independent Variables								Statistics		
	GRP	GEP	GDPNP	GCNP	GDP	DUMP		RHO	r^2	F	DW
(1)	0.99 (8.12)							0.28 (1.13)	0.835	65.94	1.78
(2)		0.86 (5.95)						0.76 (4.46)	0.731	35.43	1.63
(3)			1.23 (4.67)					0.70 (3.91)	0.626	21.77	1.60
(4)				0.55 (1.93)				0.85 (6.34)	0.222	3.73	1.68
(5)					-0.06 (-3.05)			0.89 (7.71)	0.417	9.30	2.12
(6)	0.63 (3.56)					0.25 (2.50)		0.65 (3.35)	0.630	10.24	1.73
(7)		1.26 (9.16)				0.22 (-2.51)		0.48 (2.15)	0.928	77.42	1.78
(8)			1.18 (3.86)			0.14 (1.57)		0.76 (4.61)	0.604	9.15	1.67
(9)				0.66 (1.71)		-0.07 (-0.48)		0.86 (6.57)	0.230	1.79	1.65
(10)					-0.05 (-2.88)	0.053 (0.53)		0.89 (2.47)	0.427	4.48	2.13

Notes: Estimations were made using Cochrane-Orcutt two-stage iteration procedure for serial correlation.
See text for definition of variables.
( ) = t statistic.
F = F statistic.
r^2 = correlation coefficient.
DW = Durbin-Watson statistic.

Table 7-10
Venezuelan Military Expenditure Elasticities, 1966-82

Equation	Independent Variables									Statistics		
	GRP	GEP	GDPNP	GCNP	GDP	DUMB	DUMP	RHO		r^2	F	DW
(1)	0.48 (18.97)							-0.27 (-1.15)		0.962	359.9	2.13
(2)		0.56 (5.41)						0.42 (1.86)		0.676	29.27	1.82
(3)			0.72 (9.32)					0.12 (0.52)		0.861	86.97	1.92
(4)				0.63 (6.31)				0.30 (1.30)		0.740	139.92	1.81
(5)					-0.05 (-0.63)			0.87 (7.08)		0.027	0.40	2.17
(6)		0.33 (2.70)				0.20 (1.75)		0.08 (0.34)		0.859	36.83	1.94
(7)				0.35 (2.48)		0.25 (2.25)		-0.11 (-0.42)		0.903	56.12	2.09
(8)					0.036 (0.92)	0.46 (5.86)		-0.17 (-0.69)		0.881	44.45	2.26

Notes: Estimations were made using Cochrane-Orcutt two-stage iteration procedure for serial correlation.
See text for definition of variables.
( ) = t statistic.
F = F statistic.
r^2 = correlation coefficient.
DW = Durbin-Watson statistic.

Increases in debt, on the other hand, appear to be associated with austerity measures reducing the level of military expenditures.

In short, from 1950 to 1982, government revenues apparently played a dominant role in influencing defense expenditures, while the link between total government expenditures and defense expenditures is not nearly as strong in the later period (1966–82) as in the earlier period (1950–65). The level of real government consumption also appears much more influential in explaining defense expenditures in the later period, with a correlation coefficient of 0.740 compared to 0.222 in the 1950–65 period. The links between both real and gross domestic product and defense appear to have declined over time (judged by the elasticity), although when corrected for the post-1973 oil price increases, the elasticity of 0.97 is slightly lower than the 1.23 for the 1950–65 period.

Impact of Military Expenditures in Other Latin American Countries

One possible factor affecting Venezuelan military expenditures could be the perceived need on the part of the Venezuelan authorities to emulate military expenditures in neighboring states. This need could reflect either an imagined threat to Venezuelan security or simply emulation of the acquisitions of new weapons systems by regional neighbors.

To test the importance of this emulation effect, real military expenditures were regressed on real military expenditures in several neighboring countries. The results in table 7–11 indicate that, except for Ecuador, no statistically significant relationships were found. The lagged values of military expenditures in the sample of neighboring countries were also regressed on Venezuelan real military expenditures; again, except for Ecuador, no statistically significant relationships existed.

It should be noted that the relationship with Ecuador's military expenditures is barely significant (2.39 t value, as shown in table 7–11). Perhaps more importantly, the relationship may well be spurious since Ecuador is also an OPEC oil producer and most likely expanded its military expenditures after the 1973 oil price increases in a manner similar to Venezuela.

The correlation pattern of Venezuelan and Ecuadorian military expenditures can also be corrected for in part by the strong time trend in the regression of real military expenditures over time. For 1955–83, time alone accounts for 66.4 percent of the fluctuations in

Table 7-11
Venezuelan Defense Expenditures' Response to Defense Expenditures in Selected Latin American Countries, 1955-82

Equation	Peruvian Defense Expenditures (PMEP)	Mexican Defense Expenditures (MMEP)	Colombian Defense Expenditures (CMEP)	Ecuadorian Defense Expenditures (EMEP)	Brazilian Defense Expenditures (BMEP)	Venezuelan Defense Expenditures Lagged (VMEPL)	Ecuadorian Defense Expenditures Lagged (EMEPL)	RHO	Statistics r^2	F	DW
Venezuelan military expenditure (VMEP) =	0.003 (1.73)							0.86 (8.81)	0.111	3.02	1.85
		-0.08 (-1.83)						0.95 (15.86)	0.112	3.35	2.02
			-0.01 (-0.41)					0.92 (12.57)	0.007	0.17	2.22
				0.22 (2.39)				0.87 (9.04)	0.193	0.159	5.75
					-0.003 (-0.50)			0.93 (13.14)	0.011	0.257	2.17
						0.42 (13.68)	0.08 (2.21)	—	0.916	0.916	1.46

Notes: Estimations were made using Cochrane-Orcutt two-stage iteration procedure for serial correlation.
( ) = t statistic.
F = F statistic.
r^2 = correlation coefficient.
DW = Durbin-Watson statistic.

Venezuelan military expenditures and 56.1 percent of the fluctuations in Ecuadorian military expenditures, as shown in table 7-12.

Introducing the effect of the 1973-74 oil price increases in the regression equations (equations 2 and 9 of table 7-12) increases the correlation coefficient to 88 percent for Venezuela and 90.7 percent for Ecuador. The oil price structural change was positive for both countries (each of which is a member of OPEC) and highly significant, indicating a break in the historical pattern of military expenditures for each country, wherein additional revenue accrued to both governments after 1973.

Note, also, the strong time trends in military expenditures for Colombia, Peru, and Mexico. Of the major oil importers examined, Colombia and Brazil experienced reductions in military expenditures following the 1973-74 oil price increases, while Peru's pattern of real military expenditures was not affected by these external shocks, as table 7-12 shows. Mexico and Argentina, both domestic producers of oil, did not experience alterations in their pattern of military expenditures following the oil price shocks. Of course, Argentina's pattern of military expenditure was greatly affected by the Falklands War. A dummy variable ($DUMW$) for this period (Values: 0 = 1955-81, 1 = 1982-82) was highly significant when regressed on that country's real military expenditures in table 7-12.

In short, one can conclude that Venezuelan military expenditures have been determined largely by developments internal to that country (oil revenues and increased gross domestic product), with military expenditure patterns of regional countries affecting allocations for Venezuelan defense marginally, if at all.

Determinants of the Deviation from Trends in Real Military Expenditures

As was noted, having corrected for the structural change associated with the post-1973 oil price increases, one finds great stability in the patterns of Venezuelan military expenditures. The linkage between government revenues and military expenditures is undoubtedly more complicated than outlined above, however. It is unlikely that there is a pure one-to-one relationship between government revenue and military expenditures in each time period. To throw more light on the matter, this section examines in detail the linkages over time between changes in government revenues (largely from oil) and the subsequent allocations for military expenditures.

Table 7-12
Determinants of Military Expenditures, Trend Analysis for Selected Latin American Countries, 1955-83

Equation	Time	DUMA	DUMB	Trend Variables DUMC	DUMD	DUMW	RHO	r^2	Statistics F	DW
Venezuela	$MEP =$									
(1)	120.01 (6.89)						0.52 (3.19)	0.664	47.58	1.81
(2)	71.97 (4.45)	913.82 (3.86)					0.30 (1.60)	0.880	81.11	1.93
(3)	70.27 (5.56)		963.51 (4.91)				-0.09 (-0.51)	0.939	172.22	2.01
(4)	87.96 (3.48)			357.07 (1.64)			0.50 (2.91)	0.723	28.72	1.89
(5)	80.81 (3.21)				454.25 (2.06)		0.53 (3.18)	0.712	27.21	1.89
Colombia										
(6)	384.87 (1.74)						0.66 (4.59)	0.110	3.05	1.70
(7)	972.38 (9.46)		-11623.0 (-7.26)				-0.13 (-0.67)	0.799	43.79	2.10
Ecuador										
(8)	190.56 (5.54)						0.52 (3.18)	0.561	30.79	2.24
(9)	92.93 (3.87)	1873.34 (4.92)					-0.07 (-0.37)	0.907	107.45	1.93
(10)	113.71 (3.25)		1395.62 (2.65)				0.19 (0.96)	0.816	48.89	2.00
Peru										
(11)	13491.6 (5.71)						0.64 (4.26)	0.576	32.62	1.82
(12)	11173.6 (4.12)	31200.3 (0.88)					0.54 (3.30)	0.673	22.67	1.72

144 · *Venezuela*

Table 7-12 continued

Equation	Time	Trend Variables DUMA	DUMB	DUMC	DUMD	DUMW	RHO	Statistics r^2	F	DW
Brazil										
(13)	1717.0 (1.35)						0.69 (4.63)	0.077	1.84	2.23
(14)	3942.5 (3.22)			-17816.5 (-1.85)			0.45 (2.53)	0.363	5.71	2.13
(15)	3904.0 (3.15)				-18792.4 (-1.89)		0.50 (2.83)	0.339	5.14	2.13
Mexico										
(16)	685.9 (13.07)						0.37 (2.06)	0.876	171.06	1.63
(17)	865.7 (7.64)	-2479.6 (-1.86)					0.62 (4.10)	0.770	36.86	1.84
(18)	665.0 (7.45)		390.9 (0.31)				0.38 (2.11)	0.874	76.73	1.63
Argentina										
(19)	575.7 (2.77)					8050.5 (8.39)	0.88 (10.02)	0.815	53.04	1.32
(20)						8358.8 (8.55)	0.97 (22.30)	0.745	73.14	1.24

Notes: Estimations were made using Cochrane-Orcutt two-stage iteration for serial correlation correction.
See text for definition of variables.
( ) = t statistic.
F = F statistic.
r^2 = correlation coefficient.
DW = Durbin-Watson statistic.

Because of the strength of the time trend in both military expenditures and their major determinants—government revenues (*GRP*), government expenditures (*GEP*), gross domestic product (*GDPNP*), and government consumption (*GCNP*)—the empirical relationships may be somewhat spurious. Military expenditures and government expenditures might, for example, be correlated with some other variable that, in turn, had a strong time trend. The high correlation between military expenditure and, for example, gross national product would have been only apparent and not indicative of any particular causal relationship.

To determine whether or not spurious correlation accounted for the high correlations of military expenditures and the independent variables examined above, all variables were regressed on time and the dummy variables associated with oil prices and political change. The deviations from the trend for each of the variables were then regressed on the deviations from the trend in real military expenditures (*MEPDT*), that is, the deviations from the regression equation of real military expenditures were regressed on time.

The various measures of deviations from the trend in real government revenues were computed from the deviations from the regression equation or real government revenues on:

1. Time (*GRPDT*),
2. Time, *DUMC, DUMP* (*GRPDCP*),
3. Time, *DUMC* (*GRPDTC*),
4. Time, *DUMP* (*GRPDTP*), and
5. Time, *DUMD* (*GRPDTD*).

The deviations from the trend in government revenues lagged one year were:

1. Time, *DUMC* (*GRPDTCL*);
2. Time (*GRPDTL*).

Similarly, deviations from the trend were computed for the macrovariables assumed to affect real military expenditures. These deviations were computed from:

1. For government expenditure, the regression of real government expenditure on time (*GEPDT*);

2. For gross national product, the regression of real gross national product on:
   a. Time (*GDPNPDT*);
   b. Time, *DUMP* (*GDPNPDT*)
3. For government consumption, the regression of real government consumption on time (*GCNPDT*);
4. For gross national product lagged one year, the regression of gross national product lagged one year on:
   a. Time (*GDNPNDTL*);
   b. Time, *DUMA* (*GDPNPDTAL*);
   c. Time, *DUMP* (*GDNPPDTPL*).

The results in tables 7–13 and 7–14 show that even after extracting the trend from military expenditures and the major independent variables selected for the analysis, the strong statistical significance of the regression equations persists. In terms of government revenues, a number of alternative specifications of the deviation from the trend were statistically significant when regressed on military expenditures with the deviations from the trend of government revenues regressed on time and *DUMD* (*GRPDTCD*), accounting for over 40 percent of the deviations from the trend in military expenditures regressed on time (*MEPDT*). (See table 7–13.) Interestingly, lagged values of the deviations from the trend (*GRPDTCL* and *GRPDTL*) in government revenues were also statistically significant in accounting for deviations from the trend in real military expenditures, as shown in table 7–13.

Lagged deviations from the trend for real gross national product were also highly significant in explaining deviations from the trend in real military expenditures, as revealed in table 7–14. In fact, lagged values for real gross national product were much more highly correlated with deviations from the trend in real military expenditures than current period values for GDP.

Conclusions

The statistically significant results obtained using lagged values, together with the stability of real defense expenditures as a share in gross domestic product, suggest that long-run forces may interact to maintain stability in the level of defense allocations. Revenue or

Table 7-13
Venezuelan Government Revenue Determinants of the Deviations from the Historical Trend in Defense Expenditures, 1950-82

	Measures of the Deviation of Revenues from the Historical Trend in Government Revenues								Statistics		
Equation	GRPDT	GRPDTCP	GRPDTC	GRPDTP	GRPDTCD	GRPDTCL	GRPDTL	RHO	r^2	F	DW
(1) MEPDT =	0.04 (3.02)							0.02 (0.10)	0.240	9.16	1.99
(2)		0.02 (2.52)						−0.04 (−0.22)	0.180	6.36	1.99
(3)			0.03 (5.37)					−0.40 (−2.44)	0.499	28.90	2.04
(4)				0.02 (3.51)				−0.20 (−1.12)	0.299	12.36	2.03
(5)					0.03 (4.65)			−0.39 (−2.40)	0.427	21.66	2.02
(6)						0.02 (2.98)		−0.08 (−0.50)	0.241	8.93	1.93
(7)							0.02 (2.86)	−0.13 (−0.73)	0.227	8.20	1.99

Notes: Estimations were made using Cochrane-Orcutt two-stage iteration process for serial correlation.
See text for definition of variables.
( ) = t statistic.
F = F statistic.
r^2 = correlation coefficient.
DW = Durbin-Watson statistic.
L = variable lagged one year.

Table 7-14
Venezuelan Government Expenditures and GNP: Determinants of the Deviations from the Historical Trend in Defense Expenditures, 1950–82

	Measures of Deviations From Historical Trend								Statistics		
Equation	GEPDT	GDPNPDT	GDPNPDTP	GCNPDT	GDPNPDTL	GDPNPDTAL	GDPNDTPL	RHO	r^2	F	DW
(1) MEPDT	0.03 (2.70)							−0.05 (−0.29)	0.201	7.33	2.02
(2)		0.01 (3.39)						−0.34 (−2.05)	0.348	15.51	2.15
(3)			0.02 (3.21)					−0.26 (−1.54)	0.262	10.33	2.11
(4)				0.08 (2.35)				−0.13 (−0.73)	0.160	5.52	2.06
(5)					0.02 (5.41)			0.02 (0.12)	0.511	29.33	1.99
(6)						0.05 (5.77)		0.04 (0.24)	0.544	33.37	1.96
(7)							0.02 (5.49)	0.04 (0.21)	0.518	30.17	1.98

Notes: Estimations were made using Cochrane-Orcutt two-stage iteration process for serial correlation.
See text for definition of variables.
( ) = t statistic.
F = F statistic.
r^2 = correlation coefficient.
DW = Durbin-Watson statistic.
L = variable lagged one year.

expenditure changes clearly impact on defense expenditures over more than a one-year time interval.

In brief, this analysis of the data for the 1970s and early 1980s indicates that the trends perceived by Heare and Schmitter have persisted but are not as strong as those found in the 1950s and 1960s. Presumably, the Venezuelan government wishes to maintain some overall proportion of GNP in defense expenditures, thus delineating the optimal level of defense expenditures. The difference between the actual level of defense expenditures at any point in time and this optimal level affects the amount of funds allocated for defense in any single year. Apparently, because of uncertainty concerning the optimal level of defense expenditures caused by oil shocks in the 1970s and early 1980s, the government has had an increasingly difficult time in delineating the speed with which actual levels of expenditures are to be adjusted to the optimal level.

Given the country's limited need for defense expenditures, it will be interesting to observe how the government scales down the optimal level of defense expenditures in response to declining oil revenues and how significant an impact this declining optimal level will have on year-to-year cutbacks in defense expenditures.

Notes

1. C. Brown, "Latin American Arms: For War? The Experience of the Period 1971-80," *Inter-American Economic Affairs* (Summer 1983), p. 61. Quoted from U.S. Arms Control and Disarmament Agency, *World Military Expenditures and Arms Transfers, 1978-80* (Washington: ACDA, 1983), p. 26.

2. *Ibid.*

3. P. Schmitter, "Foreign Military Spending and Military Rule in Latin America" in P. Schmitter, ed., *Military Rule in Latin America: Function, Consequences and Perspectives* (Beverly Hills, Calif.: Sage, 1973).

4. Gertrude E. Heare, *Trends in Latin American Military Expenditures* (Washington, D.C.: U.S. Department of State, 1971).

5. For a detailed nonquantitative analysis of an earlier period, cf. E. Baloyra, "Oil Policies and Budgets in Venezuela, 1938-68," *Latin American Research Review* (Summer 1974), pp. 28-72.

6. A general description of the use and interpretation of dummy variables can be found in P. Rao and R. Miller, *Applied Econometrics* (Belmont, Calif.: Wadsworth, 1971), pp. 88-93.

7. Cf. Cecilian M. Valentine, *The Political, Economic and Labor Climate in Venezuela* (Philadelphia: University of Pennsylvania, The Wharton School, 1979), pp. 88-93.

8
Determinants of Venezuelan Budgetary Patterns: Possible Trade-offs between Defense and Nondefense Expenditures

As noted in chapter 5, recent research in allocation policy analysis has demonstrated a fascination with two components of government spending—welfare and defense. The emphasis of the research has been the negative consequences of military spending for economic growth and social welfare, with particular focus on the modern industrial nations of North America and Western Europe. However, the problem of trade-offs between military spending and economic and social investment is perhaps even more serious in developing countries such as Venezuela.

This chapter focuses on two basic questions posed in earlier research:

1. Are substitutions likely to occur among military and economic and social spending categories?
2. Do such substitutions occur more intensely during periods characterized by the predominance of certain economic conditions?

Conceptual Issues

From an econometric point of view some trade-off occurs whenever resources are devoted to one sector rather than another. However, it is unlikely that any country will reduce allocations to its military to zero. Some trade-off will inevitably occur. Research on the guns versus butter problem must go beyond the mere identification of these trade-offs to focus on two critical issues: (1) the locus and weight of the burden of military allocations on other sectors and (2) the willingness of governments to divert money to defense and away from other nondefense sectors as economic conditions change.

Few scholars have devoted attention to developing countries.[1] Research in that context has focused rather on the comparison of policy outputs and outcomes of military governments as opposed to civilian governments, and the results have been conflicting to say the least.[2] Few scholars have attempted to compare policies in the context of exogenous factors such as the level and rate of inflation and development, or the level of political stability, which may influence policy outputs of either type of regime. In an era of long-range programming for economic development, governments of developing countries are confronted with the difficult problem of selecting the best set of policies for the allocation of resources for economic growth, while at the same time reconciling these policies to often more immediate demands of economic, social, and political realities.

These remarks should serve as a reminder that economists are a long way from understanding the interface of economy and polity. The discussion of substitution effects, particularly by political scientists, should seek to explore that interface in terms of both the social and economic consequences of chosen policies and the political rationale behind the choices.

One of the reasons why there is such conflicting evidence on the relationship between guns and butter is that research has been performed at a high level of aggregation and across sets of countries that vary widely on the crucial variables—levels of development and types of regimes. Working at this level, it is difficult to separate out the effects of individual variables. The economic focus of studies like Pryor's and Benoit's tends to overlook the role of political factors.[3] Moreover, the emphasis on macroeconomic categories (GNP aggregates) places the question of policy choice in an area which government decision makers can control only imperfectly.

Longitudinal strategies rely on summary statistics which obscure sharp yearly variations, a serious problem when dealing with the erratic growth patterns of developing countries. Those studies that do attempt to assess political impacts on policy decisions by examining types of differences between military and civilian regimes overlook a wide variation of policy orientations within these two categories and, more importantly, overlook the many other ways (besides overt intervention) in which the military may wield influence.[4]

This analysis attempts to resolve some of these conceptual and methodological problems by examining only one country—Venezuela—in detail. Trade-offs between military allocations, development-oriented allocations, and more traditional status quo and system maintenance allocations are examined. Data on these policies are derived from the International Monetary Fund's major data base on *Government, Finance and Expenditures*.[5] By restricting the analysis to trade-offs between government spending categories, economists have only a limited capability to assess the burden of policy decisions for the whole economy, but one does have greater confidence that one is examining the impact of political choices on an area over which decision makers have control. The restricted arena also provides a greater opportunity to explore the causes and consequences of yearly variations in allocations by major expenditure category.

Development-oriented policies may cover both human and capital resource development. Within the available data on Venezuelan expenditures, social development allocations to health, education, and welfare reflect human resource development policies. Allocations to transportation, communication, industry, and agriculture—infrastructural development—reflect capital resource development policies. Allocations to the federal bureaucracy for salaries and administration provide the best indicator of the weight of traditional, cliental political relationships on the budget.

To explore the relationships between these allocation categories, a variety of approaches based on different assumptions as to the nature of the allocation process are necessary. Previous research has focused primarily on the macroeconomic impact of military spending. Expenditure data were presented in ratio form (spending as a percentage of GNP); this ratio assumes a zero-sum game in which increases in one category necessarily entail decreases in other categories.

The GNP ratio was selected in order to overcome the trend effect of serial correlation in their time series. Russett explains the problem:

> The data appear as totals in current dollars but cannot be used in bivariate regressions in that form. Through a combination of inflation and real productivity increases, the dollar value of the U.S. GNP grew by nearly a factor of ten over the period examined. Since virtually all of the components also increased sharply over the same period, we would have high and, for our purposes, spurious, correlations between variables measured in current dollar amounts.[6]

Rather than a zero-sum game, most of Venezuela's allocation procedures (until the current period of austerity) can be described as an expanding-sum game. This means that negative shifts in the percent allocation figures do not necessarily entail negative shifts in the absolute levels of allocation. In an economy and polity characterized by instability and increasing demands for social improvements and increasing need for infrastructural development, distributed solutions may be the only means by which governments can postpone confrontations and keep their tenuous supporting coalitions intact. Such solutions however depend on an expanding output.

Assume, for example, a government has $100 to spend in *year 1* and $200 in *year 2*. If 15 percent of the budget is allocated to the military and welfare in *year 1*, each sector gets $15. In *year 2*, a one-to-one percent trade-off occurs and military gets 20 percent of the total while welfare gets only 10 percent. Military receives $40, a substantial increase, but welfare gets $20, still an increase over the previous year. Only in percent terms is welfare slighted. The government has given more to both categories, while giving less in percent terms. No one has "paid" in real terms for the greater amount given to the military. Only when the game fails to expand sufficiently do negative trade-offs in real terms occur.[7]

With these considerations in mind, the first step in the analysis of Venezuelan budgetary trade-offs between defense and non-defense items is to determine the main patterns and linkages of Venezuela's non-defense items. Here there are two main concerns:

1. Determining what the expected level of non-defense items would be, given the major macroeconomic trends in the economy;
2. Determining which of the macroeconomic aggregates appear to impact the greatest on nondefense allocations.

Clearly, budgetary trade-offs in an expanding economy cannot be adequately discussed until one can assess the likely level of nondefense expenditures *in the absence of any shift in defense allocations.*

Empirical Tests

As a starting point, a statistical study by Alan Tait and Peter S. Heller of international comparisons of expenditures and the forces that appear to influence them is suggestive of several variables that might be included in the time series analysis of Venezuelan expenditures.[8] That study covers the central government expenditures of some ninety countries, including nearly all the industrial countries and a large number of less-developed countries. Most of the data are for 1977.

By regression analysis, the authors related expenditures by functional and economic categories to variables thought likely to influence them. They tested for differences between countries with high and low per capita income. Where discontinuities were found, they reported results separately for each group. Expenditures were measured as ratios to gross domestic product (GDP). Although the statistics do not establish norms for expenditures, they are enlightening and they may suggest areas to examine in the analysis of the Venezuelan budgets.

The Tait-Heller study was most successful in statistically explaining the expenditure ratio for social security and welfare. This category includes expenditures for social security, other sickness, old age and disability payments, military and civil government pensions, and other welfare expenditures. The per capita income of the country, the percentage of the population over age 65, and the share of the labor force employed in industry were all positive and statistically significant influences. No discontinuity between high- and low-income countries was discovered, which suggests that the low expenditures for this function in most developing countries reflect mainly demographic and economic factors, rather than other social and political forces.

The health expenditure ratio was related positively to the percentage of the population over age 65 and negatively to the population per hospital bed ($r^2=0.62$). The latter factor may indicate only that countries with few hospital beds in relation to their population avoid spending for hospitals and do not substitute other health expenditures.

The ratio of educational expenditures to GDP was less well explained ($r^2=0.28$). For low-income countries, it was strongly associated with per capita income and also positively associated with the enrollment ratio in secondary schools. Surprisingly, the percentage of the population under age 15 was not statistically significant in influencing the ratio.

Expenditures for roads and other forms of transportation and for communications were positively related to the rate of growth of the urban population and negatively related to both the share of manufacturing and the share of agriculture in GDP. The ratio for housing and community amenities was positively related to per capita income in low-income countries, but not in high-income countries.

Expenditures for other economic services and for defense were well explained by the Tait-Heller study, with all r^2s below 0.20.

Because of the generally mixed results obtained by Tait and Heller in using a variety of social and demographic variables, it was felt that the analysis below could safely confine itself to a limited number of macroeconomic variables. Furthermore, it is assumed that the ability and the willingness of the Venezuelan government to divert money away from defense to other activities or vice versa can, to a certain degree, be gleaned from an examination of the stability of non-defense items with regard to these major macroeconomic indices.

Are there very stable patterns between non-defense items and such macroaggregates as:

1. Real government revenues (GRP),
2. Real government total expenditures (GEP),
3. Real gross domestic product ($GDPNP$),
4. Real government consumption ($GCNP$),
5. Real public debt (GDP),
6. Real central bank credit to the government ($CBCGP$),
7. Real government domestic borrowing ($GDBP$),
8. Real government deficit ($GDEFP$),
9. Real government foreign borrowing ($GFBP$), and
10. Real credit to the government from the monetary system ($MSCGP$).

As noted above, one can argue that the greater the correlation between non-defense budgetary items and these aggregates, the less the scope possessed by the government to expand defense expenditures rapidly in the short term.

General Public Services

In general, the government has maintained a fairly stable link between expenditures on general public services and the overall expansion in the economy, with real gross domestic product accounting for slightly over 85 percent of the fluctuation in real general public services (equation 1 in table 8-1). Interestingly, there is no statistically significant relationship between general public services and such aggregates as real government revenues (GRP) or overall real government expenditures (GEP). General public services are, however, fairly closely linked to real government consumption ($GCNP$) with increases in real government consumption accounting for nearly 63 percent of the fluctuations in real general public services (equation 2 in table 8-1). Expenditures on general public services are apparently cut back sharply when the government must rely on central bank credit (equation 3 in table 8-1).

Health Expenditures

Health expenditures are largely determined by overall movements in real government consumption (equation 5 in table 8-1). The government has also appeared willing to step up its domestic borrowing to maintain and expand the nation's health programs (equation 6 in table 8-1). In addition, health expenditures are closely linked to the overall expansion and contraction of the government's budget (equation 4 in table 8-1).

In short, given the government's willingness to borrow internally to support health programs, but its lack of willingness to borrow from the central bank to maintain general public services, one could likely expect that trade-offs between defense expenditures and general public services are possible and, indeed, likely to occur. Health expenditures, however, appear to be a major government priority, with the government willing to incur additional debt to maintain them. (Note that in this analysis the government was shown to be unwilling to incur additional debt, through either the central bank, domestic lenders, or foreign sources, to expand military expenditures.) There are likely to be few cutbacks in health expenditures if the government decides to expand military allocations.

Social Security and Welfare

Allocations for social security and welfare show a certain stability with overall government expenditures (GEP) (equation 8 in table 8-1) and real gross domestic product ($GDPNP$) (equation 9 in table 8-1). The sector's allocations are, however, negatively related to government revenue—indicating a fairly wide scope on the part of the government for allocating revenues to this sector. The willingness of the government to incur greater debt (equation 11 in table 8-1) and increase its deficit (equation 12 in table 8-1) in order to maintain social security and welfare, shows that this sector has a fairly high priority in the overall government budget. It is likely that only during periods of fairly rapid increases in government revenues would significant amounts of additional funds be allocated to defense at the expense of potential increases in social security and welfare expenditures. Clearly, in times of declining revenues, social security

Table 8-1
Venezuela: Budget Analysis, 1973-82

Equation	Independent Variables							Statistics		
	GRP	GEP	GDPNP	GCNP	CBCGP	GDBP	RHO	r^2	F	DW
General Public Services										
(1)			0.047 (6.33)				-0.48 (-1.64)	0.851	40.18	1.37
(2)				0.21 (3.41)			-0.06 (-0.19)	0.624	11.64	1.64
(3)					-0.83 (-5.02)		0.79 (3.89)	0.783	25.26	2.97
Health										
(4)		0.03 (3.09)					0.54 (1.95)	0.577	9.58	1.51
(5)				0.11 (6.69)			0.10 (0.34)	0.864	44.76	1.86
(6)						0.05 (4.41)	0.63 (2.46)	0.710	17.15	2.23
Social Security and Welfare										
(7)	-0.04 (-2.75)						0.26 0.83	0.520	7.60	1.37
(8)		0.04 (5.61)					-0.85 (-5.02)	0.818	31.49	1.96
(9)			0.01 (2.86)				-0.66 (-2.67)	0.540	8.22	1.51

Determinants of Budgetary Patterns · 159

Social Security and Welfare								
(10)						—	0.857	42.21	1.64
(11)	0.08 (6.49)					-0.44 (-1.49)	0.689	15.52	1.88
(12)		0.03 (3.93)				0.17 (0.53)	0.579	9.64	1.89
(13)			-0.06 (-3.10)			0.01 (0.03)	0.344	3.68	2.35
(14)				0.27 (1.92)		0.51 (1.80)	0.444	5.59	1.99
(15)					0.06 (2.36)	-0.10 (-2.61)	0.70 (2.93)	0.494	6.82	1.78
Housing and Community Services								
(16)						0.13 (2.15)	-0.38 (-1.25)	0.398	4.63	2.32
Other Community and Service Activities								
(17)	0.01 (5.12)						-0.44 (-1.50)	0.789	26.30	1.69
(18)		0.03 (3.55)					-0.20 (-0.63)	0.643	12.66	1.27

Table 8-1 continued

Equation	Independent Variables										RHO	Statistics		
	GRP	GEP	GDPNP	GCNP	GDP	GDEFP	CBCGP	GFBP	GDBP	MSCGP		r^2	F	DW
Other Community and Service Activities														
(19)						-0.01 (-1.92)					0.91 (7.03)	0.346	3.71	2.37
(20)							0.10 (3.93)				-0.09 (-0.28)	0.688	15.49	2.18
(21)										0.01 (5.78)	0.18 (0.54)	0.826	33.43	2.62
(22)					0.008 (3.14)						0.32 (1.01)	0.585	9.87	1.66
(23)								0.01 (4.93)			—	0.776	24.32	2.24
(24)									-0.01 (-1.88)		0.90 (6.55)	0.336	3.54	2.36
Economic Services														
(25)		0.99 (9.46)									0.79 (3.95)	0.927	89.64	2.49
(26)								-0.43 (-2.85)			-0.46 (-1.65)	0.538	8.17	2.25
(27)									1.59 (4.96)		-0.34 (-1.17)	0.778	24.63	1.85

Determinants of Budgetary Patterns · 161

					r^2	F	DW
Education							
(28)	0.09 (4.72)			-0.17 (-0.53)	0.761	22.29	1.29
(29)		0.56 (4.11)		0.44 (1.50)	0.707	16.93	1.93
(30)			-0.74 (-2.14)	0.84 (4.79)	0.396	4.58	2.48
(32)			0.01 (2.85)	0.32 (1.02)	0.538	8.17	2.02
(31)			0.18 (2.18)	0.74 (3.37)	0.530	7.92	1.87
Other Expenditures							
(33)	0.32 (2.92)			-0.08 (-0.02)	0.550	8.57	1.55
(34)			2.54 (4.34)	0.34 (1.10)	0.729	18.88	2.64
(36)			0.27 (4.07)	0.14 (0.43)	0.703	16.58	2.61

Notes: Estimations were made using Cochrane-Orcutt two-stage iteration process for serial correlation.
See text for identification of variables.
( ) = t statistic.
F = F statistic.
r^2 = regression coefficient.
DW = Durbin-Watson statistic.

and welfare might be expected to maintain their allocations at the expense of defense expenditures.

Housing and Community Services

Housing and community service expenditures have a poor correlation on all the main macroeconomic indicators other than the government's foreign borrowing (*GFBP*). Lack of any particular stability for this budgetary item suggests that it might be fairly vulnerable to increased defense allocations (or increased allocations to any other sector for that matter).

Other Community and Service Activities

As with social security and welfare, government expenditures on other community and service activities appear to be quite stable. This stability holds in particular for the overall government budget (*GEP*), which accounts for over 78 percent of the fluctuations in these activities' allocations (equation 17 in table 8-1). The government also appears willing to increase its deficit (equation 19 in table 8-1) to support allocations to other community and service activities, while credit to the government from the financial system accounts for over 82 percent of the fluctuations in expenditures in this sector.

Clearly, unless the government is constrained in terms of its domestic borrowing or ability to run increased deficits, this sector can be expected to grow in line with overall expansion in the government's budget. If defense expenditures were to expand over their historical rate, it is unlikely that they would be funded at the expense of this sector.

Economic Services

Economic services are largely a function of the overall level of government expenditures (*GEP*), with real government expenditures (equation 25 in table 8-1) accounting for over 92 percent of the fluctuations in economic services. The government also appears willing to increase its domestic borrowing (*GDBP*) to stabilize this type of expenditures in light of revenue fluctuations as shown in equation 27). It is quite unlikely, therefore, that defense expenditures could have a major expansion at the expense of the normal budgetary pattern of expenditures usually provided for economic services.

Education

Budgetary allocations for education appear to be largely related to the overall level of gross domestic product and real government consumption. Surprisingly, there are no close direct links with overall government expenditures (GEP) or revenues (GRP). The government does not seem willing to step up its domestic borrowing ($GDBP$) or borrowing from the financial system ($MSCGP$) (equations 31 and 32 in table 8-1). Because of the lack of any close relationship between GEP and educational expenditures, this may be an area where negative trade-offs could occur with defense expenditures.

Other Expenditures

As might be imagined, government expenditures for purposes other than those listed above follow no particular pattern. There is a slight correlation with overall government expenditures (equation 33 in table 8-1), while the government has increased its borrowing from the central bank (equation 34 in table 8-1) and the financial system (equation 35 in table 8-1) to fund these expenditures. In all likelihood, therefore, this type of expenditure must be reduced to fund any major expansion in defense expenditures.

Longer-Term Determinants of Nondefense Allocations

A major share of expenditures in oil-based economies such as Venezuela is undertaken by the government, which is the sole recipient of oil revenues. Furthermore, higher oil revenues not only permit greater public investment outlays but, in addition, exert considerable political pressure on the respective ministries to increase investment expenditures. Thus, the magnitude of oil revenues appears to be of critical importance in determining the volume of public investment outlays.

Government expenditures are assumed to be a linear stochastic function of the country's revenues. However, since the oil component of Venezuelan government revenues attained its present-day magnitude only recently and in a fairly discontinuous manner, one might expect adjustments over time to the altered level of revenues to be at different speeds for different sectors. The same differential speed of adjustment is likely to hold for budgetary reductions during periods of suddenly imposed austerity.

This analysis of the direct linkages between nondefense budgetary allocations and the major macroeconomic allocations identified several sectors whose allocations appeared to be quite stable and, therefore, unlikely to be contracted in light of a major increase in defense allocations. In particular, it was argued that health and other community services were unlikely to suffer budget reductions in order to increase defense allocations, whereas the budget allocations to public services, housing, and other purposes might be vulnerable to an expanded defense program.

As noted in the section on distributed lags, many longer-term expenditure patterns may also be present in the Venezuelan economy. These longer-term adjustments of government budgetary allocations to changes in such aggregates as real gross domestic product (*GDPNP*), real government revenues (*GRP*), real government consumption (*GCNP*), real government debt (*GDP*), real central bank credit to the government (*CBCGP*) and the monetary system's credit to the government (*MSCGP*) may also act to delineate the scope for trade-offs with the defense sector.

Clearly, any firm and stable long-term adjustment patterns between these macroaggregates and individual budgetary items would most likely be indicative of the unwillingness of the authorities to make major budgetary reductions for these expenditure categories for the sake of facilitating an expansionary defense program.

The regressions performed were of the form in equation 8.1 below:

$$y = ax + byL + z$$

where y = sectoral allocations in the current time period; x = macrovariable; yL = lagged value (previous year's expenditure) of the budgetary item; and z = a disturbance term.

Defense

An estimation of the distributed lags associated with adjustments over time in defense allocations indicates that defense expenditures adapt over time to increased government revenues and higher levels of gross domestic product.

During the 1970s and early 1980s, the government also seemed willing to borrow from the central bank (equation 7 in table 8–2) to maintain the trends in defense expenditures. In short, the picture of defense expenditures seems to be a rather predictable adjustment over time to the government's revenue position. Also, policymakers in Venezuela clearly desire to maintain some fixed proportion of overall gross domestic product allocated to this sector. While not willing (or perhaps able) to borrow externally for the purpose of facilitating those longer-run adjustments, the government appears quite willing to tap the central bank for defense sector financing.

Clearly any sector adversely affected by the government's borrowing from the central bank (due to the government's need to

Table 8-2
Venezuela: Determinants of Public Expenditures on Defense: Distributed Lag Estimates, 1973-83

	Independent Variables									Statistics		
Equation	Lagged Defense Expenditures	GRP	GEP	GDPNP	GCNP	GDP	GDEFP	CBCGP	RHO	r^2	F	DW
(1)	0.43 (1.96)	0.029 (2.68)							-0.14 (-0.46)	0.984	512.62	2.33
(2)	0.45 (1.78)		0.03 (1.91)						0.28 (0.93)	0.953	165.07	2.64
(3)	0.075 (0.21)			0.014 (2.55)					0.22 (0.72)	0.969	253.51	2.20
(4)	0.31 (0.93)				0.07 (1.88)				0.30 (1.02)	0.949	150.56	2.40
(5)	0.94 (5.53)					0.003 (0.18)			0.12 (0.41)	0.956	176.79	2.57
(6)	0.88 (9.56)						-0.036 (-1.16)		0.26 (0.86)	0.946	141.47	2.73
(7)	0.30 (2.13)							0.44 (3.09)	0.88 (5.18)	0.660	15.54	2.80

Source: Data were compiled from International Monetary Fund, *Government Finance Statistics Yearbook*, 1983 and 1984.
Notes: Estimations were made using Cochrane-Orcutt two-stage iteration procedure for serial correlation.
See text for identification of variables.
( ) = t statistic.
F = F statistic.
r^2 = correlation coefficient.
DW = Durbin-Watson statistic.

prioritize its borrowing within an overall ceiling on total borrowing) would experience a negative budgetary trade-off with the defense sector.

Nondefense Sectors

Tables 8-3 through 8-10 show the results of the distributed lag impacts experienced by the nondefense sectors. For several of the nondefense allocations, they reveal a great deal of stability between individual allocations and their major macro or policy determinants.

General Public Services

General public services do not show much stability over time to movements in the country's major macroaggregates. There is not a stable pattern of adjustment over time to, say, increases in the government's revenues. The only macrovariable statistically significant in the distributed lag formulations is government credit from the monetary system ($MSCGP$) (equation 7 in table 8-3). This variable had a negative sign, however, indicating government unwillingness to expand public services while simultaneously tapping the financial system for funds earmarked for other programs. Again, this budgetary area seems quite vulnerable to negative trade-offs with the defense sector.

Education

The only stable long-run adjustment variable for education was central bank credit to the government (equation 6 in table 8-4). Similar to public services, the sign on the independent variable (this time central bank credit to the government) was negative, indicating an inclination on the part of the government to allocate funds away from education during period of stepped-up borrowing from the central bank. Clearly, the government's priorities for education appear to lack a firm commitment to adjusting them systematically over time to improved economic conditions. There may exist for education, as with public services, sufficient lack of government commitment to provide some scope for negative trade-off during periods of expanded defense allocations. This picture is consistent with the positive sign for central bank credit to the government in the defense equations and the negative signs in the education and public service distributed lag estimations.

Table 8-3
Venezuela: Determinants of Public Expenditures on General Public Services: Distributed Lag Estimates, 1973-83

	Independent Variables									Statistics		
Equation	Lagged General Public Services Expenditures	GRP	GEP	GDPNP	GCNP	GDP	CBCGP	MSCGP	RHO	r^2	F	DW
(1)	0.70 (3.52)	0.022 (1.60)							0.034 (0.096)	0.970	259.12	1.85
(2)	0.45 (0.98)		0.044 (1.17)						0.024 (0.65)	0.949	150.19	1.97
(3)	0.34 (1.31)			0.014 (2.58)					0.04 (0.12)	0.976	331.91	1.82
(4)	-0.28 (-0.69)				0.19 (2.97)				0.51 (1.85)	0.928	103.38	1.77
(5)	1.10 (4.39)					-0.014 (-0.48)			0.10 (0.34)	0.953	162.92	2.28
(6)	1.21 (6.83)						-0.40 (-1.40)		0.12 (0.40)	0.959	190.81	2.53
(7)	0.85 (14.98)							-0.042 (-3.72)	-0.27 (-0.90)	0.988	663.07	2.47

Source: Data were compiled from International Monetary Fund, *Government Finance Statistics Yearbook*, 1983 and 1984.

Notes: Estimations were made using Cochrane-Orcutt two-stage iteration procedure for serial correlation.
See text for identification of variables.
( ) = t statistic.
F = F statistic.
r^2 = correlation coefficient.
DW = Durbin-Watson statistic.

Table 8-4
Venezuela: Determinants of Public Expenditures on Education: Distributed Lag Estimates, 1973-83

		Independent Variables							Statistics		
Equation	Lagged Education Expenditures	GRP	GEP	GDPNP	GCNP	GDP	CBCGP	RHO	r^2	F	DW
(1)	0.55 (0.91)	0.033 (0.38)						0.58 (2.23)	0.586	11.33	0.85
(2)	-0.56 (-0.60)		0.24 (1.56)					0.20 (0.67)	0.853	46.66	1.20
(3)	-0.007 (-0.01)			0.04 (1.73)				-0.02 (-0.06)	0.900	72.51	1.25
(4)	-0.32 (-0.56)				0.38 (2.18)			-0.13 (-0.40)	0.924	97.37	1.38
(5)	1.64 (3.52)					-0.21 (-1.79)		0.35 (1.19)	0.820	36.66	0.70
(6)	1.77 (4.54)						-2.93 (-2.27)	-0.03 (-0.09)	0.917	89.26	1.78

Source: Data were compiled from International Monetary Fund, *Government Finance Statistics Yearbook*, 1983 and 1984.
Notes: Estimations were made using Cochrane-Orcutt two-stage iteration procedure for serial correlation.
See text for identification of variables.
( ) = t statistic.
F = F statistic.
r^2 = correlation coefficient.
DW = Durbin-Watson statistic.

Health

The picture with regard to health expenditures is similar to that obtained from the direct impact analysis: great stability and predictability between health expenditures and the major macroeconomic aggregates. Health expenditures show a rather consistent pattern of gradual adjustment over time to expanded levels of government revenue (*GRP*), government expenditures (*GEP*), gross domestic product (*GDPNP*), and government consumption (*GCNP*). In each case, the relationships are highly significant as seen in equations 1 through 4 in table 8-5. On the other hand, increased public debt (GDP), central bank credit to the government (*CBCGP*), and government credit from the monetary system (*MSCGP*) tend to put a damper on health expenditures (equations 5 through 7). Tentatively, one can conclude that allocations to health have historically been of high priority in the government's allocation process. On the other hand, the debt position of the government has tended to limit somewhat the allocations received by this sector. During periods of high government borrowing from the central bank, health as well as allocations to public services and education may suffer at the expense of the defense budget.

Social Security and Welfare

As with health, social security and welfare appears quite stable in adjusting to higher levels of *GRP* and *GEP*, *GCNP*, and *GDPNP*, as seen in equations 1 through 4 in table 8-6. Although not as strong as in the case of health, government debt and borrowing appear to impact negatively on social security and welfare over periods of time. Tentatively, therefore, one might expect a negative impact on social security and welfare expenditures to be caused by an expanded military program.

Housing

Housing allocations do not appear to follow any predictable or stable pattern of adjustment to the major macroeconomic indicators, as evidenced in table 8-7. Instead, allocations to this sector show a slight short-run association to government revenues and the other macrovariables. These correlations are not high, however, indicating, perhaps, opportunities for cutbacks in lieu of expanded expenditures in defense.

Table 8-5
Venezuela: Determinants of Public Expenditures on Health: Distributed Lag Estimates, 1973-83

		Independent Variables								Statistics		
Equation	Lagged Health Expenditures	GRP	GEP	GDPNP	GCNP	GDP	CBCGP	MSCGP	RHO	r^2	F	DW
(1)	0.65 (9.83)	0.026 (5.89)							-0.21 (-0.67)	0.998	4743.97	1.47
(2)	0.32 (1.58)		0.06 (3.33)						0.25 (0.83)	0.995	1480.32	1.62
(3)	0.41 (2.42)			0.012 (3.60)					-0.09 (-0.29)	0.997	2614.23	1.64
(4)	0.05 (0.43)				0.13 (7.24)				0.37 (1.29)	0.997	2607.66	2.06
(5)	1.23 (16.84)					-0.03 (-3.09)			-0.06 (-0.18)	0.996	2235.46	2.24
(6)	1.18 (17.42)						-0.28 (-2.69)		0.08 (0.26)	0.996	1861.45	1.43
(7)	0.94 (24.98)							-0.02 (-2.36)	-0.27 (-0.06)	0.995	1746.29	1.82

Source: Data were compiled from International Monetary Fund, *Government Finance Statistics Yearbook*, 1983 and 1984.

Notes: Estimations were made using Cochrane-Orcutt two-stage iteration procedure for serial correlation.
See text for identification of variables.
( ) = t statistic.
F = F statistic.
r^2 = correlation coefficient.
DW = Durbin-Watson statistic.

Table 8-6
Venezuela: Determinants of Public Expenditures on Social Security and Welfare: Distributed Lag Estimates, 1973-83

		Independent Variables								Statistics		
Equation	Lagged Social Security and Expenditures	GRP	GEP	GDPNP	GCNP	GDP	CBCGP	MSCGP	RHO	r^2	F	DW
(1)	0.68 (8.16)	0.02 (4.69)							-0.50 (-1.83)	0.995	1477.72	1.92
(2)	0.30 (1.72)		0.05 (4.22)						-0.25 (-0.85)	0.993	1148.40	1.72
(3)	0.60 (4.24)			0.007 (3.30)					-0.35 (-1.17)	0.991	885.82	1.91
(4)	0.45 (2.78)				0.068 (3.80)				-0.27 (-0.89)	0.992	1007.51	1.86
(5)	1.46 (5.61)					-0.04 (-1.63)			-0.28 (-0.95)	0.983	479.31	2.12
(6)	1.41 (5.66)						-0.51 (-1.62)		0.06 (0.20)	0.973	292.38	1.97
(7)	0.95 (15.05)							-0.02 (-2.07)	0.21 (-0.67)	0.984	519.13	1.94

Source: Data were compiled from International Monetary Fund, *Government Finance Statistics Yearbook*, 1983 and 1984.
Notes: Estimations were made using Cochrane-Orcutt two-stage iteration procedure for serial correlation.
See text for identification of variables.
( ) = t statistic.
F = F statistic.
r^2 = correlation coefficient.
DW = Durbin-Watson statistic.

Table 8-7
Venezuela: Determinants of Public Expenditures on Housing: Distributed Lag Estimates, 1973-83

		Independent Variables							Statistics		
Equation	Lagged Housing Expenditures	GRP	GEP	GDPNP	GCNP	GDP	CBCGP	RHO	r^2	F	DW
(1)	0.24 (0.74)	0.02 (2.02)						-0.19 (-0.62)	0.722	20.81	2.01
(2)	-0.04 (-0.10)		0.03 (2.43)					-0.08 (-0.25)	0.715	20.10	1.99
(3)	0.004 (0.01)			0.007 (2.38)				-0.03 (-0.10)	0.688	17.61	1.93
(4)	(-0.23)				0.05 (2.68)			-0.02 (-0.06)	0.713	19.96	1.95
(5)	0.08 (-0.21)					0.41 (2.02)		0.21 (0.69)	0.494	7.81	1.89
(6)	0.23 (0.67)						0.38 (1.74)	0.02 (0.06)	0.583	11.21	1.94

Source: Data were compiled from International Monetary Fund, *Government Finance Statistics Yearbook*, 1983 and 1984.
Notes: Estimations were made using Cochrane-Orcutt two-stage iteration procedure for serial correlation.
See text for identification of variables.
( ) = t statistic.
F = F statistic.
r^2 = correlation coefficient.
DW = Durbin-Watson statistic.

Other Community and Social Services

Government expenditures for other community and social services show a distributed lag to increased government debt (GDP) and the government's ($GDEFP$) deficit in table 8-8. Presumably, the government's debt and budgetary policy are linked positively to this sector's allocation. The high statistical significance on the lagged value of this expenditure indicates also a high degree of continuity in these programs. All in all, one probably would not expect major cutbacks in this area in times of expanded defense efforts.

Economic Services

As indicated in the analysis of the trends in economic services, allocations (particularly investment) in this area are extremely erratic. In part, the large fluctuations are due to the government's willingness to allocate a large proportion of expanded revenues to capital formation in new projects. Similarly, during periods of austerity, potential programs and projects are postponed and existing projects sharply scaled back. The only distributed lag of statistical significance is with the government's domestic borrowing ($GDBP$), as shown in table 8-9. Apparently, during revenue shortfalls, the government is willing to borrow rather than suspend work on ongoing projects. It is unlikely, given the boom-or-bust nature of expenditure in this area, that defense expenditures would interact systematically in any particular negative way on allocations to the sector.

Miscellaneous Items

The government's allocation for miscellaneous items shows some regularity in adjustment over time to changed economic conditions, with a rather strong adjustment to movements in government revenues (GRP), government expenditures (GEP), gross domestic product ($GDPNP$), and government consumption ($GCNP$). These results (equations 1 through 4 in table 8-10), together with the insensitivity of miscellaneous allocations to increases in government borrowing, may indicate that limited negative trade-offs exist with the defense sector.

Conclusions

The purpose of this chapter was to determine the factors that effect the major Venezuelan government expenditure categories. It was

Table 8-8
Venezuela: Determinants of Public Expenditures on Other Community and Social Services: Distributed Lag Estimates, 1973-83

		Independent Variables									Statistics		
Equation	Lagged Expenditures on Other Community and Social Services	GRP	GEP	GDPNP	GCNP	GDP	GDEFP	CBCGP	GFBP	RHO	r^2	F	DW
(1)	0.97 (8.65)	0.0008 (1.46)								-0.45 (-1.61)	0.985	543.39	2.26
(2)	0.85 (6.07)		0.002 (1.94)							-0.39 (-1.33)	0.986	580.40	2.18
(3)	0.94 (7.30)			0.0003 (1.44)						-0.42 (-1.46)	0.984	516.92	2.23
(4)	0.91 (6.69)				0.002 (1.61)					-0.40 (-1.39)	0.985	531.52	2.22
(5)	0.21 (0.73)					0.008 (2.72)				0.38 (1.32)	0.933	111.85	1.89
(6)	0.86 (9.49)						-0.01 (-3.28)			0.35 (1.19)	0.951	156.02	1.86
(7)	0.52 (1.62)							0.07 (1.91)		-0.40 (-1.40)	0.986	588.38	2.08
(8)	1.08 (13.78)								0.007 (2.22)	0.14 (0.42)	0.978	312.34	1.43

Source: Data were compiled from International Monetary Fund, *Government Finance Statistics Yearbook*, 1983 and 1984.

Notes: Estimations were made using Cochrane-Orcutt two-stage iteration procedure for serial correlation.
See text for identification of variables.
( ) = t statistic.
F = F statistic.
r^2 = correlation coefficient.
DW = Durbin-Watson statistic.

Table 8-9
Venezuela: Determinants of Public Expenditures on Economic Services: Distributed Lag Estimates, 1973-83

Equation	Lagged Expenditures on Economic Services	GRP	GEP	GDPNP	GCNP	GDP	GDBP	RHO	r^2	F	DW
(1)	0.05 (0.19)	0.23 (3.77)						0.10 (0.33)	0.909	80.55	1.80
(2)	-0.31 (-1.24)		0.37 (5.09)					0.06 (0.17)	0.946	140.89	1.51
(3)	-0.07 (-0.23)			0.75 (3.25)				-0.06 (-0.19)	0.919	91.26	1.97
(4)	-0.13 (-0.42)				0.56 (3.51)			-0.10 (-0.34)	0.931	107.95	1.83
(5)	0.04 (0.11)					0.32 (1.78)		0.56 (2.12)	0.500	8.00	1.68
(6)	0.61 (4.67)						1.98 (3.89)	0.08 (0.25)	0.920	81.37	2.03

Source: Data were compiled from International Monetary Fund, *Government Finance Statistics Yearbook*, 1983 and 1984.

Notes: Estimations were made using Cochrane-Orcutt two-stage iteration procedure for serial correlation. See text for identification of variables.

( ) = t statistic.
F = F statistic.
r^2 = correlation coefficient.
DW = Durbin-Watson statistic.

Table 8-10
Venezuela: Determinants of Public Expenditures on Miscellaneous Items: Distributed Lag Estimates, 1973–83

Equation	Lagged Miscellaneous Expenditures	GRP	GEP	GDPNP	GCNP	GDP	RHO	r^2	F	DW
(1)	0.78 (7.59)	0.06 (3.08)					−0.51 (−1.88)	0.989	713.24	2.52
(2)	0.57 (4.10)		0.11 (3.72)				−0.42 (−1.47)	0.990	825.97	2.44
(3)	0.69 (5.02)			0.02 (2.89)			−0.44 (−1.58)	0.987	631.27	2.51
(4)	0.62 (93.91)				0.18 (2.94)		−0.38 (−1.30)	0.987	602.47	2.45
(5)	0.48 (1.21)					0.19 (1.36)	0.18 (0.58)	0.938	122.03	1.85

Statistics columns: r^2, F, DW.
Independent Variables: GRP, GEP, GDPNP, GCNP, GDP, RHO.

Source: Data were compiled from International Monetary Fund, *Government Finance Statistics Yearbook*, 1983 and 1984.

Notes: Estimations were made using Cochrane-Orcutt two-stage iteration procedure for serial correlation. See text for identification of variables.
( ) = t statistic.
F = F statistic.
r^2 = correlation coefficient.
DW = Durbin-Watson statistic.

argued that if a nondefense category showed a high statistical correlation with major economic variables, it was less likely to be affected by movements in defense expenditures than if a weak statistical relationship existed. In general, both the short-term and longer-term relationships between government expenditures and Venezuela's major macroeconomic variables indicate that a number of major areas of government expenditures (with the exception of economic services) may be susceptible to negative trade-offs associated with changes in defense expenditures. At most the results indicate that possible trade-offs between defense and nondefense are likely and may result from either budgetary or financial considerations. At the least, negative trade-offs observed between defense and any of the major noneconomic government allocations would not be inconsistent with the results presented above.

Notes

1. Notable studies in this area include: Joel Verner, "Budgetary Trade-offs between Education and Defense in Latin America: A Research Note," *Journal of Developing Areas* (October 1983), pp. 77-92; Margaret Daly Hayes, "Policy Consequences of Military Participation in Politics: An Analysis of Tradeoffs in Brazilian Federal Expenditures," in Craig Liske, ed., *Comparative Public Policy* (New York: Wiley, 1976) pp. 21-52; and Barry Ames and Ed Goff, "Education and Defense Expenditures in Latin America 1948-1968" in Liske, *op. cit.*, pp. 210-23.

2. For example, Terry Weaver, "Assessing the Impact of Military Rule: Alternative Approaches," in P. Schmitter, ed., *Military Rule in Latin America: Function, Consequence and Perspectives* (Beverly Hills, Calif.: Sage, 1973), pp. 58-118.

3. F.L. Pryor, *Public Expenditures in Communist and Capitalist Nations* (Homewood, Ill.: Richard D. Irwin, 1968); E. Benoit, *Defense and Economic Growth in Developing Countries* (Lexington, Mass: D.C. Heath, 1973).

4. Weaver, *op. cit.*, pp. 94-95.

5. Data are taken from International Monetary Fund, *Government Financial Statistics Yearbook,* various issues and International Monetary Fund, *International Financial Statistics Yearbook,* various issues.

6. B.M. Russett, "Some Decisions in the Regression of Time Series Data" in J.F. Herndon, ed., *Mathematical Application in Political Science* (Charlottesville: University of Virginia Press, 1971), p. 30.

7. Hayes, *op. cit.*, p. 28.

8. Alan Tait and Peter S. Heller, *International Comparisons of Government Expenditure,* "Occasional Paper 10" (Washington, D.C.: International Monetary Fund, 1982).

9
An Optimal Control Forecast of Venezuelan Defense and Socioeconomic Budgetary Expenditures

The main purpose of this chapter is the creation of a logical and empirically sound framework for forecasting the likely movement in Venezuelan defense and socioeconomic expenditures through 1990. For this purpose a macroeconomic model of the economy is constructed, and linkages between the overall rate of economic growth and military expenditures are made. Finally, the pattern of military expenditures forecast by the model is checked in terms of its consistency with the country's likely overall level of debt and borrowing capacity, its policymakers' concern with inflation, and any potential trade-offs between military expenditures and allocations to the social section.

In this context, a secondary purpose of the analysis below is to examine the feasibility and budgetary ramifications of various stabilization programs on the Venezuelan economy from 1984 through 1990.

Economic Priorities and Constraints

A cursory look at the recent trends in the major macroeconomic indicators (see table 9-1) confirms the severity of the country's current economic crisis.[1] Clearly, the current Lusinchi government will have to define its policies and actions to respond to an economic environment whose dominant features are: (1) the need to reschedule public and private debt in arrears and short-term maturities; (2) a low volume of exports and low international oil prices; (3) severe restraints on the amount of resources available to the public sector for executing programs and reviving the nonpetroleum economy; (4) a foreign exchange budget with little room for imports needed to

Table 9-1
Venezuela: Major Macroeconomic Trends, 1979-83
(macro variables in millions of 1980 bolivares)

	1979	1980	1981	1982	1983	Average Annual Growth 1979-83	1980-83	1983
Gross Domestic Product	252418	254200	245871	228806	210835	-4.4%	-6.0%	-7.9%
Government investment	19860	20675	36005	33025	25159	6.1	6.8	23.8
Government consumption	33730	35120	36758	33456	30465	-2.5	-4.6	-8.9
Private consumption	134058	135380	138388	143158	139364	1.0	1.0	-2.7
Private investment	59787	43465	24150	22088	14559	-29.8	-30.6	-34.1
Public expenditures	53590	55795	72763	66482	55625	0.9	-0.1	-16.3
Private expenditures	193846	178845	162538	165246	153924	-5.6	-4.9	-6.9
Government revenue	61832	66405	83993	65754	56809	-2.1	-5.1	-13.6
Government deficit	1037	-3617	-6677	-13213	-3093	-41.3	5.1	76.6
Government debt	40089	38829	42609	50089	55250	8.4	9.2	10.3
Balance of payments	-10482	14978	16952	-15078	-4523	18.9	-62.8	70.0
Imports	68138	64550	66840	76168	55307	-5.1	-5.0	-27.4
Exports	72678	85459	82069	68115	66476	-2.21	-8.03	-2.41
Private expenditures/ public expenditures	3.61	3.21	2.23	2.48	2.77	-6.4	-4.81	11.7
Government debt/GDP	0.159	0.153	0.173	0.219	0.262	13.3	12.7	19.6
Government deficit/GDP	0.004	-0.014	-0.0272	-0.0577	-0.0147	-67.2	0.0	074.5
Private consumption per capita	9916	9732	9671	9732	9217	-1.8	-1.8	-5.3
Consumer price index	0.823	1.000	1.160	1.273	1.353	13.23	10.6	6.3
Central bank credit to government	3216	2082	3291	5386	4048	5.9	24.8	-24.8
Defense expenditures (constant price)	3636	3893	3922	3770	3739	0.7	-1.3	-0.8
Defense expenditures (current prices)	2933	3893	4550	4800	5060	14.6	9.13	5.4

Sources: Macro variables are derived from International Monetary Fund, *International Financial Statistics*, various issues. Military expenditures are derived from Stockholm International Peace Research Institute, *World Armaments and Disarmament Yearbook*, 1984.

restore domestic economic activity; (5) a growing number of price increase applications not resolved by the administered price system; and (6) high unemployment and depressed real income of persons capable of exerting pressure on the new government to act swiftly and take significant measures.

Given this group of constraints, the outlook for economic and social progress in the near term is not very bright. The earnings in the oil sector will probably not experience any important gains. Crop and livestock production, even though the declared target of special policies to encourage sector development, will take some time to show a positive response. Manufacturing will probably continue to be buffeted, on the one hand by the stimulating effects of conditions favoring import substitution, and on the other by the dampening effects of lower real private consumer spending and public and private investment. In view of weak domestic demand, significant responses from the construction, transportation, and commercial sectors are unlikely. Since the central government has little control over oil revenues and only a weakly developed domestic tax base to replace lost oil revenues, it will probably have to further reduce its investment expenditures and transfer payments to other public sector agencies.

In addition, domestic prices, which had been frozen since late 1983, were adjusted during the first half of 1984 and the exchange system was modified. The inevitable side effect of this adjustment was renewed inflationary pressures. A resurgence of inflation could heighten worker demands for wage increases to regain some of the real income they lost in recent years. Any granting of wage increases, coupled with price controls, could discourage private production, despite the higher consumer spending this would produce. Large wage hikes in the public sector would substantially reduce the savings of the sector and thus compromise its ability to finance investment.

The following analysis rests on the presumption that Venezuela can be characterized as a country with sufficient oil to create problems, but not enough—at least so far—to solve them. Since the 1973–74 oil price increases, the central feature of the government's long-term development policy has been the need to utilize petroleum export revenues in a manner capable of placing the economy on a high-growth trajectory consistent with the public sector's long-standing income distribution objectives.

This orientation assumes that the current financial crisis is not a temporary aberration, but rather the culmination of monetary and fiscal policies pursued by successive administrations since the oil price increases of 1973–74. These past public policies will continue to dictate the options open to the Venezuelan government in the foreseeable future. The resolution of the financial crisis in the long term will come not from modification of energy policies or recovery in world petroleum markets, but rather from monetary and fiscal policies designed to achieve stable growth in the Venezuelan economy.

The impact of energy policies and the current administration's monetary and fiscal policies on the Venezuelan economy are analyzed in terms of an econometric optimal control model of the economy developed in the following section.

Description of the Model

The model constructed below is an econometric time series model, which was designed to use the available Venezuelan national accounts statistics. It aims at explaining the structural changes in the Venezuelan economy, particularly those during the 1970s and 1980s, as well as projecting values for certain macroeconomic variables and their link with budgetary expenditures over the 1984-90 period. The model is of the classical Keynesian econometric type, variations of which have been used for different countries.[2]

Ordinary least squares regression was used in the exploratory stage of model building, when much experimentation with various possible explanatory variables was undertaken to decide on the choice of variables and the form of the structural equations included. However, a two-stage least squares technique was used for the final estimation of the parameters of the model to correct for any simultaneous equation bias in the estimates.[3] The estimation procedure was carried out using the national account statistics of the International Monetary Fund for the years 1950-83 and budgetary statistics for the 1972-83 period.[4] The national account and budgetary figures were deflated using the IMF consumer price index (1980=1.0). The central government debt was deflated using the U.S. export unit price deflator (1980=1.0), as was the level of exports and imports, to obtain the constant price series used in the regressions.

The model, shown in table 9-2, contains 41 equations with 28 of the variables endogenous and 8 of the variables exogenous (or predetermined). Eight of the equations are definitions and identities, while 20 of the equations are structural, consisting of an inflation block, two consumption functions, two investment functions, two government fiscal policy functions, and six budget composition relationships. Four dummy variables representing oil price changes were included to account for external shocks associated with changing

Table 9-2
Venezuela: Macroeconomic Forecasting Model
(two-stage least square estimates)

Equation	Macroeconomic Block
(1)	Central bank reserve money (nominal): $CBRM$ $CBRM = 5.51\ CBCGL + 12464.2\ DUMA$ $\qquad\qquad (13.37) \qquad\qquad (10.41)$ $r^2 = 0.960,\ F = 363.48,\ DW = 2.56$
(2)	Money supply (nominal): $M1$ $M1 = 2.10\ CBRM + 0.287\ GDEFL - 701.95$ $\qquad\quad (40.25) \qquad\quad (2.88) \qquad\quad (-0.63)$ $r^2 = 0.992,\ F = 1862.95,\ DW = 2.56$
(3)	Consumer price index: CPI $CPI = 0.0000162\ M1 + 0.00000705\ GDEFL + 0.0000366\ CBCGP - 0.156\ DUMA + 0.297$ $\qquad\quad (15.93) \qquad\qquad (3.32) \qquad\qquad (3.56) \qquad\qquad (-5.71) \qquad (30.69)$ $r^2 = 0.988,\ F = 606,\ DW = 2.06$
(4)	Exports (real): ENP $ENP = 0.455\ ENPL + 122.12\ CPP + 315.0\ WCP$ $\qquad\quad (2.61) \qquad\quad (3.39) \qquad\quad (2.83)$ $r^2 = 0.855,\ F = 57.23,\ DW = 2.51$
(5)	Government revenue (real): GRP $GRP = 0.352\ ENP + 0.166\ GDPNP$ $\qquad\quad (3.03) \qquad\quad (3.22)$ $r^2 = 0.939,\ F = 249.51,\ DW = 3.00$
(6)	Government budgetary expenditures (real): GEP $GEP = 0.623\ GRP - 0.729\ GDEFPL + 2.88\ CBCGP + 3121.17$ $\qquad\quad (12.83) \qquad\quad (-3.46) \qquad\quad (2.38) \qquad\quad (2.19)$ $r^2 = 0.952,\ F = 195.46,\ DW = 2.76$
(7)	Central government debt (real): GDP $GDP = 0.867\ GDPL - 0.806\ GDEFP + 1.9\ CBCGPL - 1416.85\ DUMP + 734.27$ $\qquad\quad (17.49) \qquad\quad (-8.49) \qquad\quad (2.54) \qquad\quad (-2.83) \qquad\quad 0.98$ $r^2 = 0.984,\ F = 436.27,\ DW = 2.64$
(8)	Central government consumption (real): $GCNP$ $GCNP = 0.289\ GRP - 0.233\ GDEFPL + 0.187\ GDP + 4777.60$ $\qquad\qquad (11.59) \qquad\quad (-2.12) \qquad\quad (4.20) \qquad\quad (7.35)$ $r^2 = 0.960,\ F = 234.64,\ DW = 2.27$

Table 9-2 continued

Equation	
Macroeconomic Block	

(9) Central government investment (real): IGP

$$IGP = 0.329\ GRP - 0.516\ GDEFPL + 61.58$$
$$(13.37)\quad\quad (-4.11)\quad\quad\quad (0.06)$$

$r^2 = 0.902, F = 139.46, DW = 1.51$

(10) Financial sector credit to private sector (real): MSCPP

$$MSCPP = 1.02\ MSCPPL - 0.38\ MSCGP + 1.82\ CBCGP - 1067.91$$
$$(20.94)\quad\quad\quad (-6.62)\quad\quad (2.30)\quad\quad\quad (-1.28)$$

$r^2 = 0.990, F = 981.29, DW = 2.28$

(11) Private consumption (real): PCNP

$$PCNP = 0.60\ PCNPL + 0.152\ GDPNPL + 0.23\ MSCPP + 4168.55$$
$$(9.91)\quad\quad\quad (3.71)\quad\quad\quad (2.73)\quad\quad (3.06)$$

$r^2 = 0.996, F = 2926.84, DW = 2.79$

(12) Private investment (real): IPP

$$IPP = 0.85\ IGPL + 1.16\ IPPL - 0.16\ KPL$$
$$(4.82)\quad\quad (14.17)\quad\quad (-5.89)$$

$r^2 = 0.934, F = 124.38, DW = 2.54$

(13) Imports (real): ZNP

$$ZNP = 0.87\ IGP + 0.47\ IPP + 0.23\ PCNP - 3406.03\ EXAA + 12514.2$$
$$(5.10)\quad\quad (9.09)\quad\quad (4.85)\quad\quad\quad (-2.94)\quad\quad\quad (3.55)$$

$r^2 = 0.985, F = 473.57, DW = 2.72$

(14) Net factor payments (real): NFPNP

$$NFPNP = 0.657\ NFPNPL + 0.06\ GDPNPL - 0.186\ ENP - 0.229\ GNP + 4340.2\ DUMC - 2342.86$$
$$(5.89)\quad\quad\quad\quad (-2.83)\quad\quad\quad (-2.42)\quad\quad (-4.03)\quad\quad\quad (2.45)\quad\quad\quad (-5.89)$$

$r^2 = 0.419, F = 3.25, DW = 2.89$

Budget Block

(15) Defense expenditures (real): MESIP

$$MESIP = 0.009\ GDPNP + 0.409\ MESIPL + 224.81$$
$$(2.28)\quad\quad\quad (3.81)\quad\quad\quad (2.32)$$

$r^2 = 0.952, F = 298.14, DW = 2.71$

(16) Social Security and welfare's share of government expenditures: GSSWE

$$GSSWE = -0.409\ GSSWEL - 0.718\ GDEE - 0.0000\ GEPOP + 0.21$$
$$(-3.69)\quad\quad\quad (-2.60)\quad\quad (-3.05)\quad\quad (0.34)$$

$r^2 = 0.738, F = 7.51, DW = 2.11$

An Optimal Control Forecast

(17) Public service's share of government expenditures: *GPSE*

$$GPSE = -0.85\ GDEE - 0.00049\ GEY - 0.258$$
$$(-2.28)\quad (-2.50)\quad (-3.70)$$

$r^2 = 0.419, F = 3.25, DW = 2.89$

(18) Education's share of government expenditures: *GEDE*

$$GEDE = -1.17\ GDEE - 0.0003\ GEPOP + 0.469\ GPSE + 0.35$$
$$(-4.25)\quad (-5.65)\quad (2.91)\quad (8.11)$$

$r^2 = 0.827, F = 12.83, DW = 2.41$

(19) Health's share of government expenditures: *GHE*

$$GHE = 0.329\ GHEL + 0.405\ GDEE + 0.32\ GEDE - 0.0235$$
$$(2.81)\quad (2.37)\quad (2.98)\quad (-0.68)$$

$r^2 = 0.600, F = 4.00, DW = 2.81$

(20) Other community services' share of government expenditures: *GOCE*

$$GOCE = -0.381\ GDEE - 0.00000795\ GEPOP + 0.685$$
$$(-2.57)\quad (-2.35)\quad (3.02)$$

$r^2 = 0.427, F = 435, DW = 2.61$

Identities

(21) Government deficit (real): *GDEFP*

$$GDEFP = GRP - GEP - LMRP$$

(22) Government expenditures – national accounts (real): *GENANP*

$$GENANP = GCNP + IGP$$

(23) Private expenditures – national accounts (real): *PENANP*

$$PENANP = PCNP + IPP$$

(24) Total investment (real): *INP*

$$INP = IPP + IGP$$

(25) Capital stock (real): *KP*

$$KP = INPL + INPL2 + INPL3$$

(26) Gross domestic product (real): *GDPNP*

$$GDPNP = PCNP + GCNP + ENP - ZNP + IPP + IGP + ICNP$$

Table 9-2 continued

Equation	Macroeconomic Block

Transformations

(27) Government expenditures per $GDP = GEP/GDP$: GEY

(28) Government expenditures per capita = GEP/POP: $GEPOP$

Exogenous Variables

(29) Population: POP
  $POP = 2.8$ percent increase per annum

(30) Real exports: ENP
  $ENP = -5.0, -2.5, 0, 2.5$ percent increase per annum

(31) Government credit from financial system (real): $MSCGP$
  $MSCGP = 5$ percent increase per annum

(32) Change in stocks (real): $ISNP$
  $ISNP = 0.0$

(33) Exchange rate: $EXAA$ bolivares = 7.5a per US $

(34) Crude petroleum production: CPP (constant)

(35) Wholesale price index for crude petroleum: WCP (constant)

(36) Government lending minus repayment: $LMRP$ (1.0 percent real increase)

Dummy Variables

(37)   DUMA — oil price effect: 0, 1950–73; 1, 1974–83

(38)   DUMB — oil price effect: 0, 1950–72; 1, 1973–83

(39)   DUMC — oil price effect: 0, 1950–73; 1, 1974–78; 2, 1979–83

(40)   DUMD — oil price effect: 0, 1950–73; 1, 1974–78; 2, 1979–83

(41)   DUMP — political administration effect: Dictatorship = 0, 1950–57
                                                                    AD = 1, 1958–68, 1974–78
                                                                    COPEI = 2, 1969–73, 1979–83

Notes: Estimated over 1950–83.
( ) = t statistic.
F = F statistic.
r^2 = correlation coefficient.
DW = Durbin-Watson statistic.
L = lagged variable.
GDEF = nominal government deficit.
CBRM = central bank reserve money.
CBCG = nominal credit to the government from the Central Bank.
CBCGP = real credit to the government from the Central Bank.
GDEE = share of defense in government budget.

world oil markets. A final political dummy was included to account for shifts in government policy associated with changing political regimes.

In the consumption and investment functions, government sector was separated from private sector, as the two were found to be associated with much different factors.

Structural Equation Estimates

Since the model was designed largely for the purpose of examining the impact of government fiscal activity under altenative stabilization programs, a relatively large number of public sector variables appear in the final estimated equations. More specifically, the model formulation allows the problems of government deficits, debt accumulation, and inflation to be examined within the context of a simultaneous set of macroeconomic equations. Central bank credit to the government is assumed to be the main policy variable at the disposal of the authorities.

As noted, in estimating the parameters of the model, I utilized time series observations covering 1950–83, a period characterized in its first half by stable growth in a tranquil world environment and in its second half by significant structural changes in the government's revenue and expenditure patterns. Consequently, uncorrected for structural changes, the parameter estimates based on these series would provide a description of what happened in the economy during this period only in an average sense. To correct for the structural shifts in the 1970s and 1980s, a number of dummy variables were introduced in each of the estimated equations. As noted below, they were statistically significant in a number of the structural equations. Therefore, major structural shifts affecting Venezuela in the 1970s and 1980s have, to a certain extent, been systematically accounted for with the estimated parameters providing a more reliable basis for forecasting over the 1984–90 period.[5]

Inflation (CPI)

In terms of the individual equations in table 9–2, the first three sets of relationships (equations 1 through 3) attempt to capture the inflationary impact that lagged central bank lending to the government ($CBCGL$) and the lagged government budgetary deficits ($GDEFL$) have on the money supply (and, in turn, on the overall increase in the consumer price index). Equation 1 indicates a strong link between central bank lending to the government and reserve money of the central bank (*CBRM*). Reserve money and lagged government deficits (*GDEF*) are largely responsible for movements in the nominal stock of transaction balances held by the public (*M1*) (equation 2). The consumer price index itself is in turn determined by the stock of transaction balances (*M1*), the government deficit lagged one year (*GDEFL*), and the real volume of central bank credit to the government (*GBCGP*).

Exports (ENP)

As might be imagined, real exports in an oil-dominated economy such as Venezuela are largely affected by events in the oil sector. Developments in the world oil market are assumed to act on overall real exports with a slight lag due to the fact that changes in these variables do not necessarily coincide with the annual value of real exports. (For example, the oil price increases in 1973–74 did not impact much on real exports in 1973.) Real exports are estimated by a Koyck distributed lag formulation.[5] They are assumed to be largely a function of lagged real exports (*ENPL*), crude petroleum production index (*CPP*) and the wholesale price of crude petroleum (*WCP*).

Petroleum production in 1984 averaged 1.86 million barrels per day, including condensates and natural gas liquids. This was virtually the same as in 1983, although down from 1981–82 rates. Increased condensate production in 1984 balanced the reduction in crude oil output mandated by the OPEC production ceilings. Crude and product exports totalled 1.5 million barrels per day, the same as in 1983. Export revenues of $14.9 billion were up from $13.9 billion in 1983, reflecting increased exports of high-value light products and better prices for heavy crudes and residual fuel oil. The reduction in domestic consumption (from 385,000 b/d in 1983 to 343,000 b/d in 1984 including oil industry consumption) also facilitated maintenance of export levels. This reduction reflected increased natural gas use, higher domestic product prices, and the economic recession.

Venezuela's wide variety of crude types and its ability to export refined products give it a high degree of flexibility in marketing its oil. Proven and probable reserves of 55 million barrels provide production capacity of about 2.5 million barrels per day. In addition, the country has huge natural gas reserves and untapped heavy oil deposits in the Orinoco Heavy Oil Belt.

Clearly, the country has been able to stabilize its export earnings from oil to a certain extent. Forecasting the differential impact of world prices and production levels on the country's export earnings is possible with the estimated equation 4 in table 9-2, but the uncertainties surrounding each development (production level and price) make it more realistic to simply forecast an overall aggregate movement in export earnings. For purposes of simulation, four forecasts of real export earnings are made:

1. Optimistic—export earnings increase at an average annual rate of 2.5 percent over the 1984–90 period;
2. Moderately optimistic—real export earnings remain stable at their 1983 levels over the 1984–90 period;
3. Moderately pessimistic—real export earnings decline at an average annual rate of 2.5 percent over the 1984–90 period;
4. Pessimistic—real export earnings decline by an annual average rate of 5 percent over the 1984–90 period.

The simulations described below are intended to map out a general matrix of environments in which government fiscal policy can be conducted.

Government Revenue (GRP)

In an oil-based economy, the government normally relies almost exclusively on export revenues (ENP). In fact, the continuing dependence on petrodollar financing and the increasing role of the state have been the two most prominent features of the Venezuelan development model promoted by successive Venezuelan governments since the early 1970s. Annual revenues from oil exports averaged around 95 percent of total export earnings. While the contribution of petroleum revenues to the gross national product fell from nearly 40 percent in 1974 to 21.5 percent in 1978, and while the percentage of total government income derived from petroleum sales dropped from 71.6 percent in 1976 to 49.6 percent in 1978, oil income continued to sustain the major role of the state in the country's economy. The declining proportion of government income derived from petroleum revenues does, however, suggest some progress has been made in the country's tax reform efforts. When gross domestic product ($GDPNP$) was regressed on real government revenue (GRP), it was found to be statistically significant in addition to real exports (equation 5 in table 9-2).

Real Government Budgetary Expenditures (GEP)

Overall government expenditures (GEP) (line 82 of International Monetary Fund, *International Financial Statistics*) are determined in equation 6 of table 9-2 by the level of real government revenues (GRP), real government deficit lagged ($GDEFPL$), and the central bank's real volume of credit to the government ($CBCGP$). As noted in table 9-1, the government's level of real deficits increased rapidly from 1979 to 1983, averaging slightly over a 40 percent per annum increase throughout this period. The rate of expansion has been quite erratic, however, with a substantial reduction of 76.6 percent in the deficit during 1983. The government, therefore, does have considerable discretion over its expenditure policies and is able to finance them from widely differing sources of funds.

Real Government Debt (GDP)

The real level of government debt (GDP) is assumed to adjust marginally over time in a distributed lag fashion to the changes in the deficits ($GDEFP$) and central bank lending to the government ($CBCGPL$). A political variable ($DUMP$) was also found to be significant with a negative sign in equation 7 of table 9-2,—indicating a decreasing inclination on the part of COPEI administrations to increase the overall level of debt. Given the country's current debt problems, the government will undoubtedly be much more constrained than in the past in financing its expenditures through increased indebtedness. Over 1980–83, the level of real government debt grew at an average annual rate of 9.2 percent, and increased to 10.3 percent in 1983. It is likely, however, given the current concern expressed by international bankers over the country's debt situation, that rates of expansion in this range will not be possible to duplicate in the foreseeable future.[6] In the simulations that follow, it is assumed that the central government's level of real outstanding debt will increase between 5 and 7.5 percent per annum at the maximum.

Central Government Consumption (GCNP)

Real government consumption ($GCNP$) has decreased fairly rapidly, falling by 2.5 percent between 1979 and 1983, and 4.6 percent between 1980 and 1983, as shown in table 9-1. During 1983, however, real consumption expenditures decreased by 8.9 percent, indicating considerable scope for austerity measures still remains. Statistically, equation 8 in table 9-2 shows how government consumption is highly influenced by the volume of real government revenue (GRP), the lagged real deficit ($GDEFPL$), and the overall level of government real debt (GDP). Clearly, assumptions concerning the tolerable levels of deficits and the overall feasible expansion of the stock of real debt will largely determine future levels of government consumption.

Central Government Investment (IGP)

As might be expected, the pattern of government investment has behaved much more erratically over time than has the pattern of government consumption. The government's capital expenditures have increased particularly rapidly following hikes in oil revenues, only to be cut back rather severely during periods of declining revenues. Overall, real government investment increased by 6.1 percent during the post-1979 oil boom years (1979–83), but was cut back by 23.0 percent in 1983. Statistically, the flow of real government investment was found in equation 9 of table 9-2 to be highly influenced by the level of real government revenue (GRP) and the lagged real deficit ($GDEFPL$). These two variables accounted for over 90 percent of the fluctuations in real government capital formation.

Private Consumption (PCNP)

As noted, the level of private sector expenditures was broken down into private consumption and private investment for purposes of analysis. Preliminary analysis indicated that real private consumption was highly influenced by the amount of credit made available to the sector by the financial system ($MSCPP$). In equation 10 of table 9-2, $MSCPP$ was in turn found to be determined by another distributed lag relationship, real private sector credit ($MSCPP$), adjusting to increases in the financial sector's credit to the government ($MSCGP$) and the central bank's real credit to the government ($CBCGP$). Historically, the government has been a net lender to the financial system as a whole (thus resulting in $MSCGP$ having a negative value). Based on past trends, it was assumed that the government's net credit to the financial system would increase at 5 percent per annum in real terms. Private consumption ($PCNP$) itself was hypothesized to be a function of personal disposable income (as proxied by real gross domestic product, $GDPNP$). Again, a distributed lag function was found in equation 11 of table 9-2, with private consumption lagged being statistically significant. This formulation implies that past consumption, as well as present disposable income, affect present consumption, a formulation of the consumption function implied by Milton Friedman's "permanent income" hypothesis.[7]

Private Investment (IPP)

Private sector investment has been particularly depressed in recent years, declining at an average annual rate of nearly 30 percent between 1979 and 1983. (See table 9-1.) In 1983, private investment declined by 34.1 percent. Clearly any explanation of the determinants of private capital formation will have to explicitly take this decline into account and also be capable of indicating the point at which capital formation by this sector will bottom out and again resume its upward trend. (Real private investment increased at an average annual rate of 17.4 percent per annum between 1970 and 1978.) The equation for private investment used in the model assumes that private investors undertake investment to bring the actual capital stock in line with their perception of an optimal ordained capital stock. The optimal capital stock is, in turn, a function of profitability of investment. As a proxy for profitability, I have used the capital stock (*KP*) (that is, the larger the existing stock of capital at the beginning of a period, the less profitable investment will be). No series on the capital stock exists for Venezuela, but following Chenery and Eckstein, the capital stock was approximated as the sum of total investment over the three previous years.[8] The optimal capital stock is also determined by profitable investment opportunities opened up by the government's lagged investment in infrastructure (*IGPL*) and the like. The speed of adjustment of the private sector's actual to optimal capital stock takes place in a distributed lag fashion as evidenced by the high t value for the lagged (*IPPL*) private sector investment in equation 12 of table 9-2.

Imports (ZNP)

In a country such as Venezuela with limited capital good capability, investment will consist of a large imported equipment component. Both private investment (*IPP*) and government investment (*IGP*) were highly significant when regressed on imports. Private consumption was also highly significant and, thus, was included in the regression equation. The extent to which the government continues to restrict luxury consumption imports may, however, result in a slight overestimation of future imports using equation 13.

Budgetary Items

Equation 15 estimates real military expenditures (*MESIP*)—the adjustment of real military expenditures over time to changes in the level of real gross domestic product—as a function of lagged real military expenditures (*MESIPL*) and real gross domestic product (*GDPNP*). This information allows military expenditures to expand over time to changes in, for example, government revenues as they impact on gross domestic product or contract as a result of declining export earnings, reduced levels of government expenditures and, thus, (*GDPNP*). It should be noted that this formulation produced a very good fit of estimated to actual values of real military expenditures over the 1950–83 period. The regression equation accounted for over 95 percent of the fluctuations in real military expenditures.

This formulation is consistent with much discussion of the economics of national security policy and military expenditures which has an implicit "rational" or "neoclassical" model of defense.[9] According to this line of argument, social welfare is a function of civilian output and an unobserved variable, security; security depends among other things on military expenditure. The role of the state is then to balance the welfare benefits of extra security derived from military expenditure with its opportunity cost in foregone civilian output.

An examination of official Venezuelan documents does not throw much direct light on the manner in which the government authorities or populace at large value defense expenditures. The distributed lag formulation of defense expenditures does, however, show that, in general, the country feels it necessary to maintain a fairly stable pattern between overall economic production and allocations for defense purposes. Presumably, the relationship between military expenditures and gross national product breaks down when military expenditures expand too much at the expense of other budgetary items. In general, the Venezuelan government has not allowed defense expenditures to expand significantly at the expense of historical shares of social expenditures in the government's overall budget.

In the case of Venezuela, there appears to be a negative trade-off between military expenditures and a number of other major social expenditures. Given the high priority for social expenditures in Venezuela and the distributed lag nature of defense expenditures, expenditures in these areas may expand relative to military allocations during periods of budgetary ease. Both expansion and contraction of government expenditures following this interpretation would produce a negative sign for military expenditures when the share of military expenditures in the overall government budget is regressed on the share of nonmilitary expenditures in the budget. A control variable must be included in the regressions along with the share of military expenditures in the budgets to obtain less biased estimates of the budgetary trade-offs. Evidence in the area of public finance indicates that such factors as increased government expenditures per capita and public expenditures per gross domestic product are important in the rise of public spending and are significant in budgetary trade-offs. Moreover, real increases in either public expenditures per capita or public expenditures per GDP are measures of the level of economic development and the growing resources available to the public sector.

The final estimated budgetary equations show:

1. A negative relationship between military expenditures as a share of government budget (*GDEE*) and social security and welfare expenditures as a share of the budget. Social security and welfare expenditures also contract as a share of the budget as the overall level of government expenditures per capita (*GEPOP*) increases (equation 16 in table 9-2).
2. Public services' share in the government's budget (*GPSE*) is also a negative function of the share of military expenditures in the budget. Public services' share of the budget also declines with increases in government expenditures as a percentage of gross domestic product (*GEY*) (see equation 17 in table 9-2);
3. Education allocations also show a negative relationship to increases in the share of military expenditures in the government's budget and government expenditures per capita. The share of education allocations in the overall government budget does, however, increase with the share of funds allocated to public services (*GPSE*) (equation 18 in table 9-2);
4. In contrast to the other budgetary items examined, health expenditures' share in the budget increases with increases in the budget shares of both military (*GDEE*) and education (*GEDE*)—a positive trade-off indicating a complementary relationship between military allocations and the government's health programs (equation 19 in table 9-2);
5. Other community services show a negative pattern with their share in government budget declining with an increased share of military expenditures and government expenditures per capita (equation 20 in table 9-2).

Identities

The first twenty equations described in table 9-2 provide the endogenous section of the macroeconomic model. Given various assumed values for real export growth (*ENP*) and the growth of central bank credit to the government (*CBCGP*), values for these variables are determined through the estimated relationships. The model also contains a number of identities:

1. The government deficit (*GDEFP*) is simply *GRP* (government real revenue) less *GEP* (real government expenditures) and *LMRP* (lending minus repayments) (line 83, International Monetary Fund, *Financial Statistics*) as seen in equation 21 in table 9–2. Lending minus repayments has not followed any particular historical pattern. For model purposes the variable is set to increase at 1 percent in real terms over the 1984–90 period.
2. Total private (*PENANP*) and government (*GENANP*) expenditures are simply the sums of their respective consumption and investment figures (equations 22 and 23 in table 9–2).
3. Total investment is the sum of private and government capital formation (equation 24 in table 9–2).
4. The capital stock in any time period is assumed, for lack of a series on the capital stock, to be the sum of past investment. Due to the high depreciation of capital in a country such as Venezuela, a proxy for the capital stock was assumed to consist of the sum of the past three years' total investment (equation 25 in table 9–2).
5. The model is a national income accounting model; therefore, the sum of the various accounts must add to gross domestic product. Gross domestic product is, therefore, determined by overall aggregate demand considerations and is generated as the outcome of decisions to consume and invest (*PCNP, GCNP, IPP, IGP*), together with changes in stocks (*ICNP*) and the balance of payments (*ENP – ZNP*) (equation 26 of table 9–2).

The Model's Use in Forecasting

The model is driven by the values assigned to variables assumed to be exogenous to the Venezuelan economy—the population growth (*POP*) assumed to follow its historical growth of 2.8 percent per annum, real exports (*ENP*) simulated from values ranging from an annual decline of 5 percent per annum to an expansion of 2.5 percent per annum, government credit to the financial system assumed to expand at 5 percent per annum, and the exchange rate set at 7.5 percent.

A fixed exchange rate is assumed since Venezuela cannot gain much short-run stimulus from any exchange depreciation vis-à-vis Germany, Japan, or other Latin American countries, because of its relatively small export markets in those countries. Futhermore, since oil exports are denominated in dollars, at least 90 percent of the country's exports would not be affected in any case by a devaluation.

In order to stabilize the exchange rate at the current 7.5 value, the simulations of the economy assume that there is some inflation barrier such that, if the country is able to keep inflation under the given amount, the authorities will be able to maintain par value of their currency with the dollar. The maximum rate of domestic inflation consistent with the maintenance of a stable exchange rate was set at 20 percent per annum. Admittedly, rates close to 20 percent may result in the eventual overvaluation of the bolivar at the 7.5 rate. However, the country was capable of maintaining a fixed exchange rate while inflation averaged 12.32 percent annually over the 1976–82 period. The Lusinchi government has also indicated officially that it intends to pursue whatever measures are necessary to contain inflation under 20 percent per annum.

In sum, the main features of the model include:

1. A series of endogenous variables capable of determining the major macroeconomic relationships over time;
2. A series of exogenous variables—mainly the expansion or contraction of real exports, reflecting developments in the world oil markets;
3. An objective function for military expenditures linking the adjustment in military expenditures to movements in the overall level of the economy;
4. An implicit constraint on military expenditures limiting the extent to which military expenditures can expand their share of the government budget at the expense of social and economic expenditures;
5. A limit on the amount of real (constant price) debt the government will be able to contract for over the near term—a limit set at between 5.0 and 7.5 percent in real annual growth;
6. An inflation barrier limiting the rate of increase in domestic prices to 20 percent per annum.

Preliminary Optimal Control Simulations

A series of preliminary optimal control simulations of the economy was performed in an effort to determine the sensitivity of the forecasts to alternative government policies and stabilization programs. In all of the simulations, the model was set to optimize the level of real gross domestic product in 1990. The loss function was inflation; that is, the optimal control model steered the economy on a path over time that resulted in a minimal rate of inflation consistent with the values of the government's policy variables and the overall rate of growth of real gross domestic product. The chief policy variable (the design variable in optimal control terminology) assigned to the Venezuelan authorities was the increase in real central bank credit to the government. As noted in the discussion of the model, this variable is particularly significant in a statistical sense in affecting the rate of inflation, the level of government expenditures (and thus real gross domestic product), and the balance of payments. To get an idea of the policy mix available to the authorities, real central bank credit was set in general ranges, varying from a little over zero (the most severe austerity package) to around 20 percent (the most expansive fiscal policy considered to be at all realistic). To gain some idea of the inflationary impact of these alternative central bank credit policies, the model's only constraint was an inflation barrier of 25 percent.

In general, the results of these preliminary runs indicate that the debt barrier posed a greater constraint on government fiscal expansion than the inflation barrier. Over most of the range of real export values, it would be difficult for the government to increase its borrowing from the central bank at rates over 12.5 percent per annum before the 7.5 percent average annual increase in real government debt barrier was exceeded.

The main findings of this exploratory analysis indicate that:

1. As the rate of increase in real exports declines, the share of defense in the government budget also declines (for each rate of increase of real central bank credit to the government).
2. Real defense expenditures would decline from the 1983 level if real exports declined at rates over 2.5 percent per annum and if the government were forced to pursue an austerity program of holding its real debt at the 1983 level.
3. In general, inflation reaches 20 percent at real rates of increase in central bank credit to the government of over 15 percent per annum.

4. There is less inflationary pressure at each rate of increase in real central bank credit to the government at the rate of real export growth declines.
5. As the government is forced to pursue increasingly harsh austerity measures, the share of defense expenditures in the overall government budget increases at each rate of change in exports. For example, at a rate of credit expansion of 7.3 percent, the share of defense in the budget is 6.67 percent for a constant value in growth in real exports, while at a 12.35 percent rate of credit expansion to the government, the share of defense in the budget falls to 5.64 percent for the constant level of exports.

Under conditions of a moderate increase in real export growth, the expanding resources available to the government could be allocated in a way such that all of the major sectors of the economy would be able to have their real allocations increased. Note that, in this environment, as the government's fiscal policy given a debt constraint becomes more expansive, a high proportion of incremental allocations would go to economic services and not to defense. This finding is consistent with the greatly stepped-up government investment programs immediately following the oil price increases of 1973–74 and 1978–79, periods in which defense expenditures declined as a proportion of GDP.

Final Optimal Control Forecasts

Given the rough delineation obtained by the previous optimal control forecasts, the final optimal control forecasts were calibrated to come as close as possible to the 7.5 percent average annual increase in external public debt barrier, while at the same time maximizing the overall rate of growth in real gross domestic product. Real central bank credit to the government was set at a 12.5 percent average annual increase, beginning with a low of 7.5 percent annual increase and extending to 15.0 percent. Real exports were assumed to decline slightly—an average annual decline of 1 percent per annum, reflecting the government's flexibility in adapting to likely changes in world oil market conditions and its resolve to stabilize the overall level of crude oil production.

Given these assumptions, the final optimal control forecasts in table 9-3 indicate that the optimal expansion of the economy over the 1984–90 period occurs with a government fiscal policy entailing a 12.4 percent average annual increase in credit from the central

Table 9-3
Venezuela: Final Macroeconomic Defense Expenditures Forecast, 1984-90
(millions of 1980 bolivares)

	1983 Value	Absolute Values 1990 Average Rate of Growth of Central Bank Credit to the Government, 1984-90				Average Annual Rate of Growth 1984-90: Central Bank Credit to the Government (average annual growth 1984-90)			
		7.3	10.0	12.4	14.7	7.3	10.0	12.4	14.7
Gross Domestic Product	210,840	257,460	271,810	278,960	291,210	2.9%	3.7%	4.1%	4.7%
Government investment	251,160	22,111	25,800	28,192	31,823	-1.8	0.4	1.6	3.4
Government consumption	30,466	34,948	41,169	45,203	51,151	2.0	4.4	5.8	7.7
Private consumption	139,360	172,490	178,750	181,740	186,210	3.1	3.6	3.8	4.2
Private investment	14,560	22,333	27,657	29,320	33,112	6.3	9.6	10.5	12.5
Government revenue	56,809	64,549	66,931	68,117	70,151	1.8	2.4	2.6	3.1
Government deficit	-3,093	-3,564	-10,351	-16,353	-23,801	-2.0	-18.8	-26.9	-33.8
Government debt	55,251	57,140	78,274	90,535	109,910	0.5	5.1	7.3	10.3
Balance of payments	-4,523	2,051	-11,739	-18,285	-29,945	5.5	-14.6	-22.1	-31.0
Imports	55,308	56,374	63,527	66,964	73,047	0.3	2.0	2.8	4.1
Private expenditures/ public expenditures	2.77	3.41	3.08	2.87	2.64	3.0	1.5	0.5	-0.7
Government debt/GDP	0.262	0.222	0.288	0.324	0.377	-2.3	1.4	3.1	5.3
Government deficit/GDP	-0.015	0.014	-0.038	-0.58	-0.082	9.9	-14.2	-21.3	-27.5
Private expenditures per capita	9,215	9,403	9,744	9,879	10,151	0.3	0.8	1.0	1.4
Consumer Price Index	1.353	3.846	4.378	4.539	5.038	16.1	18.3	18.9	20.7
Central bank credit to government	4,048	6,644	7,888	9,146	10,546	7.3	10.0	12.4	14.7
Defense expenditures (real)	4,126	4,185	4,366	4,446	4,594	1.6	2.2	2.5	3.9
Defense expenditures (nominal)	5,060	16,098	19,117	20,179	23,145	18.0	20.9	21.9	24.3

Note: All simulations assume an average annual decline of one percent per annum in real exports over the 1984-90 period.

Table 9-4
Venezuela: Final Forecast of Major Budgetary Items, 1990
(millions of 1980 bolívares)

	1983 Value	Absolute Values 1990 Average Annual Rate of Growth in Central Bank Real Credit to the Government 1984-90				Average Annual Rate of Growth 1984-90: Average Annual Growth in Central Bank Credit to the Government 1984-90			
		7.3%	10.0%	12.4%	14.7%	7.3%	10.0%	12.4%	14.7%
Share in Budget									
Defense	6.78	6.59	6.01	5.57	5.14	-0.4%	-1.7%	-2.8%	-3.9%
Public services	6.53	5.90	6.39	6.77	7.13	-1.4	-0.3	0.5	1.3
Education	19.40	18.21	17.37	16.69	15.54	-0.9	-1.6	-2.1	-3.1
Health	8.12	9.23	8.56	8.06	7.36	1.8	0.8	-0.1	-1.4
Social services and welfare	7.27	7.39	6.99	6.64	6.13	0.2	-0.6	-1.3	-2.4
Economic services	21.10	21.50	24.22	26.42	29.97	0.3	2.0	3.3	5.1
Other community services	1.98	1.59	1.41	1.26	1.02	-3.1	-4.7	-6.3	-9.0
Other government expenditures	28.82	29.61	28.96	28.59	27.71	0.4	0.1	-0.1	-0.6
Value									
Defense	3,740	4,185	4,366	4,446	4,594	1.6	2.2	2.5	3.0
Public services	3,634	3,748	4,649	5,408	6,373	0.4	3.6	5.8	8.4
Education	10,811	11,568	12,629	13,334	13,896	1.0	2.3	3.0	3.7
Health	4,519	5,869	6,222	6,442	6,577	3.8	4.7	5.2	5.5
Social services and welfare	4,043	4,694	5,080	5,310	5,477	2.2	3.3	4.0	4.4
Economic services	11,740	13,661	17,608	21,102	26,778	2.2	6.0	8.7	12.5
Other community services	1,098	1,008	1,026	1,013	910	-1.2	-1.0	-1.1	-2.7
Other government expenditures	16,040	18,794	21,115	22,828	24,761				
Total government expenditures	55,625	63,527	72,695	79,883	89,366	1.9	3.9	5.3	7.0

Note: All simulations assume an average annual decline of one percent per annum in real exports over the 1984-90 period.

bank. This fiscal policy results in a 7.3 percent average annual increase in the central government's debt, a rate of inflation of 18.9 percent, and an overall expansion of 4.1 percent per annum in real gross domestic product. This rate of real gross domestic product will result in an average annual increase in real military expenditures of 2.5 percent per annum.

This growth path does not create any particularly severe budgetary trade-offs, according to table 9–4. By 1990, defense expenditures will have contracted to 5.57 percent of the government budget (from a 1983 figure of 6.78). Note again the budgetary trade-off pattern—even though defense has a negative impact on the shares of: (1) social security and welfare, (2) public services, (3) education, and (4) other community services, all of these sectors are able to sustain healthy increases in their real allocations despite the expansion in defense expenditures. This phenomenon is clearly the result of the fact that defense expenditures expand at a rate (2.5 percent) considerably below the overall rate of expansion in government expenditures (5.3 percent).

In short, given this fiscal policy, the trade-offs between defense expenditures and socioeconomic expenditures is more apparent than real. If the government is particularly concerned with the social and economic welfare of the population, it has a great incentive to pursue as expansive a fiscal policy as possible. For example, at a central bank credit to the government averaging 14.7 percent (generating a government debt at an annual rate of 10.3 percent), overall real government expenditures increase from 5.3 to 7.0 percent. Because this expansion in real government expenditures of 1.7 percent results in an increase in defense expenditures of only 0.5 percent, there are ample funds available for expanding all other expenditures (except other community expenditures). On the margin (over the rate associated with an increase of government debt of 12.4 percent), this fiscal policy results in an expansion of:

1. Public services—2.6 percent;
2. Education—0.7 percent;
3. Health—0.3 percent;
4. Social services and welfare—0.4 percent;
5. Economic services—3.8 percent;

with public services and economic services clearly the major beneficiaries of this high-growth strategy.

The critical assumption in these forecasts involves the ability of the government to increase its level of debt. Forecasts would be lower if the government were forced to pursue a mild austerity program, that is, holding its expansion of real debt to around 5 percent per annum. On the other hand, the forecasts would be higher if the government were able to restore its creditworthiness with foreign bankers to the extent that its real debt could expand at an average annual rate of around 10 percent. Since it is most likely that the government will only be able to expand its debt at around 7.5 percent a year, this figure establishes the medium forecast of military expenditures expansion at 2.5 percent per annum.

The forecasts imply that:

1. Real defense expenditures will expand at an average annual rate of 2.5 percent over the 1984–90 period, with a low of 2.2 percent and a high of 3.0.
2. The overall expansion of the economy should be around 4.1 percent per annum, with a high of 4.7 percent and a low of 3.7 percent.
3. Defense expenditures as a proportion of the budget should be around 6.0 percent, with a low of 5.57 percent and a high of 6.5 percent.

Further insights into the likely pattern of economic and military developments can be obtained by examining the year-to-year movements in the leading economic-military indices.

At the 12.4 percent rate of central bank credit expansion to the government, real economic growth continues to be stagnant until around 1987, as seen in table 9–5. Beginning in 1988, the economy begins a fairly healthy expansion continuing through 1990. Real military expenditures remain rather constant over the 1984–86 period, with a gradual expansion in 1987, and acceleration throughout the remainder of the decade.

In sum, the final forecasts for military expenditures presented in the previous section were based on an assumed 1 percent decline in real exports over the 1984–90 period. Within this environment, real military expenditures, given the additional assumption of a moderately expansive fiscal program (defined in terms of the real government debt increasing at 7.3 percent per annum), were forecast to expand at an average annual rate of 2.5 percent over the period. On the assumption of increased creditworthiness and access to external capital, the highest rate of real military growth considered

Table 9-5
Venezuela: Time Profile of Major Macroeconomic Variables and Defense Expenditures, 1983-90
(millions of 1980 bolivares)

	1983 Actual	Generated				Forecast		
		1984	1985	1986	1987	1988	1989	1990
Gross Domestic Product	210,840	215,990	194,490	190,440	199,410	219,390	246,660	281,920
Private consumption	139,360	137,390	140,550	144,476	150,450	158,140	168,270	181,240
Government debt	55,251	52,907	50,705	50,953	54,618	62,213	74,025	90,535
Government deficit	-3,094	729	1,509	2,731	-2,566	-6,255	-10,955	-16,353
Government expenditures	55,625	55,379	54,016	55,201	58,782	64,041	71,191	79,883
Private consumption per capita	9,217	8,839	8,796	8,813	8,910	9,110	9,430	9,880
Military expenditures (real)	3,740	3,778 (1.02)	3,777 (0.0)	3,789 (0.32)	3,849 (1.58)	3,973 (3.22)	4,172 (5.01)	4,446 (6.57)
Military expenditures (nominal)	5,060	6,875	7,739	8,571	9,400	12,283	14,654	20,179
Defense expenditures/ government expenditures	6.72	6.82	6.99	6.86	7.54	6.20	5.86	5.57
Private expenditures/ government expenditures	2.76	2.74	2.87	2.90	2.89	2.88	2.87	2.87
Government debt/GDP	0.262	0.235	0.228	0.227	0.237	0.258	0.287	0.324

Notes: Based on a 12.4 percent average annual expansion of central bank credit to the government and a 7.3 percent average annual increase in government debt, 1984-90.
( ) = average annual yearly growth.

feasible was 3.0 percent. In contrast, the government might, due to increased international scepticism regarding Venezuela's ability to manage its economy, limit the increase in real government borrowing to 5 percent per annum. In this case, the low figure of 2.2 percent annual increase in real military expenditures could be expected.

Given the fact that the inflationary impact of increasing government debt from 5.1 to 10.3 percent is only 2.4 percent per annum (20.7 percent minus 18.3 percent in table 9-3), and given the fact that social and economic programs could increase relative to defense expenditures as the budget is expanded over this range (defense falling from 6.01 percent of the budget with debt increasing at 5.1 percent per annum to 5.14 percent with debt increasing at 10.3 percent per annum, according to table 9-4), it would seem that the government would be inclined to push for as large an increase in debt as international capital markets would allow. In lieu of the fact that real government debt increased at an average annual rate of 9.21 percent between 1980 and 1983 and 10.3 percent in 1983, the 10.3 percent high forecast must be considered the absolute maximum that an expansive fiscal policy could achieve. In short, the 7.3 percent real debt expansion, given only a slight decline of 1 percent per annum in real exports, provides the most likely and feasible fiscal policy open to the government.

Conclusions

Using optimal control exercises, this analysis attempted to:

1. Optimize the growth in real gross domestic product over the period 1984–90;
2. Determine the inflationary and budgetary deficit impacts of this expansion in real gross domestic product;
3. Set maximum ranges for inflation and the government debt associated with expansion in real gross domestic product;
4. Revise the real gross domestic product forecast to be consistent with the assumed inflation and real government debt restraints;
5. Given this feasible rate of expansion in real gross domestic product, compute the allocations likely to be made on defense activities.

From the results, it is apparent that there are no quick fixes for the Venezuelan economy. There are no panaceas in tax reform or petroleum revenues that will permit the country to pursue monetary and fiscal policies inconsistent with the productive capacity of the economy.

The Lusinchi government has introduced monetary and fiscal reforms designed to restore stability and financial credibility to the Venezuelan economy. Government spending has been reduced to levels more consistent with Venezuela's financial resources. Commitment to monetary stability has accompanied more conservative fiscal policies.

While the outlook for Venezuela under the Lusinchi administration is promising, formidable obstacles stand in the way of success. The foreign debt must be serviced sooner or later; rescheduling that debt has averted a financial crisis but not the financial constraints imposed by that debt. In the near term, Venezuela will have to make every effort to halt the secular decline in its crude petroleum production even if it means continuing to produce over the OPEC quota.

The real test of the Lusinchi government is in the strength of its commitment to more stable monetary and fiscal policies. If the government can hold the growth of public spending and monetary expansion in balance with the growth of productive capacity, it can probably pull the country out of its financial crisis and onto a slower, but more stable path of expansionary growth by the end of the decade.

In terms of military expenditures, the analysis found that, by adjusting in a distributed lag fashion to changes in the country's real gross domestic product, Venezuela's military budgets have historically remained fairly stable over time. The examination also showed that during periods of austerity, military expenditures were less subject to severe cutbacks than other types of social and economic programs (and similarly expanded less rapidly in the face of increased government resources).

Notes

1. An excellent chronology of the deteriorating economic situation in Venezuela is given in the annual reports of the Inter American Development Bank, *Economic and Social Progress in Latin America*.

2. A description of the validity of this type of model together with several examples for Latin America are given in Tere Behrman and James Hanson, eds., *Short Term Macroeconomic Policy in Latin America* (Cambridge, Mass.: Ballinger, 1979). In particular, see Tere Behrman and James Hanson, "The Use of Econometric Models in Developing Countries" and Abel Beltran del Rio, "Econometric Forecasting for Mexico: An Analysis of Errors in Prediction" in this book.

3. Estimations were made using the TSP program developed at Stanford University. See B. Hall and R. Hall *Time Series Processor, Version 3.5 User's Manual* (Stanford, Calif.: B. Hall and R. Hall, 1980) for a description of the estimation procedure. The rationale for two-stage estimations in this context is given in J.R. Prindyck and D. Rubinfeld, *Econometric Models and Economic Forecasts* (New York: McGraw-Hill, 1976) pp. 144-46, 276-78, 298-302.

4. International Monetary Fund, *International Financial Statistics*, various issues and International Monetary Fund, *Government Statistics Yearbook*, various issues. Venezuela's military expenditures in current prices were taken from the Stockholm International Peace Research Institute, *World Armaments and Disarmament: SIPRI Yearbook* (Philadelphia: Taylor and Francis), various issues.

5. See the previous section on distributed lags for a discussion of this specification and the assumptions underlying the estimation.

6. See, for example, A. Robinson, "The End of the Illusion in Latin America," *Euromoney* (September 1982), p. 77.

7. For a description of this permanent-income-type consumption function together with alternative specifications of the private sector's consumption pattern, cf. Michael K. Evans, *Macroecnomic Activity: Theory, Forecasting and Control* (New York: Harper and Row, 1969), chapters 2-3.

8. H. Chenery and P. Eckstein, "Development Alternatives for Latin America," *economic development report no. 29* (Cambridge, Mass.: Harvard University, Project for Quantitative Research in Economic Development, 1967).

9. R.P. Smith, "The Demand for Military Expenditure," *Economic Journal* (December 1980), p. 811.

Part III
Argentina

Analysis of Venezuelan defense expenditures confirmed that the major patterns of budgetary allocation for defense and defense–nondefense budgetary trade-offs identified in the cross-section analysis for Latin American arms producers as a whole have also characterized that country's budget.

In sharp contrast to Venezuela, Argentina's political and economic climates have been much more unstable during the period under examination. Clearly, a question arises as to whether political crises and regime changes in Argentina have dominated the country's budgetary process and defense–nondefense allocations (together, of course, with the Malvinas War) so as to make longer-run economic trends and constants irrelevant considerations in analyzing the country's defense sector.

The main finding of part III is that, despite the markedly different priorities given to defense by various types of regime in Argentina, the country's military allocations can still be most effectively analyzed within the framework developed in parts I and II. Admittedly, political change and instability have had a major impact on the patterns of budgetary allocation over time. However, as the following analysis demonstrates, the impact of Argentinian political change on defense allocations is best seen as modifying budgetary patterns stemming from longer-term economic trends rather than as a major explanatory variable.

10
The Impact of Recent Developments on Argentinian Military Expenditures

Elected in 1983, the democratic regime of Raul Alfonsin is currently facing a major economic crisis with hyperinflation, a severe foreign debt, and, at the same time, falling real wages and serious industrial decline. Even so, Argentinian public opinion seems to have been more patient with President Alfonsin than it was with the military regimes of March 1976–December 1983. Expectations have been lowered by recent political experiences and Alfonsin has taken some strong measures to restore the economy.

However, as a democratically elected leader, he has not found it easy to take drastic austerity measures. In this sense, his performance will be a good test for the Latin American structuralist thesis that a mixture of controls and restrictions offers the chance of reducing inflation without imposing excessive pain on the main social groups.[1] Before coming to office, he indicated that the military budget was one of the few areas where major economies could be made. This chapter examines the general policies President Alfonsin has taken with regard to the military and, in particular, the manner in which he has dealt with the defense budget.

Initial Reforms

Initially after the Alfonsin government assumed office, it was expected that the armed forces would be significantly reduced in size and that they would be required to become much more professional, perhaps with the ending of compulsory military service for all males. It was generally conceded, however, that it would be much more difficult to end the extensive special privileges enjoyed by professional officers, despite the fact that their inflation-proof salaries and pensions and other benefits had grown increasingly resented during the years of recession, inflation, and misdemeanors by the military corps that has just past.[2]

During the election campaign, Alfonsin repeatedly stated that the first one hundred days of his administration would be critical for setting down the institutions of a democratic Argentina. In contrast to previous constitutional leaders, upon assuming office Alfonsin immediately set out to prosecute the military hierarchy for its errors and crimes. Less than one month after taking office, he drummed one-half of the generals out of the army, the only branch of the armed forces that had avoided a post-Malvinas self-purge. He also retired nearly as many admirals and air force brigadiers. Alfonsin then restructured the military high command, abolishing the highly politicized position of armed forces commander-in-chief and bringing the three services under civilian control.[3]

The government also took symbolic steps meant to signal the military's change in mission from internal security to defending national territory from outside attack. The senior general commanding troops, for instance, has been stationed in the far south, where tensions occasionally flare with British and Chilean forces, rather than in Buenos Aires, a post from which many coup attempts in the past had been launched.[4]

In addition to changes in the armed forces code, Alfonsin early on indicated that he wanted to slash defense expenditures from 5 percent of GNP to 2 percent. Early in 1984, the Radicals indicated that they planned ultimately to cut the 150,000-strong army in half. Initially, the government's personnel reductions for 1984 were to total 12 percent, with a programmed 1984 military spending cut of 40 percent. These measures, however, prompted criticism within more reformist sectors of the Alfonsin government, which argued that the relatively small 1984 personnel cuts would probably result in many undertrained and underequipped conscripts. Finally, these critics pointed out, Alfonsin's goal of professionalizing the services would require an initial outlay of cash to modernize the forces. Yet budget constraints were already drawn even tighter by the discovery of tens of millions of dollars in arms contracts already in the pipeline.[5] During its closing months in office, the military regime had spent heavily on arms, partly to replace material lost in the Malvinas War, but also to preempt the expected cuts in arms budgets by the incoming civilian regime.

In short, the new government found a number of constraints associated with its plan to significantly reduce military expenditures. Past orders placed by the military regime were still being filled, while the restructuring of the military, in and of itself, presented added budgetary demands.

The Cost of the Malvinas War

The military establishment is reckoned to have spent some U.S. $20 billion in 1976-80.[6] Ministry of Economy figures show a 200 percent increase in the military budget in real terms from 1972 to 1980. (In the same period, spending on education fell by 50 percent and on health by 30 percent.) Defense expenditures by the post-1976 military regime increased to 8 percent of GDP—against an average of 2.2-2.5 percent of GDP in past civilian, military and Peronist governments.

The cost of the Malvinas War itself has not been officially stated by Argentina, but unofficial estimates place it at about $850 million.[7] By the end of 1982, Argentina had already committed itself to more than $1 billion in arms purchases, with special commissions set up with the Argentinian army, navy, and air force to work out new programs of armament. Just before the end of the hostilities, the Argentinian air force received 10 Mira V aircraft from Peru and 22 Dagger/Nesher aircraft from Israel, the stock of bombs having been replenished by Libya and Israel. The shipment of French Super Etendard aircraft and Exocet missiles resumed in November 1982, in spite of strong British objections. Later, a contract was signed with France for the acquisition of 15 Super Puma helicopters. Some Soviet assistance in the expansion of Argentina's early warning system may have been provided in the latter stages of the war.

The Argentinian navy was to receive 2 submarines under construction in West Germany, in addition to 4 others planned to be assembled in Argentina. Also, 4 highly sophisticated frigates were being built in West Germany for future delivery.[8] The cost of this reequipment program was estimated at U.S. $2 billion, plus a further U.S. $1 to $2 billion remaining to be paid for orders placed before 1982.[9]

Finally, the Argentinian army had committed itself to reconstruct the system of air defense with the assistance of the Swiss Oerlikon company and to buy some 40 French-produced Panhard armored vehicles, as well as 255 Kurassier tanks from the Austrian Steyr-Daimler-Puch company.

In short, despite the perilous state of the economy in late 1983 and early 1984, purchases of new equipment to replace that lost during the Malvinas fighting were quickly arranged. France, the United States, and West Germany very soon dropped their embargoes on sales of arms and by late 1982, some important deliveries had been made. The air force, which had lost 35 aircraft during the war, had by early 1983 already regained its full combat capability and had more Mirage fighters than it had at the start of the war (65 in all). The army was seeking to acquire many more helicopters and, like the other services, more modern and sophisticated weaponry.[10]

Argentina's military build-up following the Malvinas War has been characterized as "careful and sophisticated."[11] As of early 1985, a comparison of prewar, postwar, and current force dispositions in its air force and naval air force indicated that:

1. The air force now has enhanced strike potential. The country now has 28 Exocet missiles compared with 5 before the war.
2. The 80-strong Mirage/Dagger force is being equipped with aerial-refueling probes to increase their operational range.
3. The naval air force is modifying 7 newly acquired Lockheed L-188 Electra aircraft for reconnaissance, antisubmarine, and other roles.
4. Following plans drawn up before the 1982 war, Argentina is planning to increase its modern submarines from 2 to 8, while the number of modern escorts—destroyers, frigates, and corvettes—will increase from 5 to 15.[12]

Budgeted military spending in Argentina in 1984 and 1985 still, therefore, reflected the war economy of 1982, although President Alfonsin announced a commitment to spending on education and health while reducing the military budget. But even if some of the most recent orders for aircraft, armored vehicles, guided missiles, or warships could be reduced or cancelled, the bill has yet to be paid for Argentina's rearmament program in the later half of the 1970s and in the aftermath of the Malvinas conflict. The central bank estimated early in 1983 that at least $5 billion in foreign debt had been incurred for arms purchases between 1978 and the end of 1982 and that the figure was still growing.[13]

Alfonsin's Record

Perhaps due to past commitments and the cost of restructuring the military, by April 1984, President Alfonsin seemed to be retracting his plans to slash military spending by as much as 20 percent. In fact, the defense minister indicated at that time that the first Alfonsin budget would be characterized by a reallocation rather than a reduction of military expenditure, the rationale being that security must not be affected.

Part of the answer as to how far President Alfonsin is willing to go in curtailing the military budget and reforming the services was made clear in the summer of 1984, when the government submitted to Congress its draft budget. The chiefs of the three services claimed they would be quite constrained if the budget were passed.

1. The air force, which played a key role in the Malvinas War, was allocated 26 percent of the military budget. The air force chief of staff indicated that the service needed at least U.S. $250 million merely to maintain its operational capacity.
2. Half of the navy's service allocation will be absorbed by salaries, the other half by the annual training exercises. President Alfonsin lifted part of the service's debt burden (repayments of principal on the U.S. $1.3 billion borrowed to purchase hardware) by shifting it to the treasury department, but the navy will still have to cover interest payments from its own budget.
3. Most of the army budget goes to personnel costs which do not pose too much of a problem within the existing structure, where numbers of soldiers are all-important. However, if professionalization and modernization are to go ahead, the army will find itself facing an entirely new pattern of expenditures.[14]

Despite their misgivings, the service chiefs appeared willing to go along with the reduced 1984 budget, rationalizing it as a transitional situation while plans were being drawn up for a new defense structure, drawing on the experiences of the 1982 war.

Furthermore, on October 20, 1984, two days after the Beagle Channel dispute had been resolved with Chile, President Alfonsin signed a new decree dissolving several armed forces installations. Interpreted at first as a drive to introduce military budget cuts and democratize the military, the current plan also aims to decentralize the armed forces (both geographically and in their internal structures) and to remove them from the center of power.

The decree introduced the following changes:

1. The first army corps' installations in Buenos Aires were handed over to the University of Buenos Aires. Some of its units were dissolved and others transferred to the interior.
2. Some fifty thousand conscripts (75 percent of the land troops) were discharged from active service.
3. The coast guard agency, Prefectura Nacional Maritima, is no longer to be controlled by the navy high command. It will be

headed by a prefect named from within the institution and will come under defense ministry supervision;
4. The frontier police corps, Gendarmeria Nacional, was made independent of the army. Like the Prefectura Nacional Maritima, it is to be run by a prefect under defense ministry jurisdiction, the minister being a civilian.
5. For the first time since it was set up, the military-industrial conglomerate, Fabricaciones Militares, which has always been run by generals, will have as its director a civil engineer.
6. Plans were initiated to end military control of civilian airports.[15]

In November, the Argentinian government put the proposed Beagle Channel treaty to a referendum which resulted in a strong vote of approval; the vote can also be construed as an expression of confidence in the government and a warning to the military that the public remains strongly in favor of President Alfonsin's administration, despite the economic and other problems it faces.[16]

A recent study of the Argentinian military since the Malvinas War of 1982 found that:

1. Whereas 60–80,000 soldiers had been conscripted annually under the military regime, this rate has declined, probably to a 30–40,000 level in 1985. Furthermore, it is not expected that many of these conscripts will serve beyond the 180-day minimum period allowed by law, whereas the army government had usually kept conscripts for a full year.
2. Complete replacement of war losses may not occur. Since the war, reports have frequently suggested that these losses have been fully made up or even more than made up to prewar levels. The government has denied this and the regime is adamant that only orders placed before the democracy was reestablished have been received.
3. As early as 1983–84, the defense budget was cut to 5.98 percent of GDP. This compares with about 8 percent before the Malvinas War. However, under the civilian defense minister, the defense budget fell to only 3.71 percent of GDP, with President Alfonsin indicating that he hopes to cut defense expenditures still further, perhaps down to only 2 percent of GDP.[17]

These massive blows have been felt throughout the forces in operational and training activities but nowhere more than in forces' development programs with no likely export spin-offs. The vast military complex of Campo de Mayo is to be reduced by over two-thirds in area. The land and facilities are to be sold, as are many other valuable properties held by the forces, particularly by the army.

With a budget cut to half that of 1983, it is not surprising that Argentina's suppliers are beginning to complain about delays in payment.

Conclusions

One of the main provisions of the September 1984 agreement with the IMF was that military expenditures be reduced, whereas spending on social services, health, housing, and education be increased. The current economic situation of increased austerity, together with the Radicals' resolve to cut military spending, should result in additional real budgetary cutbacks. Argentina's success in demilitarizing under Alfonsin holds open hope to other authoritarian Latin American states that are approaching democracy that it is possible for a popularly elected government to make major cutbacks—over military objections—in the share of resources allocated for defense purposes.

Notes

1. George Philip, "The Fall of the Argentine Military," *Third World Quarterly* (July 1984), p. 635.
2. Cf. Economist Intelligence Unit, *Quarterly Economic Review of Argentina* (no. 1, 1984), p. 7; and Andrew Graham-Tooll, "Argentina: The State of Transition 1983-1985," *Third World Quarterly* (July 1985), pp. 573-593.
3. Martin Anderson, "Dateline Argentina: Hello, Democracy," *Foreign Policy* (Summer 1984), p. 159.
4. *Ibid.*
5. *Ibid.*, p. 161.
6. Latin America Regional Reports, *Southern Cone* (April 13, 1984), p. 3.
7. Stockholm International Peace Research Institute, *World Armaments and Disarmament: SIPRI Yearbook, 1983* (Philadelphia: Taylor and Francis, 1983), p. 486.
8. *Ibid.*, p. 487.
9. Stockholm International Peace Research Institute, *World Armaments and Disarmament: SIPRI Yearbook, 1984* (Philadelphia: Taylor and Francis, 1984), p. 100.
10. Economist Intelligence Unit, *Quarterly Economic Review of Argentina* (no. 1, 1983), p. 9.
11. Latin America Regional Reports, *Southern Cone* (February 1, 1985), p. 3. The report quotes a study undertaken at Bradford University by Paul Rogers.

12. *Ibid.*
13. *World Armaments and Disarmament: SIPRI Yearbook, 1984, op. cit.,* p. 100.
14. Latin America Regional Reports, *Southern Cone* (April 13, 1984), p. 3.
15. Latin America Regional Reports, *Southern Cone* (November 6, 1984), p. 3
16. Economist Intelligence Unit, *Quarterly Ecomomic Review of Argentina* (no. 1, 1985), p. 6.
17. H.A. Klepak, *Continuity and Change in the Argentine Army since the Falklands* (Weybridge, England: Ian Allan, 1985) as summarized in Latin America Regional Reports, *Southern Cone* (August 2, 1985), p. 5.

11
Impact of Regime Type on Argentinian Central Government Budgetary Priorities, 1961-82: A Test of the O'Donnell Thesis

A sharp change in general economic policies appears to be taking place in Argentina following the demise of the March 1976-December 1983 military regime and the restoration of democracy.

The changes apparently are not merely ideological—a shift from neoliberal macroeconomic policies to more conventional Keynesian-type policies—but also involve budgetary priorities with a shift in emphasis away from military-related expenditures toward social and welfare-related allocations. Clearly implied in this shift is the presumption that civilian regimes in Argentina tend to pursue markedly different economic policies than their military counterparts.

While it is early to determine whether the Alfonsin government will be able to carry through on its rhetoric to modify the way macroeconomic policy is pursued and to shift the relative priorities attached to the government's major functional expenditure categories, some insights can undoubtedly be gained through an examination of the budgetary priorities of recent civilian and military regimes. The purpose of this chapter, therefore, is to examine through statistical analysis the patterns of budgetary allocation associated with regime type in Argentina over the period 1961-82.[1] The main thrust of the analysis is to determine the possible existence and nature of structural changes in the government's budgetary priorities associated with the change of regime.

The O'Donnell Thesis

A wide body of literature on Argentina suggests that transitions from military to civilian regimes bring about fundamental changes to policy-making, in general, and in socioeconomic and military priorities, in particular. This view has been developed by Guillermo O'Donnell in his path-breaking thesis about the emergence of new forms of authoritarianism in Latin America. According to O'Donnell, particular types of economic and social crises tend to be associated with each phase of modernization. Each phase tends to bring a new dominant coalition to power and produce a distinct type of authoritarian rule. Each alliance comes to power imbued with a distinct sense of what should be done at whose expense, consolidates its control, centralizes power and authority, seals off the arena to non-coalition members, exercises unconstrained control over the policy process, and translates the goals and interests of the members of the coalition into public policies. Coalition members benefit from public policies; non-coalition members bear the costs.[2] Authoritarianism in general and populist and bureaucratic authoritarianism in particular are seen as the response that different sets of elites take in reaction to crises engendered by different phases of modernization.[3]

A causal relationship exists among economic stages, politics, and public policies; the "elective affinity" is close. As a consequence, questions of possible disjunctures between economics and politics, or between politics and policies, never arise. Indeed, different types of authoritarianism are defined jointly on the basis of certain economic stages, coalitions, and public policies.[4]

The bureaucratic authoritarian model has the following characteristics:

1. Economic state: capital/durable consumer goods production, import substitution industrialization;
2. Coalition: segments of the military, large and efficient domestic industrialists, foreign capital, and technocrats in public sector;
3. Policies:
   a. Promotion of capital (basic) and durable consumer goods industries as well as modernization of their infrastructure;
   b. Conservative budgetary and restrictive monetary policies, combined with efforts to increase tax revenues;
   c. Decreases in overall public spending;
   d. Decreases in public employment;
   e. Efforts to impose a rational calculus on policy-making;
   f. Efforts to stop or regress political redistribution of wealth to the popular sector in order to provide sufficient investment capital;

g. Decreases in social welfare benefits;
h. Efforts to demobilize and exclude the popular sectors both economically and politically;
i. Increases in military spending to control actual or expected social unrest and threats to domestic security.[5]

The critical variable as conditioning the development of bureaucratic authoritarianism is the level of perceived threat to the existing socioeconomic order generated by the precoup crisis.[6] The level of prior threat not only represents its originating circumstances; it shapes subsequent features of the bureaucratic authoritarian state and accounts for differences among cases. The economic and political crises that precede the bureaucratic authoritarian administrations have variations from one case to another that have repercussions on the specific characteristics of the government that results.

Of interest here is that O'Donnell also argues that threat levels explain variations in economic policies and economic performance. The short-term consequences of a higher threat level that he has specifically identified include:

1. More careful adherence to orthodox economic policies;
2. More immediate inflows of external public assistance to help stabilize the economy;
3. More difficulty in reducing the rate of inflation to acceptable levels;
4. Less capacity of the state to invest;
5. Less probability of rapidly restoring economic growth;
6. Slower restoration of investor confidence;
7. By implication, less immediate success in attracting long-term private investment.[7]

Clearly, the post-1966 Argentinian military regime was a low-threat bureaucratic authoritarian case, while the post–March 1976 regime was a high-threat case.

O'Donnell has observed that the economic policies of the military incorporate fundamental components. Disinflation through fiscal-monetary orthodoxy is used in part to break the political mobilization of labor unions through the creation of additional slack in labor markets. Disinflation is also necessitated by the second characteristic of economic policy under military authoritarianism, a trend toward transnationalization of the production structure, particularly heavy industry. Because of the greater dependence of heavy industry on external sources of capital, stabilization is a necessary precondition for the extension of additional foreign loans; at the same time, the successive phases of import substitution require higher rates of capital accumulation because of the capital intensity of industry and consequent reductions in real wages.[8]

The similarity of the orthodox economic policies introduced by authoritarian regimes in the 1970s has been well documented.[9] If, in fact, similar macro policies carry over to a similar approach toward budgetary allocations and priorities, the O'Donnell thesis would predict cutbacks in social services and welfare in bureaucratic authoritarian regimes to aid the stabilization efforts with increased military expenditures to shore up domestic security. One would predict, therefore, that based on the change in regimes from a high-threat bureaucratic authoritarian regime to a civilian regime in 1984, a marked shift downward in military expenditures could be expected in Argentina over the next few years.

Previous Empirical Examinations of Regime Type and Budgetary Priorities

The above predictions also have some empirical validity. In a recent examination of civilian and military regimes in ten Latin American countries, Thomas Dickson found that:

1. Military regimes appear to have been more fiscally conservative than civilian ones.
2. Civilian regimes appear to have been more developmentally oriented than military ones.
3. Military regimes were inclined to spend less and run lower deficits, even though they spent more on the military.
4. Military regimes also showed a lower rate of increase in the cost of living and maintained stronger international liquidity positions for the central bank.
5. Civilian regimes spent more, did more for education, and effected higher savings and investment ratios.[10]

On the other hand, a number of empirical studies along these lines have provided little empirical support for the O'Donnell thesis or for the general proposition that military regimes tend to expand military budgets over and above what one might predict a civilian regime would do. Bernard Most for example found little change in military expenditures or most other socioeconomic variables in Argentina during the post-1966 transition to bureaucratic authoritarian rule from a civilian regime.[11] Other studies also concluded that governments dominated by the military produce socioeconomic results quite similar to those produced by civilian regimes.[12] As Philippe Schmitter commented in summarizing this research:

> The conclusions have tended to be similar whether arrived at by statistical inference from synchronic correlations across units or descriptive evaluation based on diachronic counter-factual assumptions within units. We have been led to believe that the relatively constant features of ecological setting and underlying class interests and/or the persistence of subtle machinations by informal cliques and patron-client dyads impose such narrow and fixed parameters upon performance that it makes no "real" difference if political structures are more or less centralized, more or less competitive, or more or less participatory. Such an overdetermined system (provided the three layers of determinism are self-reinforcing) will produce the same outputs and outcomes—i.e., benefit the same interests—in any case short of violent revolution.[13]

A number of other studies have found the same pattern.

Jackman examined seventy-seven Third World countries using covariance analysis, concluding that "military intervention in the politics of the Third World has no unique effects on social change, regardless of either the level of economic development or geographic region."[14]

Two cross-national aggregate data studies by Robert McKinlay and Arthur Cohan based on an initial sample of 115 countries reached conclusions similar to Jackman's. In the first of these studies, McKinlay and Cohan compared the performance of military and civilian governments over the 1951–70 period, using indicators of annual change in per capita GNP, cost of living, food production, exports, primary education, military spending, and military size. They found that military regimes perform significantly better than civilian ones in the poorest countries, although their evidence also suggests that in Latin America, military regimes perform somewhat better than civilian ones. However, McKinlay and Cohan concluded that military regimes do not in the aggregate form a distinctive regime type in terms of performance. They found that the rate of growth of primary education was the only overall significant performance difference between military and civilian regimes.

The second study by McKinlay and Cohan covering the 1951–70 period used different data and statistical techniques to arrive at the same basic conclusion. In this study, McKinlay and Cohan found evidence that military regimes tend to occupy a weaker international trading position than their civilian counterparts but that their economic performance rates, measured in terms of the rate of growth of per capita GNP, cost of living, and exports, compared favorably with nonmilitary regimes. Military regimes were clearly distinguished from civilian regimes only by their lower levels of political activity and higher levels of political change.[15]

The most extensive study to date of the consequence of regime differences in Latin America was by Philippe Schmitter. It partially confirms the findings of these cross-regional studies. Using both cross-sectional and longitudinal data, Schmitter concluded that no regime type was exclusively linked with developmental success as measured by such indicators of performance as average annual percentage increases in inflation, exports, industrial production, and per capita GNP.

Military and noncompetitive regimes were slightly more successful in curtailing inflation, increasing foreign exchange earnings, and promoting economic growth, especially in industry. However, environmental factors, particularly dependence on foreign capital, aid, and trade were more important in understanding the performance variations than was regime type.

Regime type only appeared relevant for understanding variations in governmental allocations (outputs) as distinct from system performance (outcomes). In particular, Schmitter found that military regimes in Latin America tend to spend less on social welfare, rely more heavily on indirect taxation as a source of government revenue, and extract fewer resources for the pursuit of public policies than civilian regimes. However, most correlations between regime type and policy outputs were weak, supporting the view that regime differences are relatively unimportant for understanding policy differences in Latin America.[16]

A major study of Brazil also cast doubt on the relevance of regime differences. Margaret Daly Hayes's detailed work on longitudinal changes in Brazilian national expenditures, for example, indicates that military and civilian regimes in Brazil have not differed extensively in their economic goals and policy outputs. Compared to their military counterparts, civilian governments in the 1950–67 period were more likely to spend money on social development and the civilian bureaucracy, while being less likely to spend funds on military equipment. But all regimes in this period gave priority to national development with an emphasis on infrastructural development. Moreover, economic constraints (particularly GDP, political conflict, primary export earnings, inflation, and debt service) explain a high proportion of the variation in expenditure patterns over time.[17]

Finally, Ames and Goff have noted, "If students of Latin American politics were to inventory verified propositions regarding the performance of Latin American regimes, the resulting list might not exceed zero."[18] In summary, while there is some evidence that the more recent bureaucratic authoritarian regimes in Latin America tend to pursue similar macroeconomic policies, recent research on budgetary priorities clearly suggests that underlying socioeconomic conditions may impose such basic constraints on political actors that it makes little difference whether they are civilian or military. Similar conclusions have been reached by studies employing very different units of analysis and research strategies.

Why do experts on Latin America argue that history has shown regime type to be irrelevant in affecting budgetary priorities? One version of this position stresses economic constraints and suggests that socioeconomic variables are more important in explaining policy differences than political variables. In particular, the dependency literature has emphasized that the dynamics and structure of economic development in Latin America cannot be understood without taking into account factors such as imperial domination, foreign investment and technology, foreign aid, and export demand—factors that domestic policymakers cannot control directly.[19]

A major variant on this argument suggests that civilian and military regimes do not even have different policy orientations, either because the civilian–military dichotomy is totally artificial or because the same class, sectoral, or status group interests control the government no matter who occupies the top positions.

Finally, the policy relevance of system-level characteristics has been questioned on the grounds that factors such as operational systems and formal institutional arrangements which may account for policy variations are not systematically related to regime type or regime orientation.[20]

Before concluding that experts on Latin America, who have expended considerable time and effort explaining the causes of regime variations, have been totally misguided, it should be noted that all of the above-mentioned empirical studies suffer from a fundamental weakness. By assuming that regime type has the same meaning across political units, time periods, and even cultural regions, existing studies of public policy have built their conclusions into their questions. Obviously, military regimes do not form a homogenous group. Military governments are reformist as well as reactionary, populist as well as authoritarian, personalist as well as corporatist. By aggregating all types of military regimes together, much of the research to date has ensured that differences in regime type will appear irrelevant. Moreover, the use of the civilian military dichotomy has obscured possible overlaps between civilian and military governments. Officers may exercise substantial influence even if civilians are in top positions, and vice versa.[21]

In short, the literature is deeply divided on the basic theoretical question: Do the policies and performance records of military regimes differ from those of civilian regimes? Much of the literature suggests that they do, but disagrees on the nature of the differences, while another sizable body of literature suggests that they do not. In such a situation, empirical tests taking into account some of the limitations noted above must ultimately be performed to throw additional light on the matter.

Empirical Evidence for Argentina

Is there some statistical evidence for Argentina linking the pattern of military expenditures to regime type? Simple and multiple regression analyses were performed on time series data of the level of real military expenditures to determine the statistical significance of regime type in accounting for fluctuations in military expenditures over time.[22]

The regime type variables were treated dichotomously through the use of dummy variables. During the period under examination, there were four governments:

1. 1961–1965: democratic administrations;
2. 1966–72: first military regime;
3. 1973–1975: Peronist regime;
4. 1976–82: second military regime.

There is sufficient reason to believe that regime type does not have the same meaning over time; the first and second military regimes might in fact have few similarities with regard to economic policy, with the same to be said for the elected Peronist civilian regime (1973–76) and the non-Peronist civilian regime (1961–65). At least eight different representations of the 1961–82 regime types make sense (table 11–1) with:

1. *DUMPB* representing the standard civilian-military dichotomy;

Table 11-1
Argentinian Political Dummy Variables, 1961-82

	DUMP	DUMPA	DUMPB	DUMPC	DUMPD	DUMPE	DUMPF	DUMPG
1961	0	0	0	0	1	1	1	1
1962	0	0	0	0	1	1	1	1
1963	0	0	0	0	1	1	1	1
1964	0	0	0	0	1	1	1	1
1965	0	0	0	0	1	1	1	1
1966	0	1	1	2	2	2	1	3
1967	0	1	1	2	2	2	1	3
1968	0	1	1	2	2	2	1	3
1969	0	1	1	2	2	2	1	3
1970	0	1	1	2	2	2	1	3
1971	0	1	1	2	2	2	1	3
1972	0	1	1	2	2	2	1	3
1973	1	2	0	1	0	0	0	0
1974	1	2	0	1	0	0	0	0
1975	1	2	0	1	0	0	0	0
1976	2	3	1	2	2	3	2	2
1977	2	3	1	2	2	3	2	2
1978	2	3	1	2	2	3	2	2
1979	2	3	1	2	2	3	2	2
1980	2	3	1	2	2	3	2	2
1981	2	3	1	2	2	3	2	2
1982	2	3	1	2	2	3	2	2

Note: 1961-65: period of democracy.
1966-72: first military regime.
1973-76: Peronist regime.
1977-82: second military regime.

2. *DUMP* depicting structural shifts upward over time between the 1960s regimes to the Peronists and finally to the second military regime. If *DUMP* is statistically significant, the country would have experienced two sharp breaks upward in the amount of funds allocated to military expenditures during the 1961-82 period;

3. *DUMPA* similiar to *DUMP* with three upward structural shifts produced with regime changes, that is, increased militarization with regime change;

4. *DUMPC* assuming military regimes in Argentina to allocate significantly more resources to defense than their civilian counterparts, with the Peronists more inclined to increase defense expenditures than their civilian counterparts in the early 1960s;

5. *DUMPD* similiar to *DUMPC*, but with the first civilian regime more prone to step up military spending than the Peronists;
6. *DUMPE* assuming the Peronists to be least likely to give priority to defense, followed by the first civilian regime, then the first military regime, with the second military regime most heavily increasing military spending;
7. *DUMPF* assuming no real change in military allocation priorities in the 1960s, a sharp fall-off under the civilian Peronist regime, and a major shift upward under the second military regime. This interpretation is often implicitly assumed in the qualitative literature;
8. *DUMPG* assuming again the Peronists to be least likely to undertake military expenditures, followed by the first civilian regime. It is used to test whether the first military regime was more inclined to allocate funds to defense purposes than the second military regime.

Again, by themselves, these dummy variables are used to test whether any structural shifts occurred with changes in regime type. Real central government revenues are used as a control variables to account for any movements in military expenditures that may have resulted simply from corresponding revenue increases or declines.

Regressions were performed for each dummy individually and for three time periods:

1961–75,

1961–82, and

1966–82

to determine the extent to which the second military regime affected the pattern of military expenditures. The Cochrane-Orcutt iterative procedure was employed to correct for serial correlation in the error term and dependent variable.[23] Once the correlation was made (as indicated by the Durbin-Watson statistic), the coefficients in the regression equations could be interpreted normally as is done in ordinary least squares regression.

In general, the results in table 11–2 indicate that:

1. Regime type is highly important in explaining the pattern of military expenditures over time (based on the high statistical significance of the dummy variable).

Table 11-2
Argentina: Impact of Political Change on the Level of Defense Expenditures: Shift Analysis, 1961-82

	Political Shift Variable	Central Government Revenues	RHO	r^2	Statistics F	DW
	DUMP					
1961-75	(-8.02)	(5.51)	(-0.39)	0.856	29.86	1.94
1961-82	(-0.87)	(2.04)	(1.06)	0.218	2.52	1.32
1966-82	(-1.03)	(2.17)	(0.26)	0.289	2.44	1.53
	DUMPA					
1961-75	(-1.45)	(1.08)	(0.61)	0.172	1.04	1.67
1961-82	(-1.17)	(2.18)	(0.63)	0.285	3.57	1.23
1966-82	(-1.03)	(2.17)	(0.26)	0.289	2.44	1.53
	DUMPB					
1961-75	(12.43)	(-2.71)	(-0.79)	0.934	71.75	2.27
1961-82	(1.19)	(1.46)	(0.34)	0.285	3.57	1.23
1966-82	(4.50)	(4.53)	(0.01)	0.774	20.62	1.49
	DUMPC					
1961-75	(7.57)	(-4.21)	(-0.73)	0.842	26.64	2.40
1961-82	(0.49)	(1.33)	(0.98)	0.201	2.26	1.22
1966-82	(4.50)	(4.53)	(0.01)	0.774	20.62	1.49
	DUMPD					
1961-75	(14.47)	(3.16)	(-0.90)	0.951	97.14	1.89
1961-82	(2.37)	(2.63)	(-1.72)	0.504	9.16	1.33
1966-82	(4.50)	(4.53)	(0.01)	0.774	20.62	1.49
	DUMPE					
1961-75	(14.47)	(3.16)	(-0.90)	0.951	97.14	1.89
1961-82	(2.37)	(2.63)	(-1.72)	0.504	9.16	1.33
1966-82	(4.50)	(4.53)	(0.01)	0.774	20.62	1.49
	DUMPF					
1961-75	(8.02)	(5.51)	(-0.39)	0.856	29.86	1.94
1961-82	(2.55)	(2.26)	(-3.17)	0.558	11.39	1.32
1966-82	(1.28)	(1.24)	(-0.97)	0.369	3.51	1.26
	DUMPG					
1961-75	(14.55)	(0.69)	(-0.85)	0.951	98.26	2.03
1961-82	(1.52)	(2.27)	(0.34)	0.316	4.16	1.25
1966-82	(3.24)	(4.46)	(-3.96)	0.649	11.10	1.42

Notes: Estimates were made using Cochrane-Orcutt iterative estimation procedure to correct for serial correlation.
Defense expenditures are nominal defense expenditures deflated by consumer price index 1974 = 100).
See text for definition of political dummy variables.
( ) = t statistic.

2. Military regimes are much more inclined (given central government revenues) to allocate funds for defense (as indicated by high statistical significance and positive sign for dummy variables in 1961–75 and 1966–82 subperiods).
3. The Peronists were clearly the least likely to allocate funds for defense (as shown by high statistical significance of *DUMPD* and *DUMPE* for 1961–75).
4. There has not been a progressive upward shift in military expenditures over time (as shown by the statistical insignificance of *DUMPA*).
5. Military allocations are not based simply on the dichotomy between civilian and military regimes (as shown by the statistical insignificance of *DUMPB* over 1961–82 period).
6. It is not clear whether the second military regime was more inclined to allocate funds for defense than the first military regime (as shown by the generally lower t values for 1961–82 than for either subperiod and insignificance of *DUMPF* for 1966–82).

A structural shift in defense expenditures (a shift in the intercept of the regression equation) is one possible way to test for changing military priorities of alternative regime types. Another test would be to determine whether the propensity to spend out of revenues differed by regime type, that is, whether the slope of the regression line was statistically different for alternative regimes. To test for this possible phenomenon, an interaction variable was created by multiplying each dummy variable by the level of real central government revenues.[24] The result is depicted by an X at the end of each dummy (for example, *DUMPX*). Here, new variables are referred to as modification variables.

Each modification variable was regressed together with the central government revenues. The results in table 11–3 indicate that:

1. Again, regime type was highly important in accounting for the observed fluctuations over time in military expenditures.
2. For the period as a whole, the rankings in ascending order of propensity to spend on defense are Peronists, first civilian regime, first military regime, and second military regime (as shown by the high significance of *DUMPEX* for the period as a whole).

Table 11-3
Argentina: Impact of Political Change on the Level of Defense Expenditures: Modification Analysis, 1961-82

	Political Modification Variable	Central Government Revenues	RHO	r^2	Statistics F	DW
	DUMPX					
1961-75	(-8.77)	(5.96)	(-0.50)	0.876	35.63	1.77
1961-82	(-0.37)	(1.51)	(1.05)	0.192	2.15	1.27
1966-82	(-0.77)	(1.76)	(0.42)	0.257	2.08	1.48
	DUMPAX					
1961-75	(-2.89)	(2.60)	(2.02)	0.444	3.93	1.85
1961-82	(-0.54)	(1.38)	(0.98)	0.203	2.29	1.29
1966-82	(-0.11)	(1.76)	(0.42)	0.257	2.08	1.48
	DUMPBX					
1961-75	(12.94)	(-3.06)	(-0.40)	0.939	77.59	2.34
1961-82	(2.00)	(0.75)	(-0.91)	0.433	3.70	1.28
1966-82	(5.29)	(2.67)	(0.10)	0.822	27.71	1.47
	DUMPCX					
1961-75	(8.83)	(-5.70)	(-0.463)	0.878	36.21	2.58
1961-82	(1.03)	(0.44)	(0.20)	0.251	3.02	1.23
1966-82	(5.29)	(2.67)	(0.10)	0.522	27.71	1.47
	DUMPDX					
1961-75	(12.57)	(0.32)	(0.05)	0.936	73.15	1.91
1961-82	(3.64)	(1.42)	(-5.68)	0.671	18.78	1.36
1966-82	(5.29)	(2.67)	(0.01)	0.822	77.71	1.47
	DUMPEX					
1961-75	(12.57)	(0.32)	(-0.05)	0.936	73.15	1.91
1961-82	(7.20)	(0.57)	(-0.01)	0.884	66.57	1.63
1966-82	(6.38)	(0.67)	(0.01)	0.868	39.53	1.62
	DUMPFX					
1961-75	(8.77)	(2.84)	(0.50)	0.833	35.63	1.77
1961-82	(3.20)	(0.95)	(-5.81)	0.638	15.86	1.32
1966-82	(3.21)	(0.16)	(0.01)	0.670	12.19	1.38
	DUMPGX					
1961-75	(13.31)	(-0.96)	(-0.17)	0.942	82.12	2.04
1961-82	(1.83)	(1.62)	(-0.03)	0.369	5.28	1.68
1966-82	(3.32)	(3.55)	(-4.21)	0.658	11.58	1.44

Notes: Estimates were made using Cochrane-Orcutt iterative estimation procedure to correct for serial correlation.
See text for definition of variables.
Political modification variables were formed by multiplying respective political variables by the level of central government revenues in constant (1980) prices.
Defense expenditures are nominal defense expenditures deflated by the consumer price index (1974 = 100).
( ) = t statistic.

3. The first military regime was less inclined to increase military expenditures with increasing revenues than the first (as shown by the insignificant value *DUMPGX* for the period as a whole).
4. The country has not been more inclined over time to allocate existing funds for defense (as shown by the insignificance of *DUMPX* and *DUMPAX* for the period as a whole).

Finally, tests were performed to determine whether regime change was more effective in influencing military expenditures through (1) shifting the regression line keeping the propensity to spend out of the government revenues constant, (2) shifting the regression line with no structural shift in the pattern of defense expenditures, or (3) some combination of both a shift in propensity to spend and an overall structural shift in the inclination to increase or decrease military expenditures out of a given amount of revenues.

The results in table 11–4 indicate:

1. A general tendency to increase the propensity of military expenditure with the second military regime (as shown by the consistently higher t values for the modification variables for the 1961–82 period over the 1961–75 period);
2. The interaction variable, in general, is more indicative of structural change with regime type than the dummy shift variable. There appears to be more of an inclination for the propensity to increase military expenditures to grow larger as regimes shift from civilian to military (as shown by the generally higher t values for the modification variable compared with the shift variable);
3. Political change appears more important than changes in government revenues in affecting military expenditures, particularly when the second military regime is included in the analysis (as indicated by the generally insignificant t values for government revenues for the period as a whole).

Clearly, if in fact regime change is so important in accounting for movements in the level of military expenditures, the share of the public sector's budgetary allocations to defense ought to depict the same general pattern. Using government expenditures as a percent of gross domestic product as a control variable, regressions were performed using the political shift dummy. Again, three time periods were considered: 1961–75, 1961–82, and 1966–82.

Table 11-4
Argentina: Impact of Political Change on the Level of Defense Expenditures: Shift and Modification Analysis, 1961-82

	Political Modification Variable	Political Shift Variable	Central Government Revenues	RHO	Statistics		
					r^2	F	DW
	DUMPX	*DUMP*					
1961-75	(-3.08)	(1.51)	(6.18)	(0.67)	0.895	25.60	1.81
1961-82	(2.58)	(-2.70)	(0.76)	(-0.53)	0.500	5.00	1.57
	DUMPAX	*DUMPA*					
1961-75	(-7.35)	(5.12)	(7.74)	(0.22)	0.936	28.90	1.87
1961-82	(-1.85)	(1.45)	(0.98)	(0.09)	0.388	3.17	1.51
	DUMPBX	*DUMPB*					
1961-75	(1.65)	(-0.37)	(-2.78)	(0.22)	0.936	44.7	2.32
1961-82	(4.69)	(-3.45)	(-1.08)	(0.01)	0.851	18.69	1.47
	DUMPCX	*DUMPC*					
1961-75	(3.30)	(-2.12)	(-5.09)	(0.22)	0.889	24.02	2.61
1961-82	(3.73)	(-3.23)	(-2.13)	(-5.64)	0.201	11.72	1.40
	DUMPDX	*DUMPD*					
1961-75	(0.87)	(0.30)	(0.39)	(-19.15)	0.940	47.40	1.91
1961-82	(3.60)	(-2.55)	(-1.37)	(0.01)	0.863	38.22	1.52
	DUMPEX	*DUMPE*					
1961-75	(0.87)	(0.29)	(0.39)	(-0.15)	0.940	47.60	1.91
1961-82	(2.48)	(-1.10)	(-0.56)	(0.01)	0.899	44.71	1.57
	DUMPFX	*DUMPF*					
1961-75	(3.08)	(-1.51)	(-0.20)	(0.67)	0.895	25.60	1.84
1961-82	(2.08)	(-1.81)	(-1.47)	(-3.55)	0.660	9.73	1.29
	DUMPGX	*DUMPG*					
1961-75	(0.84)	(0.37)	(-0.28)	(-0.39)	0.946	53.50	2.05
1961-82	(2.84)	(-2.44)	(-1.10)	(-5.66)	0.701	11.72	1.37

Notes: Estimates were made using Cochrane-Orcutt iterative estimation procedure to correct for serial correlation.
See text for definition of variables.
Political modification variables were formed by multiplying respective political variables by the level of central government revenues in constant 1980 prices.
Defense expenditures are nominal defense expenditures deflated by consumer price index (1974 = 100).
( ) = *t* statistics.

The results in table 11-5 show:

1. The long-run trend is for military expenditures to decline as government expenditures increase relative to overall gross domestic product (as shown by the consistently negative sign on the control variable).

Table 11-5
Argentina: Impact of Political Change on the Share of Defense Expenditures in the Total Central Government Budget: Shift Analysis, 1961-82

	Political Variable	Government Expenditures as a Percentage of GDP	RHO	Statistics		
				r^2	F	DW
1961-75		(-2.86)	(2.55)	0.405	8.18	1.58
1961-82		(-2.66)	(4.96)	0.271	7.09	1.21
1966-82		(-3.32)	(7.01)	0.440	11.03	1.04
	DUMP					
1961-75	(-1.26)	(1.22)	(1.86)	0.535	5.76	1.81
1961-82	(1.57)	(-3.09)	(3.87)	0.350	4.85	1.38
1966-82	(1.35)	(-3.42)	(4.84)	0.475	5.43	1.21
	DUMPA					
1961-75	(0.93)	(-2.29)	(3.40)	0.392	3.23	1.46
1961-82	(2.36)	(-3.77)	(4.55)	0.442	7.13	1.42
1966-82	(1.35)	(-3.42)	(4.84)	0.475	5.43	1.21
	DUMPB					
1961-75	(1.89)	(-2.58)	(3.03)	0.523	5.49	1.74
1961-82	(2.61)	(-2.99)	(4.49)	0.469	7.96	1.56
1966-82	(1.64)	(-2.52)	(4.80)	0.503	6.07	1.49
	DUMPC					
1961-75	(2.18)	(-3.07)	(3.54)	0.536	5.77	1.63
1961-82	(2.56)	(-3.29)	(5.31)	0.468	7.94	1.38
1966-82	(1.64)	(-2.52)	(4.80)	0.503	6.07	1.49
	DUMPD					
1961-75	(1.61)	(-2.03)	(2.54)	0.520	5.42	1.79
1961-82	(2.53)	(-2.68)	(3.78)	0.453	7.47	1.65
1966-82	(1.64)	(-2.52)	(4.80)	5.03	6.07	1.49
	DUMPE					
1961-75	(1.61)	(-2.03)	(2.54)	0.520	5.42	1.79
1961-82	(3.02)	(-3.39)	(3.00)	0.501	9.05	1.75
1966-82	(5.45)	(-3.83)	(-0.36)	0.727	16.01	1.56
	DUMPF					
1961-75	(1.26)	(-1.22)	(1.86)	0.535	5.76	1.80
1961-82	(3.47)	(-3.88)	(1.84)	0.536	10.43	1.75
1966-82	(5.95)	(-4.92)	(-0.50)	0.758	18.84	1.61
	DUMPG					
1961-75	(1.71)	(-2.25)	(2.73)	0.519	5.41	1.78
1961-82	(2.15)	(-2.46)	(4.80)	0.419	6.05	1.49
1966-82	(1.20)	(-2.49)	(5.89)	0.484	5.63	1.33

Notes: Regressions were made using Cochrane-Orcutt iterative technique to correct for serial correlation.
See text for definition of variables.
( ) = *t* statistic.

2. The general pattern of structural shift upward in defense expenditures when regimes change from civilian to military is confirmed by the positive signs on the shift variable.
3. The second military regime appears to have the highest inclination to increase the share of the budget going to defense, followed by the first military regime, the first civilian regime, and finally the Peronists (based on the high statistical significance of *DUMPE* for the 1961-82 period).
4. There may be little difference between the first civilian regime and the first military regime in allocating expenditures for defense, (as shown by the high overall significance for *DUMPF*).
5. The most dramatic increases in government share occurred with the shift in regimes from Peronist to second military, as revealed by the very high t values for *DUMPF* and *DUMPE* for 1966-82, compared with insignificant values for 1961-75).

In general, therefore, analysis of the share of government allocations going to defense confirms all of the patterns discovered from the statistic of structural shift obtained in the analysis of the level of military expenditures.

As with the level of military expenditures, regressions were performed to determine whether the slope of the regression line changed with regimes.[25] The results in table 11-6 confirm that regime changes have a strong impact on the manner in which the central government allocates funds for defense. In general:

1. There is a strong propensity to increase military expenditures when a shift from civilian to military regime takes place and vice versa (as shown by the statistically significant and positive t tests for the 1961-82 period in all cases).
2. The shift toward an increased propensity to spend was fairly weak and perhaps insignificant for the first change from civilian to military regime (as shown by the values of t being slightly under 2.0 for all of the dummy variables for the 1961-75 period).
3. A strong shift in the propensity to increase military expenditures under the second military regime existed, as revealed by the high and positive t values of the dummy variables for the 1966-82 period.
4. The second military regime was most inclined toward an increased tendency to spend on defense, followed by the first military regime, the first civilian regime, and finally the Peronists.

Table 11-6
Argentina: Impact of Political Change on the Share of Defense Expenditures in the Total Central Government Budget: Modification Analysis, 1961-82

	Political Modification Variable	Government Expenditures as a Percentage of GDP	RHO	Statistics		
				r^2	F	DW
	DUMPX					
1961-75	(-2.06)	(0.51)	(1.91)	0.613	7.93	1.84
1961-82	(2.11)	(-3.47)	(3.38)	0.402	6.06	1.59
1966-82	(2.05)	(-3.70)	(3.81)	0.515	6.38	1.55
	DUMPAX					
1961-75	(0.29)	(-1.43)	(2.83)	0.387	3.61	1.55
1961-82	(2.45)	(-3.80)	(3.81)	0.445	7.23	1.75
1966-82	(1.90)	(-3.57)	(3.80)	0.496	5.91	1.62
	DUMPBX					
1961-75	(1.78)	(-2.50)	(3.04)	0.510	5.20	1.83
1961-82	(3.31)	(-3.51)	(3.98)	0.540	10.59	1.91
1966-82	(5.28)	(-3.33)	(0.22)	0.722	15.62	1.69
	DUMPCX					
1961-75	(1.62)	(-3.01)	(3.23)	0.478	4.59	1.76
1961-82	(3.09)	(-3.84)	(-4.59)	0.522	9.83	1.91
1966-82	(6.03)	(-4.58)	(0.20)	0.765	19.60	1.83
	DUMPDX					
1961-75	(1.42)	(-2.23)	(2.60)	0.493	4.88	1.82
1961-82	(3.25)	(-3.42)	(3.22)	0.528	10.08	1.92
1966-82	(5.28)	(-3.33)	(0.22)	0.722	15.62	1.69
	DUMPEX					
1961-75	(1.42)	(-2.23)	(2.60)	0.493	4.88	1.82
1961-82	(3.92)	(-4.41)	(2.52)	0.589	12.91	1.99
1966-82	(7.19)	(-5.79)	(-0.41)	0.819	27.24	1.70
	DUMPFX					
1961-75	(1.02)	(-1.91)	(2.19)	0.486	4.73	1.78
1961-82	(4.48)	(-5.10)	(1.57)	0.631	15.43	1.93
1966-82	(7.09)	(-6.32)	(-0.19)	0.817	26.82	1.79
	DUMPGX					
1961-75	(1.54)	(-2.33)	(2.74)	0.498	4.97	1.83
1961-82	(2.61)	(-2.74)	(4.32)	0.467	7.90	1.74
1966-82	(1.72)	(-2.41)	(4.92)	0.514	6.36	1.64

Notes: Estimates were made using Cochrane-Orcutt iterative estimation procedure to correct for serial correlation.
See text for definition of variables.
Political modification variables were formed by multiplying respective political variables by the level of central government revenues in constant (1980) prices.
( ) = t statistic.

5. Again, there is not strong evidence that the first civilian regime and first military regime had statistically different propensities to spend on defense, as indicated by a statistically significant *DUMPX* for 1961-75 and generally insignificant dummies for 1961-75.

In table 11-7, the combined effects of the dummy (shift in slope) and modification (change in slope) were also tested to determine the overall manner in which changes in political regime impacted on defense expenditures. In general:

1. The major impact of political change appears to be in affecting the propensity to spend on military activities. (The modification variable tends to be statistically significant while the political shift variable is not.)
2. Again, the results show no real secular trend upward or downward in the propensity to change military expenditures from regime to regime. (*DUMPA* and *DUMPAX* are insignificant for 1961-82.)
3. The highest t value for the 1966-82 period was obtained assuming that the two military regimes have the same propensity to spend on defense (*DUMPBX* and *DUMPDX*), but slightly higher t values for the period as a whole (1961-82) were obtained assuming a higher propensity on the part of the second military regime (*DUMPEX, DUMPFX*).
4. The first military regime and first civilian regime were quite similar in their propensity to spend on defense (as shown by the statistical significance of *DUMPX*, 1961-75 and *DUMPFX*, 1961-82), particularly when the 1961-75 period was examined. The first military regime does tend to have a higher propensity than the first civilian regime to spend on defense in the context of the period as a whole (as revealed by the statistical significance of *DUMPBX* and *DUMPEX*).

Beginning in 1972, the share of the government budget dedicated to servicing the public financial obligation jumped dramatically from 0.1 percent in 1971 to 4.4 percent in 1972, 11.5 percent in 1976, 16.3 percent in 1980, and 37.1 percent in 1982. It must be argued that this rapid increase in debt service payments tended to affect the share of defense in government budget irrespective of regime type, thus producing a systematic bias in the result by presumably underestimating the impact of the second military regime on defense allocations.

Table 11-7
Argentina: Impact of Political Change on the Share of Defense Expenditures in the Total Central Government Budget: Shift and Modification Analysis, 1961-82

	Political Shift Variable	Political Modification Variable	Government Expenditures as a Percentage of GDP	RHO	Statistics r^2	F	DW
	DUMP	*DUMPX*					
1961-75	(1.95)	(-2.60)	(-0.15)	(2.85)	0.661	5.87	1.61
1961-82	(-0.56)	(1.36)	(-3.34)	(3.09)	0.418	3.59	1.66
1966-82	(-0.40)	(1.26)	(-3.53)	(3.53)	0.520	4.34	1.64
	DUMPA	*DUMPAX*					
1961-75	(2.42)	(-2.28)	(-0.55)	(3.62)	0.596	4.43	1.27
1961-82	(0.75)	(0.78)	(-3.80)	(4.25)	0.459	4.25	1.64
1966-82	(0.93)	(0.21)	(-3.44)	(3.90)	0.499	3.98	1.57
	DUMPB	*DUMPBX*					
1961-75	(0.60)	(-0.31)	(-2.50)	(3.00)	0.529	3.37	1.64
1961-82	(-1.32)	(2.26)	(-3.99)	(0.57)	0.585	7.50	2.17
1966-82	(-1.97)	(3.27)	(-3.97)	(0.60)	0.769	13.38	1.97
	DUMPC	*DUMPCX*					
1961-75	(1.77)	(-1.20)	(-2.58)	(3.58)	0.594	4.39	1.30
1961-82	(-0.27)	(1.51)	(-3.73)	(4.45)	0.523	5.49	1.99
1966-82	(-0.19)	(2.66)	(-3.38)	(-0.12)	0.761	12.78	1.89
	DUMPD	*DUMPDX*					
1961-75	(0.92)	(-0.61)	(-1.66)	(2.35)	0.550	3.67	1.70
1961-82	(-0.99)	(1.93)	(-3.53)	(3.02)	0.557	6.30	2.06
1966-82	(-1.97)	(3.27)	(-3.97)	(0.60)	0.769	13.38	1.97
	DUMPE	*DUMPEX*					
1961-75	(0.92)	(-0.61)	(-1.66)	(2.35)	0.550	3.67	1.70
1961-82	(-0.90)	(2.03)	(-4.37)	(2.47)	0.609	7.81	2.08
1966-82	(-1.34)	(2.87)	(-5.16)	(0.38)	0.803	16.27	1.95
	DUMPF	*DUMPFX*					
1961-75	(0.63)	(-0.18)	(0.54)	(1.79)	0.545	3.59	1.80
1961-82	(-0.85)	(2.09)	(-4.61)	(1.91)	0.627	8.43	1.99
1966-82	(-1.14)	(2.65)	(-5.67)	(0.50)	0.799	15.93	1.97
	DUMPG	*DUMPGX*					
1961-75	(0.87)	(-0.57)	(-2.08)	(2.61)	0.542	3.55	1.66
1961-82	(-1.05)	(1.73)	(-2.99)	(3.74)	0.499	4.99	1.99
1966-82	(-2.57)	(3.47)	(-2.98)	(0.86)	0.71	9.90	1.96

Notes: Estimates were made using Cochrane-Orcutt iterative estimation procedure to correct for serial correlation.
See text for definition of variables.
Debt service payments were included in budget.
Political modification variables were formed by multiplying respective political variables by the level of central government revenues in constant (1980) prices.
( ) = t statistics.

Impact of Regime Type · 239

To determine whether the results presented here were affected by the rapid build-up of debt servicing obligations, regressions were run with defense share computed as the percent of the budget that was not related to debt servicing. Again three sets of regressions were estimated: (1) the shift in military expenditures with regime change, (2) the modification of the propensity to change the propensity to increase defense expenditures and (3) a combined shift-modification analysis.

Table 11-8 shows the results of the shift analysis:

1. There is no trend upward or downward with regime change.
2. The pattern of increase in military expenditures with changes from civilian to military regimes is much clearer than was the case when government debt servicing was included in the budget for computing the share of defense. (t values and r^2 are much higher, especially in the 1966–82 period.)
3. The ranking of second military, first military, first civilian, Peronist regimes in terms of inclination to spend on defense (*DUMPE*) is extremely strong statistically but is contradicted by *DUMPF*, which assumes no difference between the first military and first civilian regimes.
4. The increase in military expenditures by the second military regime is particularly striking when the 1966–82 period is considered.

The same general results were obtained from the modification (table 11-9) and combined modification and shift analysis (table 11-10). The general picture that emerges from the past three sets of regressions (tables 11-7, 11-8, and 11-9) is that *DUMPF* provides the best depiction of military regimes, particularly over the 1961–82 period.

In summary, the analysis presented here indicates that either *DUMPE* or *DUMPF* performs best in differentiating Argentinian regimes with respect to their propensities to spend on defense. Overall, it appears that:

1. With regard to the level of military expenditures (table 11-2), *DUMPE* is the superior shift dummy, particularly with respect to the 1966–82 period and also (table 11-3), *DUMPEX* the superior modifying dummy.
2. Explanations of the share of defense in the government budget including debt servicing show little difference between *DUMPE*

240 · Argentina

Table 11-8
Argentina: Impact of Political Change on the Share of Defense Expenditures in the Non-Debt Service Central Government Budgetary Items: Shift Analysis, 1961-82

	Political Shift Variable	Government Expenditures as a Percentage of GDP	RHO	Statistics		
				r^2	F	DW
	DUMP					
1961-75	(-1.03)	(-0.86)	(1.31)	0.445	4.01	1.70
1961-82	(1.71)	(-1.45)	(4.93)	0.160	1.71	1.62
1966-82	(0.56)	(-2.72)	(13.05)	0.367	3.94	1.50
	DUMPA					
1961-75	(0.46)	(-1.64)	(2.18)	0.331	2.48	1.53
1961-82	(2.00)	(-1.99)	(6.03)	0.229	2.67	1.60
1966-82	(0.56)	(-2.72)	(13.05)	0.367	3.94	1.50
	DUMPB					
1961-75	(1.32)	(-2.13)	(2.33)	0.403	3.38	1.57
1961-82	(2.54)	(-1.66)	(10.24)	0.373	5.36	1.87
1966-82	(7.30)	(5.15)	(0.93)	0.855	35.39	1.64
	DUMPC					
1961-75	(1.52)	(-2.48)	(2.77)	0.407	3.44	1.48
1961-82	(2.23)	(-2.19)	(13.15)	0.352	4.90	1.56
1966-82	(7.30)	(5.15)	(-0.93)	0.855	35.39	1.64
	DUMPD					
1961-75	(1.15)	(-1.66)	(1.93)	0.409	3.46	1.63
1961-82	(2.65)	(-1.09)	(7.94)	0.360	5.07	2.11
1966-82	(7.30)	(5.15)	(-0.93)	0.855	35.39	1.64
	DUMPE					
1961-75	(1.15)	(-1.60)	(1.93)	0.409	3.46	1.63
1961-82	(3.85)	(-0.17)	(3.17)	0.454	7.48	2.36
1966-82	(16.83)	(4.49)	(-3.89)	0.968	186.98	1.68
	DUMPF					
1961-75	(1.03)	(-0.87)	(1.31)	0.445	4.01	1.70
1961-82	(7.41)	(-0.29)	(0.09)	0.788	33.51	2.03
1966-82	(17.81)	(0.62)	(-3.74)	0.972	208.98	2.03
	DUMPG					
1961-75	(1.22)	(-1.85)	(2.09)	0.405	3.40	1.61
1961-82	(2.27)	(-1.65)	(13.50)	0.360	5.06	1.81
1966-82	(1.71)	(-1.76)	(11.49)	0.460	5.00	2.01

Notes: Estimates were made using Cochrane-Orcutt iterative estimation procedure to correct for serial correlation.
Defense's share was computed as the proportion of the government budget excluding debt service payments.
( ) = t statistic.
See text for definition of variables.

Table 11-9
Argentina: Impact of Political Change on the Share of Defense Expenditures in the Non-Debt Service Central Government Budgetary Items: Modification Analysis, 1961-82

	Political Modification Variable	Government Expenditures as a Percentage of GDP	RHO	Statistics		
				r^2	F	DW
	DUMPX					
1961-75	(-1.87)	(-0.14)	(1.52)	0.527	5.57	1.68
1961-82	(1.60)	(-1.23)	(4.28)	0.131	1.36	1.68
1966-82	(0.19)	(-2.65)	(12.77)	0.351	3.25	1.47
	DUMPAX					
1961-75	(-1.58)	(0.25)	(1.10)	0.519	5.40	1.60
1961-82	(0.43)	(-1.92)	(11.75)	0.172	1.89	1.57
1966-82	(-0.18)	(-2.58)	(13.09)	0.354	3.28	1.34
	DUMPBX					
1961-75	(1.22)	(-2.11)	(2.27)	0.394	3.25	1.61
1961-82	(2.94)	(-0.98)	(5.59)	0.354	4.93	2.16
1966-82	(9.85)	(3.92)	(-1.42)	0.914	63.96	1.77
	DUMPCX					
1961-75	(0.92)	(-2.47)	(2.26)	0.362	2.83	1.66
1961-82	(1.85)	(-1.95)	(9.68)	0.278	3.46	1.81
1966-82	(7.42)	(1.37)	(-1.02)	0.859	36.71	2.01
	DUMPDX					
1961-75	(0.98)	(-1.90)	(1.92)	0.391	3.22	1.64
1961-82	(3.20)	(-0.37)	(4.06)	0.365	5.18	2.25
1966-82	(9.85)	(3.92)	(-1.42)	0.914	63.96	1.77
	DUMPEX					
1961-75	(-1.90)	(0.98)	(1.92)	0.391	3.22	1.64
1961-82	(4.12)	(-0.69)	(2.83)	0.491	8.68	2.31
1966-82	(13.58)	(0.62)	(-2.15)	0.952	121.26	1.96
	DUMPFX					
1961-75	(0.72)	(-1.57)	(1.60)	0.397	3.29	1.66
1961-82	(5.47)	(-1.18)	(1.35)	0.655	17.10	2.10
1966-82	(11.87)	(-1.16)	(-1.61)	0.938	92.21	1.93
	DUMPGX					
1961-75	(1.07)	(-1.97)	(92.06)	0.390	3.20	1.64
1961-82	(2.25)	(-1.52)	(10.87)	0.340	4.65	1.99
1966-82	(4.97)	(3.97)	(0.14)	0.725	15.86	1.88

Notes: Estimates were made using Cochrane-Orcutt iterative estimation procedure to correct for serial correlation.
See text for definition of variables.
Defense's share was computed as the proportion of the government budget excluding debt service payments.
Political modification variables were formed by multiplying respective political variables by the level of central government revenues in constant (1980) prices.
( ) = t statistic.

Table 11-10
Argentina: Impact of Political Change on the Share of Defense Expenditures in the Non-Debt Service Central Government Budgetary Items: Shift and Modification Analysis, 1961-82

	Political Shift Variable	Political Modification Variable	Government Expenditures as a Percentage of GDP	RHO	Statistics		
					r^2	F	DW
	DUMP	DUMPX					
1961-75	(2.77)	(-3.40)	(-0.36)	(2.60)	0.688	6.62	1.52
1961-82	(0.97)	(0.32)	(-1.44)	(5.69)	0.163	0.97	1.55
1966-82	(0.78)	(-0.57)	(-2.55)	(12.77)	0.383	2.48	1.26
	DUMPA	DUMPAX					
1961-75	(2.86)	(-3.23)	(0.28)	(2.24)	0.67	6.13	1.26
1961-82	(1.77)	(-0.80)	(-1.95)	(7.65)	0.266	1.81	1.35
1966-82	(1.02)	(-0.86)	(-2.45)	(12.14)	0.398	2.65	1.14
	DUMPB	DUMPBX					
1961-75	(0.56)	(-0.36)	(-2.08)	(2.31)	0.411	2.09	1.50
1961-82	(-0.25)	(1.08)	(-0.82)	(4.97)	0.355	2.76	2.21
1966-82	(-0.21)	(2.38)	(2.25)	(-1.36)	0.913	42.10	1.81
	DUMPC	DUMPCX					
1961-75	(1.94)	(-1.57)	(-1.98)	(2.78)	0.525	3.32	1.23
1961-82	(1.28)	(-0.40)	(-0.40)	(14.66)	0.363	2.86	1.39
1966-82	(1.91)	(1.93)	(2.47)	(-1.65)	0.908	39.78	1.76
	DUMPD	DUMPDX					
1961-75	(0.85)	(-0.63)	(-1.20)	(1.86)	0.440	2.36	1.61
1961-82	(0.17)	(0.76)	(-0.30)	(4.23)	0.363	2.84	2.26
1966-82	(0.21)	(2.38)	(-2.25)	(-1.36)	0.913	42.10	1.81
	DUMPE	DUMPEX					
1961-75	(0.85)	(-0.63)	(-1.20)	(1.86)	0.440	12.36	1.61
1961-82	(-0.36)	(0.85)	(-0.47)	(2.83)	0.494	4.89	2.35
1966-82	(-2.05)	(2.27)	(-1.41)	(-3.69)	0.972	143.80	1.82
	DUMPF	DUMPFX					
1961-75	(0.78)	(-0.40)	(-0.44)	(1.10)	0.447	2.74	1.73
1961-82	(1.69)	(0.29)	(-0.38)	(0.24)	0.778	17.60	2.04
1966-82	(2.89)	(0.64)	(0.05)	(-3.55)	0.972	141.03	2.04
	DUMPG	DUMPGX					
1961-75	(0.79)	(-0.60)	(-1.61)	(1.99)	0.434	2.27	1.54
1961-82	(0.43)	(0.13)	(-1.58)	(12.93)	0.358	2.78	1.86
1966-82	(-1.47)	(2.72)	(1.88)	(-0.24)	0.797	15.78	1.90

Notes: Estimates were made using Cochrane-Orcutt iterative estimation procedure to correct for serial correlation.
See text for definition of variables.
Defense's share was computed as the proportion of the government budget excluding debt service payments.
Political modification variables were formed by multiplying respective political variables by the level of central government revenues in constant (1980) prices.
( ) = t statistics.

and *DUMPF* for either the shift (table 11-5) or *DUMPEX* and *DUMPFX* for modification variables (table 11-6).

3. The share of defense in the non-debt service items of the budget shows that *DUMPF* outperforms *DUMPE* on the shift of military expenditures with regime change (table 11-8), but on the modification of military expenditures (table 11-9), it only outperforms *DUMPE* for the 1961-82 period, with *DUMPE* superior for the 1966-82 period.

4. Using *DUMPE* for explaining the level of military expenditures, in table 11-4 it appears that the modification influence of regime change is stronger than a structural shifting of defense expenditures to a higher level of revenues. That is, military regimes have a stronger propensity to spend out of changes in revenues over time than do their civilian counterparts, but they do not necessarily spend a higher proportion of existing revenues.

5. Again using *DUMPE* for depicting political change, it appears in table 11-10 that military regimes after 1966 not only produced a structural shift upward in the share of the budget allocated to defense but, in addition, increased the share of the defense budget as the ratio of government expenditures to GDP increased.

Conclusions

The empirical results presented here yield considerable support to the general thesis that regime type in Argentina has a major impact on the amount and share of resources devoted to defense. Military regimes consistently outspent their civilian counterparts on defense and increased the share of defense in the central government budget.

The results lend some credibility to the policy statements and policy moves throughout Alfonsin's first year and a half in power, giving economists adequate reason to believe that the present civilian regime will make significant reductions in military expenditures, both in real amounts and as a share of the central government's budget.

With respect to the O'Donnell thesis, the results lend strong support to the theory that the degree of threat preceding the assumption of power by a military regime influences its overall defense expenditures; all authoritarian regimes are not alike in the priority they place on defense, as evidenced by the second military regime's outspending the first military regime on defense. The results do not, however, give a sharp delineation between the first civilian regime and first military regime with respect to their approaches to defense.

Notes

1. The time period selected was based on data availability. The longest consistent series on government budgetary allocations has recently been compiled by the World Bank for 1961-82. Cf. The World Bank, *Argentina: Economic Memorandum, Vol. 2, Statistical Appendix* (Washington, D.C.: International Bank for Reconstruction and Development, IBRD, 1985), pp. 334-35.

2. G. O'Donnell, *Modernization and Bureaucratic-Authoritarianism: Studies in South American Politics,* Politics of Modernization Series no. 9 (Berkeley, Calif.: Institute of International Studies, University of California Press, 1973). A useful critique of the approach is given in K. Remmer and G. Merkx, "Bureaucratic Authoritarianism Revisited," *Latin American Research Review* (no. 2, 1982), pp. 3-40. See also G. O'Donnell, "Reply to Remmer and Merkx," *Latin American Research Review* (no. 2, 1982), pp. 41-50.

3. D. Collier, "Overview of the Bureaucratic-Authoritarian Model" in D. Collier, ed., *The New Authoritarians in Latin America* (Princeton, N.J.: Princeton University Press, 1979), pp. 19-32.

4. G. O'Donnell, "Reflections on the Patterns of Change in the Bureaucratic-Authoritarian State," *Latin American Research Review* (no. 1, 1978), pp. 3-38.

5. B. Most, "Authoritarianism and Growth of the State in Latin America: An Assessment of Their Impacts on Argentine Public Policy, 1930-1970," *Comparative Political Studies* (July 1980), pp. 175-76.

6. Remmer and Merkx, *op. cit,* p. 8.

7. *Ibid.*

8. Gordon Richards, "The Rise and Decline of Military Authoritarianism in Latin America: The Role of Stabilization Policy," *SAIS Review* (Summer-Fall 1985), p. 159.

9. Cf. the special November 1983 issue of *The Journal of Interamerican Studies* devoted to economic experiments in the Southern Cone, 1974-82. In particular, see M. Blejer, "Liberalization Policies in Southern Cone Countries," pp. 431-44 in that issue.

10. T. Dickson, "An Economic Output and Impact Analysis of Civilian and Military Regimes in Latin South America," *Development and Change* (1977), pp. 325-45.

11. Most, *op. cit.*, pp. 192-93.

12. For example, R.D. McKinlay and A.S. Cohan, "Performance and Instability in Military and Non-Military Regime Systems," *American Political Science Review* (September 1976), pp. 850-64.

13. P. Schmitter, "Corporatism and Public Policy in Authoritarian Portugal," *Sage Professional Paper in Contemporary Sociology* (Beverly Hills, Calif.: Sage, 1975), p. 37.

14. R. Jackman, "Politicians in Uniform: Military Governments and Social Change in the Third World," *American Political Science Review* (December 1976) p. 1096.

15. R.D. McKinlay and A.S. Cohan, "A Comparative Analysis of the Political and Economic Performance of Military and Civilian Regimes," *Comparative Politics* (October 1975), pp. 1-30; and McKinlay and Cohan, "Performance and Instability," *op. cit.*

16. P. Schmitter, "Military Intervention, Political Competitiveness and Public Policy in Latin America, 1950-67" in M. Janowitz and J. Van *On Military Intervention* (Rotterdam: Rotterdam University Press, 1971), pp. 425-506.

17. Margaret Daly Hayes, "Policy Consequences of Military Participation in Politics: An Analysis of Tradeoffs in Brazilian Federal Expenditures" in Craig Liske, ed., *Comparative Public Policy* (New York: Wiley, 1976), pp. 21-52.

18. Barry Ames and Ed Goff, "Education and Defense Expenditures in Latin America: 1948-68" in C. Liske, ed., *op. cit.* p. 175.

19. K. Remmer, "Evaluating the Policy Impact of Military Regimes in Latin America," *Latin American Research Review* (no. 2, 1978), p. 111.

20. *Ibid.*

21. Remmer, *op. cit.*, p. 47.

22. The level of nominal expenditure is taken from various issues of Stockholm International Peace Research Institute *World Armaments and Disarmament: SIPRI Yearbook* (Philadelphia: Taylor and Francis). (The series was deflated by the consumer price index (1974=100) taken from The World Bank, *Argentina: Economic Memorandum, vol. 2, Statistical Appendix* (Washington, D.C.: The World Bank, 1985), p. 398. The budgetary share of military expenditures is taken from The World Bank, *op. cit.*, p. 335.

23. Regressions were run using TSP—Time-Series Processor. Cf. B. Hall and R. Hall, *Time Series Processor, Version 3.5, User's Manual* (Stanford, Calif.: Bronwyn Hall and Robert E. Hall, 1980) for a description of the program and generated statistics.

24. An interesting application of this method is given in D. Giannaros and J. Lee, "Private Savings Behavior and Estimation of Structural Change: The Case of Korea," a paper presented at the 20th Atlantic Economic Conference, Washington, D.C., September 1985.

25. The modification variable for each dummy was formed by multiplying real government revenues by the respective dummy. For example, *DUMPX* was formed by real government revenues. *DUMPX* now indicates whether the slope of the regression line changes with regime type as government revenues change while overall government expenditures change vis-à-vis gross domestic product.

12
Consequences of Military Rule in Argentina: An Analysis of Central Government Budgetary Trade-offs, 1961-82

If military regimes in Argentina are more likely than their civilian counterparts to increase the share of defense in the overall budget, then from where does the money come? It is a truism that resources devoted to defense are unavailable for nondefense purposes. Clearly investment in defense may take place partly at the expense of either economic or social services. Defense expenditures might also be increased by reducing civilian spending on consumer and capital goods through tax rates that are higher than they would otherwise have been, as well as by reducing government spending on nondefense programs. Obviously, the funds might alternatively come from external borrowing and/or government borrowing from the central bank, that is, inflationary taxation. The purpose of this chapter is to address the issue of possible budgetary trade-offs between defense and nondefense expenditures by examining in some detail Argentina's central government budgetary allocations for the period 1961-82.[1] This period is particularly interesting because it spans a number of different political regimes, thus allowing economists to test whether defense and nondefense trade-offs occur independently of regime type or are instead specific to the type of regime in power.

Theory of Budgetary Trade-offs

One prevailing theory is that no trade-offs occurs between military and nonmilitary expenditures.[2] Proponents of this theory argue that as countries move toward a warfare state, ruling elites must buy off the populace with welfare goods. Another argument in favor of this theory is that welfare spending contributes to political order by co-opting the masses.[3]

In a more pragmatic vein, Otto Eckstein concludes:

> I think that the historical experience has been that governments are either stingy or they're spenders, and if they're stingy about defense, they're stingy about everything. I would say that the historical record suggests that the association between civilian spending and military spending is positive, not negative.[4]

This quote suggests that there is no negative relationship between defense and other policy sectors and that there may be a positive relationship. Other theorists, however, take a contrary position and view defense and welfare policy goals as mutually exclusive. They argue that military burdens drain political, technical, and economic resources from domestic programs. A related argument is that heavy defense involvement retards the establishment of new welfare or health programs. If a country supports a burdensome defense, other domestic policies or programs may not be introduced or established because policymakers perceive the cost as insupportable given present and anticipated defense sector outlays. This possibility is legitimately a substitution effect, although it cannot be empirically supported by examining current expenditure data.

In another vein, government-funded research and development may be heavily concentrated in the defense and space industries while non-defense agencies do not have research and development programs that relate broadly to their entire mission. This continued imbalance in government research efforts also retards innovations in welfare, housing, and health care programs.

Empirical findings to date are mixed. The number of studies indicating the existence of a trade-off relationship approximate the number showing that none exists.

Frederic Pryor is the only researcher to apply both cross-sectional and time series data analysis to this question.[5] His cross-sectional study of seven "capitalist" and seven "socialist" countries reveals no evidence of a substitution effect between nonmiliary and military expenditures for two different years: 1956 and 1962. (All nonmilitary expenditures were lumped together.) However, his time series analysis for 1950–62 uncovers a more varied pattern.

In those countries where defense expenditures were a relatively small proportion of the GNP, there existed no statistically significant inverse relationship between defense and current public expenditures. When defense expenditures were a relatively more important part of the government budget, a significant but small substitution effect was evident, but only when transfer payments were excluded. When transfer payments were added to current expenditures, there was no substitution effect.[6]

Similarly, in another time series analysis over the period 1950-70 for Sweden, the United Kingdom, Australia, and the United States, David Caputo found that defense did not undercut welfare expenditure.[7]

Recent research on Latin American countries also indicates no trade-off between these two categories of expenditure. In an anaylsis of the relationship between defense and education expenditures, Barry Ames and Ed Goff obtained positive and significant correlations between changes in defense and education outlays. They concluded that these two policies were not mutually exclusive.[8]

In an analysis of eighteen Latin American countries over the period 1948-79, Vener found that there was considerable variation in the defense-education spending trade-offs among the Latin American countries. Vener felt that the evidence seemed to support the conclusion of Ames and Goff that "Latin America may not have a common allocation process; instead different models may explain different groups of countries or time periods." Vener found that a negative trade-off existed in only one country (El Salvador) with a positive trade-off existing in ten countries, while there was no significant trade-off one way or the other between the two spending measures in seven countries.[9]

While the results of these studies do not strongly support theoretical argument suggesting a positive relationship between defense and social welfare spending, neither do they support the substitution hypothesis or the idea of an inverse relationship. They do suggest that major decisions about the magnitude of various public consumption expenditures are made in relative isolation from each other. In sum, empirical findings are not very consistent. Those research designs employing cross-section data show little or no support for a trade-off or substitution effect, while time series studies reveal more complex patterns.

The following analysis tests the trade-off hypothesis over the years 1961-82 for Argentina. Additionally, the analysis tests the possibility of changes in these trade-off relationships from 1961 to 1975—omitting the second military regime—and over the 1966-82 period—omitting the first civilian regime. This allows some judgements as to whether the second military regime produced, as some say, a fundamental change in the manner in which budgetary allocations were made in the country.

Empirical Tests

As in previous chapters, linear regressions using the Cochrane-Orcutt iterative technique for serial correlation correction were used. Regressions were performed using the respective budgetary shares as the dependent variables with the share of defense as the independent variable. The other independent variable was a control variable—government expenditures as a percent of GDP. The inclusion of the control variable was to improve the specifications of the regression models and obtain less biased estimates of the budgetary trade-offs. Existing evidence in the area of public finance seems to indicate the importance of this basic economic variable in the development process and as a significant factor in budgetary trade-offs. Moreover, increases in the ratio of government expenditure to GDP are a measure of the level of economic development and of the growing resources available to the public sector.

After these regressions were estimated, another set of equations was estimated by adding a third set of independent variables, the dummy variables found in table 11-1. The purpose of these variables was to determine whether or not any particular trade-offs between defense and other budgetary items were in fact not true trade-offs but simply the effects of a regime change. If this were the case, one could not infer any general budgetary patterns without first specifying the regime under which the budgets were to be drawn up. Because large numbers of regressions were run, only those with statistically significant signs on one or more of the independent variables are reported below.

The results for the period as a whole appear in table 12-1:

1. There is a fairly weak negative trade-off between defense and the share of the budget devoted to public administration, with regime changes not statistically significant in either increasing or decreasing the share of funds in the budget allocated for this activity.

2. The share of the budget allocated to domestic security appears to increase with the share of the budget allocated to defense, with regime changes not affecting this pattern.

3. At first, social services appear to have a strong negative trade-off with the share of the budget allocated to defense. Inclusion of the political variables, however, indicates that regime changes are much more important elements in affecting the share of social services than increases in the share of funds allocated to

defense per se. Clearly, the military regimes *(DUMPE* and *DUMPF)* have had the most severe effect on social expenditures.
4. The general pattern for education resembles that found for total social services—the negative trade-off between defense and education disappears when political dummies are introduced to the regression equation.
5. The share of health expenditures in the budget is not affected by the share of funds allocated to defense. Nor is regime change from civilian to military important. Instead, there is a secular trend downward in health expenditures associated with regime change *(DUMP)*.
6. The share of social security and welfare in the budget appears to be weakly related to the share of defense in the budget, with regime change having little impact on this budgetary item.
7. The share of housing in the budget appears to be negatively related to both the share of defense and regime type, with the second military regime least inclined to allocate funds for housing, followed by the first military regime, the first civilian regime, and the Peronists, who were most likely to allocate funds for this purpose.
8. Economic development is not hurt by defense expenditure and is, in fact, aided by regime change, with the military regimes showing a greater inclination to provide funds for this activity.

Are these results effected by the time period? Again, two subperiods, 1961–75 and 1966–82, were estimated to determine whether the second military regime significantly affected the pattern established before its ascension to power.

Tables 12–2 and 12–3 present the results:

1. No real changes in the impact of defense on public administration occurred between these time periods.
2. Domestic security expenditures were dramatically affected by the second military regime, increasing positively with the share of funds allocated to defense.
3. In the first period, social services' total share in the budget appears to have been negatively affected by the share of defense expenditures. This pattern changes dramatically in the second period, with a negative and highly significant political shift variable accounting for most of the reduction in social expenditures.
4. Education appears to have been unaffected by defense expenditures or regime change in the first period, but in the second period it appears to have had a negative trade-off with defense.

Table 12-1
Argentina: Impact of Political Change on Budgetary Trade-offs between Defense and Nondefense Expenditures, 1961–82

Budgetary Item	Political Variable	Share of Defense	Government Expenditures as a Percentage of GDP	RHO	r^2	Statistics F	DW
Share of General Administration							
	DUMP (1.52)	(-1.72)	(-4.24)	(0.71)	0.500	9.02	1.90
	DUMPC (0.90)	(-1.30)	(-0.93)	(-0.23)	0.632	8.61	1.90
	DUMPG (0.77)	(-2.06)	(-4.52)	(0.11)	0.576	6.81	1.70
		(-2.07)	(-4.83)	(0.02)	0.500	6.91	1.87
Share of Domestic Security							
	DUMPA (0.91)	(2.79)	(1.02)	(0.99)	0.305	3.95	1.62
		(2.73)		(0.92)	0.295	3.77	1.62
Share of Social Services							
	DUMP (-1.63)	(-2.46)	(35.06)	(0.54)	0.587	12.83	1.51
	DUMPD (-2.41)	(-0.71)	(-0.60)	(2.50)	0.411	3.49	1.50
	DUMPE (-3.30)	(-0.13)	(-2.75)	(2.07)	0.539	5.85	1.83
	DUMPF (-4.55)	(0.50)	(-1.56)	(2.09)	0.621	8.21	2.02
		(0.86)	(-1.58)	(0.36)	0.823	23.29	1.95
Share of Education							
	DUMP (-2.82)	(-2.24)	(-5.27)	(1.41)	0.607	13.93	1.66
	DUMPA (-2.32)	(-0.97)	(-0.73)	(1.96)	0.683	10.78	1.64
	DUMPB (-2.26)	(-0.28)	(-0.13)	(3.52)	0.474	4.50	1.77
	DUMPD (-2.83)	(0.08)	(-1.16)	(5.28)	0.335	2.52	1.64
		(0.12)	(-1.94)	(4.52)	0.452	4.14	1.74

Consequences of Military Rule · 253

Share of Health	DUMPE (-4.00)	(0.63)	(-1.82)	(3.77)	0.626	8.40	1.95
	DUMPF (4.99)	(0.74)	(-2.43)	(2.72)	0.765	16.43	1.98
	DUMPG (-1.81)	(-0.16)	(-0.99)	(6.83)	0.222	1.43	1.51
	DUMP (-4.31)	(-0.33)	(-1.69)	(17.52)	0.154	1.64	2.13
		(-0.30)	(-3.73)	(-0.05)	0.952	99.18	1.90
Share of Social Security and Welfare	DUMPD (-1.34)	(2.03)	(2.59)	(1.06)	0.297	2.12	1.68
Share of Housing	DUMPD (-2.51)	(-3.69)	(-2.32)	(0.93)	0.440	7.08	1.97
	DUMPE (-2.68)	(-2.54)	(-2.68)	(-0.83)	0.698	11.60	1.93
	DUMPF (-2.21)	(-1.84)	(-0.51)	(-0.98)	0.703	11.88	1.92
	DUMPG (-1.91)	(-1.35)	(-0.32)	(-0.69)	0.662	9.79	1.94
		(-3.40)	(-3.05)	(-0.19)	0.616	8.03	1.93
Share of Other Social Expenditures)	DUMP (-2.12)	(0.11)	(1.11)	(4.36)	0.078	0.76	2.04
		(0.60)	(1.54)	(8.72)	0.245	1.62	1.68

Notes: See text for definition of political variables.
( ) = t statistic.

Table 12-2
Argentina: Impact of Political Change on Budgetary Trade-offs between Defense and Nondefense Expenditures, 1961-75

Budgetary Item	Political Variable	Share of Defense	Government Expenditures as a Percentage of GDP	RHO	r^2	Statistics F	DW
Share of Public Administration	DUMPG	(-1.45)	(-1.07)	(-1.17)	0.295	1.25	1.91
	(1.72)						
Share of Domestic Security		(1.24)	(0.72)	(0.87)	0.129	0.74	1.75
Share of Total Social Services	DUMP	(-3.83)	(1.05)	(-1.60)	0.800	11.95	2.59
	(-1.53)						
	DUMPF	(-3.83)	(1.05)	(-1.60)	0.800	11.95	2.59
	(1.53)						
Share of Education		(-1.07)	(-0.84)	(1.99)	0.097	0.54	2.22
Share of Health	DUMP	(1.73)	(-2.25)	(0.50)	0.749	14.97	1.67
	(-2.0)						
	DUMPB	(1.34)	(-0.47)	(-1.70)	0.900	27.27	2.24
	(1.59)						
	DUMPD	(2.46)	(-2.48)	(-1.05)	0.871	20.29	1.97
	DUMPE						
	(1.81)	(2.25)	(-2.51)	(-1.22)	0.881	22.41	2.04

Notes: See text for definition of political variables.
( ) = t statistic.

Table 12-3
Argentina: Impact of Political Change on Budgetary Trade-offs between Defense and Nondefense Expenditures, 1966-82

Budgetary Item	Political Variable	Share of Defense	Government Expenditures as a Percentage of GDP	RHO	r^2	Statistics F	DW
Share of Housing	DUMP	(-5.57)	(-3.29)	(-0.59)	0.722	15.61	1.78
	DUMPA (1.74)	(-6.75)	(-3.33)	(-1.25)	0.811	17.23	1.90
	DUMPB DUMPC DUMPD (-2.41)	(-2.27)	(-3.58)	(-2.03)	0.860	24.69	2.07
	DUMPG (-2.69)	(-3.60)	(-5.40)	(2.07)	0.871	27.17	2.09
Share of Other Government Services	DUMP	(-0.81)	(0.54)	(3.24)	0.038	0.23	2.00
	DUMPA (3.12)	(-2.31)	(-1.82)	(-0.89)	0.506	5.67	2.00
	DUMPB DUMPC DUMPD (-1.88)	(0.93)	(1.11)	(2.10)	0.277	1.53	2.14
	DUMPE (-3.58)	(1.64)	(0.94)	(-0.12)	0.614	6.37	2.01
Share of Public Administration	DUMP DUMPA (-2.05)	(-0.87)	(-0.28)	(-1.07)	0.756	12.39	1.82

Table 12-3 continued

Budgetary Item	Political Variable	Share of Defense	Government Expenditures as a Percentage of GDP	RHO	Statistics r^2	F	DW
Share of Domestic Security	DUMPE	(3.35)	(2.16)	(-0.22)	0.529	4.50	1.95
	(-1.91)	(3.45)	(2.42)	(-0.51)	0.554	4.97	2.02
	(-2.07)						
Share of Social Services	DUMPB		(-4.94)	(-0.10)	0.659	11.64	1.58
	DUMPC						
	DUMPD						
	(-3.45)						
	DUMPE	(0.39)	(-6.21)	(-0.82)	0.859	24.45	2.01
	(-6.05)						
	3DUMPF	(2.35)	(-6.05)	(-2.56)	0.948	73.48	2.33
	(-6.86)	(2.94)	(-0.40)	(-3.11)	0.959	94.78	2.31
	DUMPG	(-0.22)	(-6.21)	(-0.21)	0.770	13.40	1.86
	(-2.28)						
Share of Education	DUMP	(-2.04)	(-4.88)	(0.76)	0.642	11.04	1.62
	DUMPA						
	(-2.35)	(-1.20)	(-1.91)	(0.23)	0.802	16.21	1.53
	DUMPB						
	DUMPC						
	DUMPD						
	(-3.30)	(0.91)	(0.36)	(10.80)	0.514	4.24	1.84
	DUMPE	(1.22)	(0.23)	(7.47)	0.607	6.18	1.98
	(-4.18)						
	DUMPF	(1.62)	(-1.81)	(0.88)	0.878	28.99	2.10
	(-4.94)						
	DUMPG	(0.54)	(0.31)	(-1.61)	0.396	2.62	1.77
	(-2.50)						

Share of Health							
DUMP		(0.32)	(-0.19)		0.031	0.19	1.63
DUMPA	(-3.95)	(-0.36)	(-3.62)	(14.45)	(-0.54)	0.98	84.63	1.89
Share of Social Security and Welfare							
DUMPB							
DUMPC							
DUMPD	(-2.15)	(2.62)	(3.32)	(0.04)	0.517	4.29	2.03
DUMPE	(-1.71)	(2.25)	(2.97)	(0.26)	0.440	3.15	1.86
DUMPF	(-1.34)	(1.94)	(2.44)	(0.59)	0.370	13.15	1.74
DUMPG	(-2.22)	(2.60)	(2.17)	(0.03)	0.526	4.44	2.04
Share of Economic Development							
DUMPB							
DUMPC							
DUMPD	(1.96)	(-1.26)	(-10.37)	(0.39)	0.912	41.48	1.76
DUMPE	(2.28)	(-1.72)	(8.43)	(0.01)	0.901	36.77	1.57
DUMPF	(2.33)	(-1.83)	(-7.31)	(0.26)	0.890	32.40	1.46

Notes: Regressions were made using Cochrane-Orcutt iterative estimation procedure to correct for serial correlation. See text for definition of political variables.
( ) = t statistics.

258 · *Argentina*

Adding the political dummies to the regression equation, however, indicates that the reduction in the share of funds in education was not necessarily to increase defense, but instead reflected budgetary priorities with regime type. *DUMPE* and *DUMPF* were highly significant, indicating an inclination on the part of the two military regimes to reduce the share of education in the overall budget.

5. In the first period, the share of the budget devoted to health appears to have increased with increases in the the share devoted to defense. There may also have been an inclination on the part of military regimes to increase resources to this area. The second time period again shows a major change in pattern, with health expenditures no longer related to defense expenditures. Instead they were more a result of secular changes in regime but not regime type.

6. The share of the budget going toward social security and welfare was not affected by defense or political change in the first time period. In the second time period, however, this expenditure category took on a positive relationship with defense and a negative relationship with regime type; that is, authoritarian regimes tended to reduce expenditures in this area but did increase them in line with defense allocations.

7. The share of the budget allocated to housing does not appear to be related to defense in the first time period and may be slightly related to regime type. In the second period, housing showed a strong negative trade-off with defense. The military regimes were also inclined to reduce expenditures for housing, in addition to cutting back housing's share with increases in defense.

8. The share of the budget going to economic development showed a positive trade-off with defense in the first period, but in the second, it was closely related to regime type—the military regimes were more willing to increase funding of this sector than were their civilian counterparts. However, there was a slight negative trade-off with defense expenditures.

What do the results indicate with regard to the questions posed at the beginning of this section?

1. For the period as a whole (not taking into account regime types), defense increased its share of the budget at the expense of public administration, total social services, education, and housing. Introducing political dummies, however, left only public administration and housing as areas where cutbacks were presumably used to finance defense expansion.

2. For the first time period (1961–75), defense increased its share only at the expense of total social services.
3. During the second time period (1966–82), defense expanded only at the expense of housing.
4. Cutting down on the number of regimes included in the analysis, therefore, reduces the negative trade-offs.

Conclusions

The results above provide several important insights into the setting of priorities in Argentina.

First, they again confirm the bureaucratic authoritarian (BA) model's thesis that military regimes were more concerned with economic development than civilian regimes and are less concerned with the provision of social services.

Second, the results indicate, however, that within a given political context in Argentina, few trade-offs occur between defense and other major budgetary categories. In fact, the trade-offs that do occur are largely complementary. For example, for the 1966–82 period (given a certain regime type), defense was positively related to domestic security, total social services, and social security and welfare.

The negative trade-offs that appear to occur between defense and other budgetary items seem to be more of a statistical aberration. That is, budget shifts (both positive and negative) are more associated with changes in regime than with stable long-term budgetary priorities. This phenomenon may help explain the actual rise and demise of regimes in Argentina.

Apparently, military regimes systematically shift budgetary priorities toward economic development and defense while civilians shift allocations toward social services. The increase in social services under civilians may, as O'Donnell and others note, result in lax fiscal policies, higher inflation, and, eventually, exchange rate collapse. Upon assuming power, the military's orthodox austerity programs begin by slashing social programs. Initially, the fiscal crisis is reduced but over longer periods of time the unwillingness of the military regimes to restore social programs weakens their popular support. Eventually, they are forced to turn over power to the civilians.

The military regimes appear unwilling to expand social programs at the expense of defense. (Again most budgetary decisions within a regime type appear to be complementary.) Similarly, civilian regimes do not appear willing to cut social expenditures as a means of austerity once inflation is out of hand.

While traditional explanations of the rise and fall of military regimes in Argentina have tended to concentrate on macroeconomic policy failures, it is suggested here that bureaucratic authoritarian regimes may become increasingly weak politically, since, as social services deteriorate, extensive civilian opposition to these regimes begins to include civilian elements previously aligned with the military.

While this conclusion must be very tentative, it seems consistent with the fact that many of the country's apparent negative trade-offs between defense and other expenditures disappear once regime type is systematically accounted for.

The high-threat situation perceived by the second military regime may also explain why it slashed social programs much more drastically than the first military regime. Once the programs were slashed, however, they did not later expand at the expense of defense, nor did defense systematically expand over time at the expense of social services. Whatever expansion of defense did occur was, in the BA context, in line with social services.

Notes

1. The time period selected was based on data availability. The longest consistent series on government budgetary allocations in Argentina has been compiled by the World Bank for 1961-82. Cf. The World Bank, *Argentina: Economic Memorandum, vol. 2, Statistical Appendix* (Washington, D.C.: International Bank for Reconstruction and Development, 1985), pp. 334-35.

2. Cf. Paul Baran and Paul Sweezy, *Monopoly Capital* (New York: Monthly Review Press, 1966).

3. A. Gouldner, *The Coming Crisis of Western Sociology* (New York: Basic Books, 1970).

4. O. Eckstein, "Discussion" in D. Abshire and R. Allen, eds., *National Security: Political, Military and Economic Strategies in the Decades Ahead* (New York: Praeger, 1963), p. 1012.

5. Frederic Pryor, *Public Expenditures in Communist and Capitalist Nations* (London: George Allen and Urwin, 1968).

6. *Ibid.*, p. 298.

7. David Caputo, "New Perspectives on the Public Policy Implications of Defense and Welfare Expenditures in Four Modern Democracies: 1950-1970," *Policy Sciences* (1975), pp. 423-446.

8. Barry Ames and Ed Goff, "Education and Defense Expenditures in Latin America, 1948-68" in Craig Liske, ed., *Comparative Public Policy* (New York: Wiley, 1976).

9. J. Vener, "Budgetary Tradeoffs between Education and Defense in Latin America: Research Note," *Journal of Developing Areas* (October 1983), pp. 77-92.

13
Impact of Increased External Debt Servicing on Government Budgetary Priorities in Argentina

The economic climate of the 1960s through the 1980s in Argentina has been particularly unstable, not only because of adverse developments in world markets, but also because of increased difficulties in stabilizing the domestic economy. One of the consequences of the country's relative economic stagnation has been an increasing difficulty on the part of the government to finance its customary budgets.

As debt service costs have risen and revenue has levelled off or declined, the government has been forced to reevaluate programs in an effort to curtail government spending. This chapter attempts to examine the character of the sectoral adjustment that has taken place in the main functional areas of government expenditures.[1] Is there evidence that particular sectors have suffered as debt service payments increased? Were the shifts in political regime particularly important in reordering budgetary priorities in light of mounting debt service payments? What are the implications for servicing increased levels of debt?

Empirical Testing

As in the previous chapters, multiple regressions with Cochrane-Orcutt correction for serial correlation were performed. The share of the budget allocated to each functional expenditure type was the dependent variable, with the share of debt service and independent variable and government expenditures as a percent of gross domestic product and control variable.

After the first set of regressions were run, each equation was reestimated with a political shift dummy variable (originally used in

Table 13-1
Argentina: Impact of Public Sector Debt Service Allocations on Major Budgetary Items, 1961-82

Budgetary Item	Political Variable	Share of Debt Service	Government Expenditures as a Percentage of GDP	RHO	r^2	F	DW
Share of Public Administration	DUMP (-1.99)	(-4.98)		(1.06)	0.566	24.04	2.08
	DUMP (-1.99)	(-2.75)	(1.59)	(-0.25)	0.721	12.95	2.06
Share of Defense	DUMPA (0.86)	(-1.99)		(4.10)	0.173	3.97	1.36
	DUMPB (2.68)	(-2.15)		(3.12)	0.205	3.98	1.57
	DUMPC (2.05)	(-2.51)		(-4.36)	0.409	6.23	1.94
	DUMPD (3.05)	(-2.25)		(-4.85)	0.327	4.37	1.67
	DUMPE (3.48)	(-2.70)		(-3.56)	0.455	7.54	2.07
	DUMPF (5.85)	(-3.45)		(-2.90)	0.506	9.24	2.23
	DUMPG (2.51)	(-5.74)		(0.44)	0.703	21.34	2.05
		(-2.19)		(-4.43)	0.386	5.67	1.84
Share of Domestic Security	DUMPE (2.25)	(-5.22) (-3.66)	(2.10)	(12.07) (2.98)	0.589 0.443	27.27 7.17	1.36 1.26
	DUMPF (3.83)	(-3.85)	(3.91)	(0.97)	0.488	4.77	1.41
		(-4.91)	(3.97)	(0.22)	0.615	7.99	1.71

Impact of Increased Debt Servicing · 263

Share of Social Services

DUMP	(-6.48)		(2.40)	0.688	42.00	1.61
(-2.52)	(-5.95)		(2.20)	0.756	28.02	1.58
DUMPA	(-6.12)	(2.12)	(2.74)	0.804	20.54	1.61
(-3.44)						
DUMPB	(-7.19)	(3.29)	(3.49)	0.819	22.71	1.94
(-3.57)						
DUMPC	(-7.22)	(4.13)	(2.31)	0.858	30.33	2.06
(-2.85)						
DUMPD	(-7.06)	(2.78)	(2.73)	0.818	22.53	1.96
(-4.12)						
DUMPE	(-6.99)	(3.04)	(1.71)	0.889	40.42	2.09
(-5.43)						
DUMPF	(-7.52)	(2.18)	(1.55)	0.921	58.80	2.28
(-6.12)						
DUMPG	(-6.56)	(3.05)	(0.88)	0.939	77.10	2.19
(-2.80)						
	(-6.66)	(2.62)	(0.40)	0.838	26.01	1.91
		(1.99)				

Share of Education

DUMPA	(-6.43)		(2.49)	0.685	41.34	1.69
(-5.08)	(-6.56)	(3.81)	(3.08)	0.860	30.75	2.75
DUMP	(-5.41)	(3.00)	(2.07)	0.874	34.80	2.04
(-4.56)						
DUMPB	(-6.13)		(3.59)	0.753	27.52	2.00
(-3.31)						
DUMPC	(-5.65)		(3.49)	0.703	21.28	2.04
(-2.43)						
DUMPD	(-6.51)		(3.57)	0.776	31.21	1.97
(-3.78)						
DUMPE	(-6.86)		(3.49)	0.849	50.73	1.88
(-5.40)						

Table 13-1 continued

Budgetary Item	Political Variable	Share of Debt Service	Government Expenditures as a Percentage of GDP	RHO	r^2	Statistics F	DW
	DUMPF (-6.16)	(-7.11)		(3.12)	0.869	67.84	1.54
	DUMPG (-2.47)	(-6.13)		(3.50)	0.704	21.44	1.81
Share of Health							
	DUMP (-7.07)	(-2.59) (-2.26)	(-1.41)	(16.93) (15.39)	0.260 0.346	6.71 4.77	2.19 2.35
	DUMPA (-5.22)	(-4.35)	(-1.85)	(-1.23)	0.983	305.83	1.98
		(-6.32)		(0.34)	0.923	108.43	1.98
Share of Social Security and Welfare							
	DUMP (2.00)	(-3.53) (-3.33)	(2.84)	(13.90) (3.70)	0.396 0.392	12.47 5.82	1.79 1.71
	DUMPF (1.45)	(-3.26)	(1.87)	(-1.53)	0.478	4.58	1.72
		(-3.35)	(3.40)	(2.19)	0.432	3.81	1.80
Share of Housing							
	DUMPB (-2.11)	(-1.52)	(1.42)	(3.15)	0.122	1.25	1.90
	DUMPC (-1.42)	(-1.53)	(1.36)	(1.37)	0.307	2.21	2.06
	DUMPD (-4.03)	(-1.67)	(1.63)	(2.43)	0.212	1.34	2.05
	DUMPE (-4.81)	(-1.10)	(0.72)	(-0.36)	0.569	6.61	1.93
	DUMPF (-5.71)	(-0.66)	(1.09)	(-0.93)	0.648	9.21	1.94
	DUMPG (-2.14)	(0.77)	(0.10)	(-1.76)	0.719	12.80	1.93
		(-1.49)	(0.90)	(1.28)	0.311	2.26	2.03

Share of Other Social Expenditures

DUMP	(-1.01)	(1.68)	(10.51)	0.286	2.01	1.75
(-2.23)						
DUMPA	(-1.26)	(2.03)	(9.72)	0.289	2.03	1.97
(-2.25)						
DUMPE	(-0.53)	(1.17)	(5.04)	(0.208)	1.31	2.24
(-1.51)						
DUMPF	(-0.39)	(0.94)	(5.64)	0.227	1.47	2.20
(-1.71)						

Share of Economic Development

	(-4.89)	(-4.48)	(1.14)	0.557	23.91	1.78
	(0.03)		(-0.35)	0.867	59.16	2.02
DUMPB	(-0.01)	(-4.77)	(-0.17)	0.878	36.14	2.14
(1.65)						
DUMPC	(0.33)	(-4.77)	(-0.15)	0.874	34.91	2.18
(1.51)						
DUMPD	(-0.35)	(-4.31)	(-0.25)	0.882	37.92	2.08
(1.63)						
DUMPE	(-0.44)	(-4.45)	(-0.27)	0.879	36.40	2.03
(1.48)						
DUMPG	(-0.06)	(-4.44)	(-0.21)	0.881	36.93	2.15
(1.68)						

Note: Estimations were made using Cochrane-Orcutt iterative procedure of serial correlation correction.

table 11-1 included as a third independent variable. Only the statistically significant results are given here due to space and limitations.

For the period as a whole, it appears in table 13-1 that:

1. The share of the budget allocated to public administration declined to help service the government's debt. This tendency has been reinforced by a secular trend downward in the share of the budget going to public administration following a shift in regimes (but not following changes from military to civilian and vice versa).

2. The defense share may be weakly affected by debt service payments. The r^2 for the debt service–defense trade-off is only 0.17 with a t value less than 2. Adding the political dummies to the equation increases the negative sign on the debt service term. It appear that whatever cutbacks have occurred in the share of defense in the budget as a result of mounting debt service payments have been more than offset by shifts to military regimes.

3. As with defense, domestic security has contracted as a share of the budget with increased debt service payments, only to be offset by shifts to military regimes.

4. Total social services have been greatly cut back with the increase in debt service—the share of debt service explains nearly 70 percent of the fluctuations in the share of the total services. Changes in regime have reinforced the country's normal tendency to service the debt at the expense of social services. The military regimes, in particular (as depicted by the dummy variables DUMPE and DUMPF) have tended to reduce share of government funds allocated to this sector of the budget.

5. The share of eduction in the budget mirrors fairly closely that of total social services, as does the share of health.

6. The share of social security and welfare appears less vulnerable to budgetary cutbacks. There is a tendency to reduce the share of the budget allocated to social security and welfare with increases in debt service's share of the budget, but, historically, there has also been a secular trend toward an increased share of the government budget to social security and welfare.

7. The share of housing in the budget has not been influenced much by developments in debt servicing. However, regime changes, particularly to military regimes, have significantly reduced the share of the budget allocated to housing.

8. The share of the budget allocated to economic services follows an interesting pattern. Regressed on the share of debt service in the budget, one finds a large negative trade-off as the share of debt service in the budget increases. Adding the control variable, however, reveals that economic development's share of the budget has contracted as a proportion of government expenditures as GNP has expanded. The longer-run trend has apparently not been offset with political change. (The sign is positive on the political dummies, but none are statistically significant.)

Contrasting the two time periods in tables 13.2 and 13.3 reveals more or less the same pattern with regard to the handling of debt service. Debt service was not a particular problem in the first period (1961–75), with service payments on the government debt not reaching a significant share (4.4 percent) until 1972. As a result, the t values and r^2 are somewhat lower for the first period when compared to those of the 1966–82 years.

Conclusions

In terms of the questions asked at the beginning of this book, it appears that social services in general (and education and health in particular) along with public administration have borne the brunt of the government's rising debt service problem. The social sectors have suffered further due to regime changes, with military regimes tending to cut back even more severely than normal debt service constraints would have warranted.

Other sectors have been negatively affected by the debt servicing problem—possibly defense, domestic security, and social security and welfare—but these sectors have found their budgets stabilized, with the military regimes inclined to raise their shares even in the light of mounting debt. Defense and economic development, on the other hand, appear to be largely unaffected by the government's increased debt burden.

By 1982, debt service was accounting for 37.1 percent of the government budget, up from 22.6 percent in 1981 and 16.3 percent in 1980. Obviously, this trend cannot continue. Given current levels of external debt, it is fairly unlikely that the government will be contracting for major net increases in debt in the near term. Given this assumption, economists can probably expect regime changes to play a more assertive role than in the past in influencing government budgetary allocations.

Table 13-2
Argentina: Impact of Public Sector Debt Service Allocations on Major Budgetary Items, 1961-75

Budgetary Item	Political Variable	Share of Debt Service	Government Expenditures as a Percentage of GDP	RHO	Statistics		
					r^2	F	DW
Share of Public Administration							
	DUMP	(-1.98)		(0.37)	0.247	3.93	2.13
	(1.76)	(-2.05)	(1.00)	(0.08)	0.299	2.13	2.11
	DUMPA	(-2.77)		(0.55)	0.416	3.53	2.11
	(1.70)						
	DUMPB	(-2.62)		(-0.25)	0.386	3.14	2.00
	(-1.47)	(-2.65)		(2.24)	0.408	3.44	2.25
	DUMPD						
	DUMPE	(-2.77)		(1.60)	0.413	3.52	2.21
	(-1.58)						
	DUMPF	(-2.77)		(0.56)	0.416	3.57	2.11
	(-1.76)						
	DUMPG	(-2.75)		(1.89)	0.415	3.54	2.23
	(-1.56)						
Share of Defense							
	DUMPB	(0.87)	(-2.55)	(3.49)	0.541	3.53	1.95
	(2.02)						
	DUMPC	(1.10)	(-3.10)	(4.20)	0.574	4.06	1.89
	(2.40)						
	DUMPD						
	DUMPE	(0.65)	(-2.01)	(2.81)	0.522	3.28	1.93
	(1.66)						
	DUMPG	(0.73)	(-2.22)	(3.05)	0.527	3.35	1.94
	(1.79)						

Share of Domestic Security

DUMP (-0.43)	(-1.96) (-2.37)		(0.85) (0.70)	0.243 0.344	3.85 2.62	1.53 1.33

Share of Total Social Services

DUMPA (1.23)	(-1.91)	(1.28)	(0.57)	0.361	1.70	1.37
DUMPB (-1.50)	(0.72) (-1.24)	(1.21)	(0.59) (0.78)	0.042 0.411	0.52 3.48	2.32 2.19
DUMPC (-1.47)	(-1.63)	(2.68)	(0.75)	0.489	2.87	2.28
DUMPD	(-1.97)	(1.16)	(1.23)	0.505	3.06	2.36
DUMPE (-1.46)	(-1.97)	(2.91)	(1.33)	0.498	2.97	2.37
DUMPF (-1.23)	(-1.91)	(3.11)	(1.08)	0.505	3.06	2.34
DUMPG (-1.49)	(-1.63)	(2.36)	(0.75)	0.489	2.87	2.28
	(-1.94)	(1.16)	(1.14)	0.505	3.07	2.35
		(2.62)				

Share of Education

DUMPB (-1.83)	(-2.65) (-2.82)	(1.12)	(2.43) (2.21)	0.370 0.442	7.07 3.65	2.00 1.82
DUMPC (-1.59)	(-3.35)		(2.76)	0.529	5.62	2.45
DUMPD	(-3.11)		(2.90)	0.503	5.07	2.53
DUMPE (-1.83)	(-3.41)		(2.60)	0.524	5.52	2.20
DUMPF (-1.50)	(-3.14)		(2.35)	0.474	4.51	1.86
DUMPG (-1.86)	(-3.42)		(2.67)	0.530	5.64	2.31

Table 13-2 continued

Budgetary Item	Political Variable	Share of Debt Service	Government Expenditures as a Percentage of GDP	RHO	r^2	Statistics F	DW
Share of Health		(-9.66) (-5.03)		(-0.45) (1.48)	0.886 0.881	93.33 37.02	1.82 1.85
	DUMP (-1.45)	(-4.25)	(-3.32)	(-0.80)	0.946	53.49	1.83
	DUMPA (-2.37)	(-8.48)	(-1.02)	(-2.61)	0.967	88.94	2.14
	DUMPF (-1.45)	(-4.25) (-4.64)	(0.44)	(-0.80) (2.04)	0.946 0.860	53.49 18.56	1.83 1.74
Share of Social Security and Welfare		(1.21) (-0.30)		(0.24) (1.03)	0.110 0.219	1.48 1.40	1.96 1.83
	DUMP (0.01)	(-0.27)	(1.54)	(1.03)	0.219	0.84	1.83
Share of Housing		(3.34) (-2.28)	(1.07)	(-1.37) (3.94)	0.481 0.483	11.15 4.67	2.19 1.51
	DUMP (3.21)	(-1.08)	(2.71)	(-0.83)	0.758	9.41	2.07
	DUMPB (-2.61)	(-2.46)	(-0.56)	(1.89)	0.651	5.61	1.74
	DUMPC (-2.40)	(-2.80)	(3.42)	(3.00)	0.653	5.66	1.73
	DUMPD DUMPE (-2.88)	(-2.10)	(3.77)	(0.26)	0.671	6.13	1.83
	DUMPF (-3.21)	(-1.08)	(2.48)	(-0.83)	0.758	9.41	2.07
	DUMPG (-2.76)	(-2.26)	(-0.56)	(1.37)	0.661	5.84	1.79

Impact of Increased Debt Servicing · 271

Share of Other Social Expenditures						
	(5.56)		(0.74)	0.720	30.99	2.02
	(3.40)	(1.97)	(0.59)	0.804	20.61	2.00
DUMPA						
(1.07)	(3.79)	(0.19)	(-0.13)	0.861	18.65	2.03
Share of Economic Development						
	(-6.02)		(-0.32)	0.751	36.24	2.33
	(-3.05)	(-2.15)	(-0.52)	0.834	25.26	2.45
DUMPA						
(-0.61)	(-3.06)	(-0.67)	(-0.69)	0.846	16.57	2.38

Notes: Estimations were made using Cochrane-Orcutt iterative procedure for serial correlation correction.
( ) = t statistic.

Table 13-3
Argentina: Impact of Public Sector Debt Service Allocations on Major Budgetary Items, 1966-82

Budgetary Item	Political Variable	Share of Debt Service	Government Expenditures as a Percentage of GDP	RHO	r^2	F	DW
Share of Public Administration							
	DUMP	(-4.72)		(0.85)	0.614	22.28	1.92
	DUMPA	(-3.06)	(0.95)	(1.17)	0.607	9.28	1.98
	(-2.78)	(-2.89)	(1.87)	(-0.21)	0.838	20.83	1.94
	DUMPF	(-2.24)	(0.64)	(0.85)	0.675	8.32	1.96
	(-1.21)						
Share of Defense							
	DUMPB	(-1.74)		(3.80)	0.178	3.05	1.34
	DUMPC	(-1.19)	(2.98)	(10.62)	0.507	6.19	1.17
	DUMPD						
	(4.99)						
	DUMPE	(-1.82)	(1.05)	(-0.27)	0.712	9.90	1.77
	(12.05)						
	DUMPF	(-4.18)	(1.79)	(-3.29)	0.932	55.14	1.79
	(14.30)						
	DUMPG	(-4.96)	(1.07)	(-3.84)	0.951	72.84	2.36
	(1.46)	(-1.50)	(-1.92)	(9.35)	0.575	5.43	1.69
Share of Domestic Security							
	DUMPB	(-5.33)		(12.74)	0.670	28.42	1.05
	DUMPC						
	DUMPD						
	(3.59)						
	DUMPE	(-4.40)	(4.25)	(-0.47)	0.650	7.44	1.78
	(4.20)						
	DUMPF	(-4.92)	(4.42)	(-0.54)	0.704	9.53	1.84
	(4.02)						
	DUMPG	(-4.89)	(4.06)	(-0.22)	0.698	9.28	1.83
	(2.19)	(-3.59)	(3.35)	(0.37)	0.530	4.51	1.69

Impact of Increased Debt Servicing · 273

Share of Total Social Services

DUMP	(-5.39)		(1.88)	0.682	29.07	1.57
DUMPA	(-5.47)	(2.47)	(2.81)	0.725	15.85	1.61
(-2.62)						
DUMPB						
DUMPC						
DUMPD	(-6.19)	(3.88)	(3.68)	0.806	16.61	1.64
(-5.10)						
DUMPE	(-5.03)	(0.85)	(-0.32)	0.947	71.62	1.95
(-7.97)						
DUMPF	(-5.94)	(1.77)	(-1.06)	0.974	149.91	2.12
(-7.97)	(-6.28)	(2.72)	(-0.82)	0.974	151.41	1.84
DUMPG	(-4.72)	(0.76)	(0.67)	0.887	31.42	1.74
(-2.83)						

Share of Education

DUMP			(2.00)	0.670	28.51	1.69
DUMPA	(-5.34)	(1.27)	(3.32)	0.583	8.39	1.99
(-5.18)	(-3.89)					
DUMPB						
DUMPC						
DUMPD	(-5.87)	(3.50)	(0.38)	0.939	62.47	1.63
(-3.44)						
DUMPE	(-3.51)	(0.41)	(4.80)	0.749	11.96	2.00
(-4.90)						
DUMPF	(-4.22)	(0.52)	(3.82)	0.850	22.69	1.90
(-6.02)						
DUMPG	(-4.82)	(0.83)	(3.24)	0.898	35.23	1.80
(-2.32)	(-3.04)	(0.60)	(5.84)	0.634	6.94	2.08

Table 13-3 continued

Budgetary Item	Political Variable	Share of Debt Service	Government Expenditures as a Percentage of GDP	RHO	r^2	Statistics F	DW
Share of Health		(-2.47)		(12.89)	0.304	6.12	1.66
		(-2.26)	(-0.13)	(13.20)	0.301	2.59	1.71
	DUMP						
	DUMPA (-7.09)	(-6.47)		(-0.83)	0.976	249.15	1.98
	DUMPB						
	DUMPC						
	DUMPD (-0.13)	(-2.38)		(12.79)	0.306	2.64	1.63
	DUMPE (-0.11)	(-2.38)		(12.82)	0.305	2.64	1.65
	DUMPF (-0.01)	(-2.39)		(12.76)	0.306	2.64	1.66
	DUMPG (-0.91)	(-2.17)		(16.09)	0.370	2.94	2.16
Share of Social Security and Welfare		(-3.02)		(12.04)	0.395	9.16	1.08
		(-2.63)	(2.99)	(1.34)	0.409	4.16	1.59
	DUMP						
	DUMPA (2.46)						
	DUMPE (1.39)	(-3.24)	(2.21)	(0.31)	0.638	7.06	2.00
	DUMPF (1.72)	(-3.01)	(3.48)	(0.85)	0.509	4.14	1.73
		(-3.20)	(3.64)	(0.65)	0.551	4.89	1.78
		(-0.76)		(2.22)	0.041	0.57	1.96
		(-1.52)	(1.79)	(3.66)	0.213	1.60	1.92
Share of Housing							
	DUMPB						
	DUMPC						
	DUMPD (-6.89)	(1.03)	(-1.76)	(-2.78)	0.839	20.86	2.10

Share of Other Social Expenditures						
DUMPE (-6.58)	(1.15)	(-1.01)		(-2.68)	0.827	19.13	2.13
DUMPF (-4.92)	(0.60)	(-0.09)		(-1.64)	0.753	11.00	1.94
DUMPG (-4.39)	(0.11)	(-1.24)		(-1.31)	0.688	8.83	1.84
DUMP	(-0.33)		(1.24)	(3.63)	0.01	0.11	2.11
DUMPA (-2.25)	(-1.02)			(3.20)	0.109	0.74	2.16
DUMPE (-1.30)	(-0.50)	(1.63)		(7.35)	0.367	2.32	1.65
DUMPF (-1.47)	(-0.51)	(0.74)		(3.54)	0.217	1.11	2.20
DUMPG (-1.32)	(-0.47)	(0.73)		(4.10)	0.241	1.27	2.21
		(0.59)		(2.01)	0.244	1.29	2.09
Share of Economic Development						
DUMPB	(-4.32)	(-4.99)		(0.64)	0.572	18.72	1.68
DUMPC	(0.90)			(-1.06)	0.913	63.13	1.71
DUMPD (1.21)	(0.19)	(-3.88)		(-1.14)	0.924	49.14	1.81
DUMPG (1.24)	(0.26)	(-3.60)		(-1.16)	0.925	49.59	1.88

Notes: Estimations were made using Cochrane-Orcutt iterative procedure for serial correlation correction.
( ) = t statistic.

Notes

1. The time period selected was based on data availability. The longest consistent series on government budgetary allocations has recently been compiled by the World Bank for the 1961-82 period. Cf. World Bank, *Argentia: Economic Memorandum, vol. 2, Statistical Appendix* (Washington, D.C.: IBRD, 1985), pp. 334-35.

14
The Future Demand for Military Expenditures in Argentina

As R.P. Smith has observed, much of the discussion of the economics of national security policy and military expenditures has implicit in it a "rational" or "neoclassical" model for defense.[1] This assumes that social welfare is a function of civilian output and an unobserved variable, security. It also assumes that security depends, among other things, on military expenditures. The role of the state is then to balance the welfare benefits of extra security derived from military expenditures against its opportunity cost in foregone civilian output.

Clearly implied here is that, ceteris paribus, military expenditures will be largely a function of economic conditions and regime type (a proxy for defense/non-defense priorities). The purpose of this chapter is to present an optimal control forecast of military expenditures in a major developing country, Argentina, under differing economic and political conditions. An attempt will be made through this analysis to determine the relative importance of economic versus political factors in affecting overall Argentinian military expenditures.

Methodology

The steps used in forecasting the main macro elements in the Argentinian economy, including military expenditures, are as follows:

1. Developing a macroeconomic model of the economy;
2. Statistically estimating the individual equations of the model using ordinary least squares;

3. Correcting the individual equations of the model by estimating them using a two-stage least squares estimation technique;
4. Assuming values for the exogenous variables and possible policy tools over the 1984–90 period and solving the model's endogenous variables for these years;
5. Examining the model for stability within various policy ranges and reestimating equations that produced infeasible results (given policy constraints such as limits on external borrowing);
6. Linking the model with an optimal control program to generate forecasts that optimize real gross domestic product in 1990, given the constraint that inflation had to be reduced on a year-to-year basis from its 1983 level;
7. Simulating optimal growth paths under various assumptions concerning external debt;
8. On the basis of the preliminary runs, and taking into account the difficulties of implementing policy in the current Argentinian environment, selecting the most effective policy tools (in both technical and political terms) available to the authorities;
9. Estimating the final optimal path of the economy and the policy mix needed for its attainment;
10. Generating, from the optimal path, governmental budget allocations by major activity, including military expenditures;
11. Determining the impact of regime change on military expenditures (for example, the Peronists in office in 1987) and the (unlikely) change of a future Malvinas situation in the late 1980s.

The Macroeconomic Model

The macroeconomic model developed for forecasting the Argentinian economy appears in table 14–1. It was estimated over the time period 1970–83.[2] Lack of comparable data, presumably due to difficulties encountered by the major data sources (the IMF and the World Bank) in developing consistent long-term real (constant price) aggregates, made longer-run estimates impossible.

Note that in table 14–1, P at the end of a symbol represents a real (constant) variable, while the absence of P depics a nominal (current price) variable. L at the end of a variable indicates that it is the previous year's value.

Table 14-1
Argentina: Macroeconomic Forecasting Model
(two-stage least squares estimates)

Equation				Statistics		
				r^2	F	DW
Estimated Equations						
(1)	Import price index	$(ZPI) =$	$0.88\ ZPIL + 3.32\ WINFIC + 3.41$ $\quad(12.30)\qquad\ (2.87)\qquad\qquad(0.68)$	0.939	78.28	2.27
(2)	Export price index	$(EPI) =$	$2.28\ WINFUS + 0.71\ ZPI + 38.17$ $\quad(2.75)\qquad\quad(7.98)\qquad(1.67)$	0.880	36.69	2.98
(3)	Exchange rate (pesos per $, end of year)	$(EXAE) =$	$3.87\ EXAEL + 0.0003\ GDPDFL - 0.15$ $\quad(9.89)\qquad\qquad(2.50)\qquad\qquad(-1.22)$	0.997	1685.71	2.60
(4)	Exchange rate (pesos per $, period average)	$(EX) =$	$2.91\ EXL + 0.0002\ GDPDFL - 0.09$ $\quad(5.35)\qquad\quad(2.24)\qquad\qquad(-1.15)$	0.994	858.87	1.70
(5)	Export volume index (1970 = 100)	$(EUV) =$	$0.14\ USYP - 219.05$ $\quad(8.75)\qquad\ (-5.4)$	0.876	76.73	2.14
(6)	Bank credit to private sector (billions of pesos)	$(BCPR) =$	$1.55\ BCPRL + 50473.7\ DUMW + 0.84\ BCPUB$ $\quad(22.82)\qquad\qquad(5.42)\qquad\qquad\quad(45.61)$ $\qquad\qquad + 1234.87$ $\qquad\qquad\quad(0.93)$	0.999	1724.1	2.37
(7)	Money supply (billions of pesos)	$(M1) =$	$0.80\ MIL + 0.26\ BCPUB + 18802.8\ DUMW$ $\quad(4.60)\qquad(24.77)\qquad\qquad(3.21)$ $\qquad\qquad + 1411.37$ $\qquad\qquad\quad(1.08)$	0.999	10634.0	2.78

Table 14-1 continued

Equation			r^2	Statistics F	DW
(8)	Rate of inflation (Consumer Price Index)	$(INFC) = \underset{(8.29)}{1.21\ GM1} \underset{(-0.34)}{-8.94}$	0.862	68.83	1.95
(9)	Rate of inflation (Wholesale Price Index)	$(INFW) = \underset{(6.29)}{1.26\ GM1} \underset{(-0.16)}{-5.76}$	0.782	39.62	2.66
(10)	Rate of inflation (GDP deflator)	$(INFG) = \underset{(7.01)}{1.10\ GM1} \underset{(-0.05)}{-1.51}$	0.817	49.25	2.61
(11)	Consumer Price Index (1974 = 100)	$(CPI) = \underset{(30.18)}{2.03\ M1} + \underset{(30.81)}{0.68\ BCPUB} + \underset{(1.30)}{1057.79}$	0.999	672510	2.29
(12)	Gross Domestic Product deflator (1980 = 1.0)	$(GDPDF) = \underset{(8.09)}{0.56\ GDPDFL} + \underset{(11.58)}{0.067\ M1} + \underset{(4.55)}{0.0066\ BCPUB} \underset{(-0.83)}{-21.32}$	0.999	260536	1.78
(13)	Wholesale Price Index (1960 = 100	$(WPI) = \underset{(7.04)}{62.69\ M1} + \underset{(4.91)}{18.69\ BCPUB} \underset{(-0.94)}{-131208}$	0.999	19368.8	1.78
(14)	Bank credit deflator (1970 = 1.0)	$(BCTDF) = \underset{(818.97)}{0.00158\ WPI} \underset{(-1.24)}{-56.29}$	0.999	670710	1.83
(15)	Government domestic debt (constant 1980 price)	$(GBDP) = \underset{(2.52)}{0.54\ GBDPL} + \underset{(2.72)}{0.037\ BCPUBP} \underset{(-0.57)}{-0.11}$	0.584	7.02	2.52
(16)	Central government tax revenue (constant 1980 prices)	$(TAXP) = \underset{(2.51)}{0.000151\ GDPNPL} + \underset{(2.61)}{0.116\ BCTP} + \underset{(1.71)}{1.94}$	0.698	11.56	2.33

(17)	Central government revenues (constant 1980 prices)	$(CGRP) = 79067.4\ TAXP + 611349$ $(5.51)\qquad\qquad(3.67)$	0.734	30.41	2.39
(18)	Central government expenditures (constant 1980 prices)	$(CGEP) = 0.57\ CGRPL + 0.72\ CGRP + 30296.7\ BCPUBP$ $(2.11)\qquad(2.70)\qquad\qquad(2.20)$ -466336 (-1.22)	0.819	13.56	2.12
(19)	Exports (BOP-FOB) (millions U.S. dollars)	$(BOPE) = 38.42\ EUV + 21.87\ EPI - 4492.25$ $(12.77)\qquad(11.68)\qquad(-12.31)$	0.987	392.55	2.75
(20)	Imports (BOP-FOB) (millions U.S. dollars)	$(BOPZ) = 0.44\ GBF + 85.97\ BCTP - 5546.98\ DUMW$ $(5.07)\qquad(2.79)\qquad\qquad(-4.93)$ -1960.36 (-2.47)	0.914	32.26	2.71
(21)	Imports (BOP-CIF) (millions U.S. dollars)	$(BOPZC) = 0.636\ GBF - 7952.27\ DUMW + 140.70\ BCPUB$ $(6.44)\qquad(-5.60)\qquad\qquad(2.39)$ -1482.46 (-1.34)	0.863	19.01	2.56
(22)	Services - net (BOP) (millions U.S. dollars)	$(BOPS) = -0.29\ GBF - 103.04\ BCPUB + 2225.64$ $(-9.32)\qquad(-2.23)\qquad\qquad(4.88)$	0.942	81.35	2.08
(23)	Capital account (BOP) (millions U.S. dollars)	$(BOPC) = 0.23\ GBF - 154.71\ BCPUBP + 719.02$ $(3.16)\qquad(-2.47)\qquad\qquad(0.69)$	0.502	5.05	2.77

Table 14-1 continued

Equation			r^2	Statistics F	DW
(24)	Gross foreign exchange reserves (millions U.S. dollars)	$(RES) = 0.88\ RESL + 0.92\ BOPC + 0.81\ BOPCA$ $\qquad\qquad\quad(10.46)\quad\ \ (7.91)\qquad\ \ (8.13)$ $\qquad\qquad\quad + 352.88$ $\qquad\qquad\qquad(1.70)$	0.979	144.18	2.17
(25)	Government consumption (national accounts, constant 1980 prices)	$(GCNP) = 0.18\ GBF + 0.0023\ CGRP + 9971.70\ DUMC$ $\qquad\qquad\quad\ (6.56)\qquad\ (4.03)\qquad\qquad(19.89)$ $\qquad\qquad\quad\ + 6332.72$ $\qquad\qquad\qquad\ (2.87)$	0.979	144.18	2.17
(26)	Government investment (national accounts, constant 1980 prices)	$(IGP) = 0.32\ GBF + 0.53\ BOPCA - 5182.4\ DUMW$ $\qquad\qquad(2.26)\qquad\ (2.36)\qquad\qquad(-3.51)$ $\qquad\qquad + 0.20\ GCNP$ $\qquad\qquad\quad\ (2.29)$	0.653	6.76	2.76
(27)	Private consumption (national accounts, constant 1980 prices)	$(PCNP) = 0.557\ GDPNPL - 0.76\ GCNP + 20767.5$ $\qquad\qquad\quad\ (4.01)\qquad\qquad(-2.80)\qquad\ \ (0.19)$	0.658	9.65	2.57
(28)	Exports (national accounts, constant 1980 prices)	$(EP) = 61.74\ EUV + 6.94\ EPI + 659.82\ DUMW$ $\qquad\quad\ (25.74)\qquad\ (5.08)\qquad\quad\ (3.33)$ $\qquad\quad\ + 1151.89$ $\qquad\qquad(4.17)$	0.995	588.61	2.79
(29)	Imports (national accounts, constant 1980 prices)	$(ZP) = 0.65\ GBF + 249.86\ BCPUBP - 9729.16\ DUMW$ $\qquad\quad(4.13)\qquad(2.56)\qquad\qquad(-4.31)$ $\qquad\quad + 2597.72$ $\qquad\qquad(1.48)$	0.756	9.34	1.60
(30)	Private investment (national accounts, constant 1980 prices)	$(IPP) = 0.13\ PCNP - 4648.96\ DUMW + 4061.14$ $\qquad\quad\ (2.03)\qquad\ (-4.91)\qquad\qquad(0.95)$	0.829	24.25	2.51

(31)	Military expenditures (constant 1974 prices)	$(MESICP) = 0.00006\ GDPNPL + 0.0193\ DUMPB$ $(2.93)\quad\quad\quad\quad (2.04)$ $+ 0.0519\ DUMZ - 0.11$ $(4.26)\quad\quad (-1.26)$	0.781	10.72 2.24
(32)	Share of debt service in central government expenditures (percentage)	$(CGSERE) = 0.0015\ GBF - 0.000012\ CGDEFP - 2.75$ $(6.69)\quad\quad\quad (-2.76)\quad\quad\quad (-2.21)$	0.959	118.70 1.98
(33)	Share of economic development in central government expenditures (percentage)	$(CGEDE) = 0.29\ CGSERE + 27.63$ $(-3.80)\quad\quad (23.74)$	0.577	15.13 2.60
(34)	Share of defense in central government expenditures (percentage)	$(CGDE) = -0.91\ GEY + 3.05\ DUMPB + 29.60$ $(-2.80)\quad\quad (2.73)\quad\quad\quad (6.52)$	0.459	4.24 2.94
(35)	Share of general administration in central government expenditures (percentage)	$(CGAE) = -0.19\ CGDE - 0.33\ GEY + 15.56$ $(-2.86)\quad\quad (-3.85)\quad\quad (5.85)$	0.612	7.91 2.09
(36)	Share of domestic security in central government expenditures (percentage)	$(GCDSE) = 0.13\ CGDE + 1.61\ YPOP - 2.92$ $(2.05)\quad\quad (2.63)\quad\quad (-0.86)$	0.487	4.76 2.50
(37)	Share of total social services in central government expenditures (percentage)	$(CGSTE) = -0.61\ CGSERE + 39.39$ $(-6.06)\quad\quad (25.24)$	0.770	36.82 2.21

Table 14-1 continued

Equation			r^2	Statistics F	DW
(38) Share of education in central government expenditures (percentage)	$(CGEE) =$	$-0.82\ CGDE\ -1.29\ GEY + 52.29$ $(-2.63)\quad (-5.02)\quad (6.62)$	0.733	13.73	1.69
(39) Share of health in central government expenditures (percentage)	$(CGHE) =$	$-0.11\ CGSERE\ -1.18\ DUMP + 7.39$ $(-5.58)\quad (-4.97)\quad (29.67)$	0.954	105.52	2.25
(40) Share of social security and welfare in central government expenditures (percentage)	$(CGSSE) =$	$-0.14\ CGSERE + .000005\ CGEP + .16$ $(-4.17)\quad (5.50)\quad (0.13)$	0.754	15.39	1.76
(41) Share of housing in central government expenditures (percentage)	$(CGHOE) =$	$-0.39\ CGDE\ -0.00007\ CGEP + 11.19$ $(-3.78)\quad (-2.31)\quad (4.96)$	0.644	9.05	1.89
(42) Share of other social expenditures in central government expenditures	$(CGOE) =$	$-0.91\ CGSERE + 0.11\ GEPOP\ -3.09$ $(-2.03)\quad (2.72)\quad (-1.29)$	0.425	3.69	2.51
(43) Net factor payments (National accounts, 1980 constant price)	$(NFPP) =$	$-0.23\ GBF\ -3744.64\ DUMW + 308.26$ $(-5.73)\quad (-5.93)\quad (4.71)$	0.873	15.92	2.63

Model Identities

(44) Total bank credit (nominal)	$(BCT) =$	$BCPR + BCPUB$
(45) Central government deficit	$(CGDEFP) =$	$CGRP - CGEP$
(46) Balance of payments current account	$(BOPCA) =$	$BOPE - BOPZC + BOPS$

The Future Demand for Military Expenditures · 285

(47)	Balance of payments trade balance	$(BOPTB) =$	$BOPE - BOPZ$
(48)	Change in reserves	$(BOPCR) =$	$BOPCA + BOPC$
(49)	Government expenditures (national accounts)	$(GENANP) =$	$IGP + GCNP$
(50)	Private expenditures (national accounts)	$(PENANP) =$	$PCNP + IPP$
(51)	Gross Domestic Product	$(GDPNP) =$	$PCNP + IPP + IGP + EP - ZP$
(52)	Gross National Product	$(GNPNP) =$	$GDPNP + NFPP$
(53)	Gross domestic savings	$(SNP) =$	$GNPNP - PCNP - GCNP$
(54)	Government expenditures per capita	$(GEPOP) =$	$CGEP/POP$
(55)	Per capita income	$(YPOP) =$	$GDPNP/POP$
(56)	Government expenditures per GDP	$(GEY) =$	$CGEP/GDPNP$
(57)	External gap	$(EGAP) =$	$EP - ZP + NFPP$

Dummy Variables

(58) DUMC 0, 1970–82; 1, 1983
(59) DUMW 0, 1970–81; 1, 1982–83
(60) DUMZ 0, 1970–81; 1, 1982–83
(61) DUMP 0, 1970–72; 1, 1973–76; 2, 1977–82
(62) DUMPB 1, 1970–72; 0, 1973–76; 2, 1977–82

Notes: WINFIC = price index industrial countries (1980 = 100.0); WINFUS = price index United States (1980 = 100.0); USTP = real United States gross national product; BCPUB = nominal central bank credit to public sector; GM1 = rate growth in M1 money; GBF = government nominal external debt; BCTP = total nominal central bank credit; POP = population; BOP = balance of payment accounts; FOB = price at factory gate; CIF = cost plus freight and insurance.

The model contains fifty-seven equations. Its major features include:

1. The first thirty equations depict the major financial and national account flows in the economy.
2. Equation 31 links military expenditures with the gross domestic product generated by the first part of the model, a political dummy variable reflecting regime change, and a final dummy variable depicting the Malvinas conflict.
3. Equations 32 through 42 depict the various central government budgetary items.
4. The model is closed with a series of fourteen national income account and balance of payments identities.
5. A series of dummy variables are included depicting:
   a. Increased public consumption ($DUMC$) in 1983;
   b. Austerity ($DUMZ$) in 1982 and 1983;
   c. Malvinas War ($DUMW$) in 1982 and 1983;
   d. Political variables reflecting shifts with regime change:
      i. The first political dummy ($DUMP$) assigns 0 to 1970–72 (the first military regime), 1 to 1973–75 (the Peronist regime), and 2 to 1976–82 (the second military regime). The second dummy variable weights the policy orientation of the regimes somewhat differently: 1=1970–72, 0=1973–75, and 2=1976–83.
      ii. The second variable was found to be highly significant in estimating the impact of regime change on military expenditures. Everything else being equal, the second military regime was most inclined to allocate funds to defense, followed by the first military regime, and finally the Peronists. As noted in a previous section, there was little difference in orientation between the first civilian regime (1960–65) and the first military regime (1966–72). Therefore the value assumed for 1970–72 by $DUMP$ or $DUMPB$ is also indicative of the orientation of the first civilian regime.
6. For reasons to be discussed, the policy variable chosen for the model was expansion of nominal bank credit to the government.

The first block of equations in table 14-1 links Argentina to the world economy with:

1. The import price index based on world inflation (*WINFIC*) assumed to remain at a 5.0 percent growth rate over the 1984–90 period (equation 1);
2. Export prices linked to import prices (equation 2);
3. Export volume determined by the expansion of the U.S. economy (*USYP*) set at 3.0 percent over the 1984–90 period (equation 5).

The financial equations are driven by nominal bank credit to the public sector:

1. Nominal bank credit to the private sector is adjusted in a Koyc distributed lag fashion to increases in nominal sector credit (*BCPUB*) (equation 6).
2. The money supply also expands in a Koyc distributed lag fashion to increases in nominal public sector credit (*BCPUB*) (equation 7).
3. The various rates of inflation are linked to the growth in money supply (equations 8, 9, and 10), while the price deflators ultimately adjust to increases in bank credit to the government (equations 11, 12, 13, and 14).

The government's fiscal operations are depicted in table 14–1 by:

1. Government domestic debt adjusting in a Koyc distributed lag fashion to injections of new bank credit (*BCPUBP*) (equation 15);[3]
2. Real central government tax revenue adjusting in a Koyc distributed lag fashion to increase in total real bank credit (*BCTP*) (equation 16);
3. Real central government revenues linked to real tax revenues (*TAXP*) (equation 17);
4. Total real central government expenditures as a function of past revenues (*CGRPL*), current revenues (*CGRP*), and real bank credit (*BCPUBP*) (equation 18);
5. The central government's deficit defined in equation 45 as the difference between its revenues and expenditures.
6. Various aspects of the country's balance of payments linked to the world economy through the nominal external debt (*GBF*), bank credit (*BDPUBP*) to the government, and total bank credit (*BCTP*) in equations 19 through 24.

288 · Argentina

The national accounts are aggregated to generate gross domestic product in equation 51 of table 14-1. The components of real gross domestic product are as follows:

1. Equation 25 shows government consumption to be determined by the nominal public external (dollar) debt (GBF) and real government revenues ($CGRP$).
2. Government investment is also a function of GBF, the current account in the balance of payments ($BOPCA$), and government consumption ($GCNP$) in equation 26. Government investment is therefore used to complement government consumption, but only to the extent facilitated by external debt and the flows of reserves generated by the external current account.
3. Private consumption expands with a lag to increases in overall GDP, but is crowded out by increased government consumption (equation 27). It appears that the government has in its debts operations preempted financial flows that would ordinarily be used to finance private consumption. This phenomenon undoubtedly accounts for the fact that real private consumption in 1983 was 80 percent of its 1974 figure, despite the fact that overall real gross domestic product was only slightly lower in 1983 than in 1974.
4. Exports (equation 28) expand with increases in their unit value (EUV), which in turn is linked to the U.S. economy (equation 5) and the export price index generated in equation 2.
5. Imports (equation 29) are linked to real bank credit to the government ($BCPUBP$) and the nominal (dollar) external debt (GBF). No distinction is made between imports of consumer goods and investment goods, but it is widely believed that a large proportion of the country's external debt was used to finance consumption, with few tangible assets financed by the debt available for aiding in debt servicing.
6. Private investment (equation 30) is assumed to respond to increased private sector consumption demand ($PNCP$) and the austerity dummy variable ($DUMW$). Private sector investment in 1983 was only 37 percent of its 1980 figure, with little chance of being revitalized unless consumer demand begins to show significant signs of revitalization.

Items 1 through 6 above, were summed to yield the real level of gross domestic product.

Real military expenditures ($MESICP$) (equation 31) are linked to the previous year's real gross domestic product ($GDPNPL$), a dummy variable depicting regime change (*DUMPB*), and a dummy variable depicting the Malvinas military build-up and replacement (*DUMZ*). As noted in the previous section, a clear statistical pattern exists between regime type and military expenditures with the second military regime more inclined to spend on military activities, followed by the regimes in the 1960s and finally the Peronists. These regime types are depicted by *DUMPB*.

The central government's budget allocations (equations 32 through 42 in table 14–1) are estimated as shares of the total government expenditure (equation 18):

1. As shown in equation 32, the share of debt service in the budget is a function of the government's nominal external debt (*GBF*) and the government's deficit *CGDEFP*.
2. Economic development is linked to debt services *CGSERE* (equation 33).
3. The military's share in the budget (equation 34) is linked—as in the analysis above—to the proportion of government expenditures to GDP and the political dummy variable *DUMPB* used to depict regime change.
4. The rest of the budgetary share analysis depicts trade-off situations with the military share of the budget (equations 35, 36, 38, and 41) or trade-offs with the share of the budget allocated to debt service (equations 37, 39, 40, and 42). The budgetary shares, therefore, depict the trade-offs found in a previous section characterizing the Argentinian budgetary process.

Since several functional areas (economic development, total social services, health, social security and welfare, and other social services) contract with increased debt service obligations, a political constraint could have been introduced into the model limiting the extent to which debt servicing (and, therefore, total nominal public sector debt) could expand without major public opposition. However, the Alfonsin government has given no clear indication as to the limits beyond which it is unwilling to cut basic social and economic expenditures in order to resume servicing the public external debt. Therefore, this constraint was not introduced into the model.

In sum, the model is designed to examine the country's growth prospects over the 1984–90 period. It is a policy-oriented model in that it is capable of examining the impact various government policy tools such as public sector consumption, investment, deficits, and credit from the banking system would have on various facets of the economy. In this sense, it is capable of depicting the trade-offs usually associated with macroeconomic policy-making and the most efficient policy package available to the authorities for resolving these trade-offs.

Policy Design

The policy design of the model is predicted on many of the ideas developed in the World Bank and Kiel reports.[4] They are also based conclusions reached by many observers that traditional orthodox monetarist and Keynesian policies are not implementable at the present time.[5]

The main policy assumptions are:

1. Inflation must be gradually reduced if the country is to be able to create some sort of stable environment conducive to expanded output.
2. Ultimately, inflation can only be controlled by reducing the increase in the money supply.
3. The government must gradually reduce its deficit to reduce inflation, but the deficit cannot be rendered too quickly without setting off a major recession.
4. External public debt will not be able to expand in real terms during the period under consideration.
5. External balance must be achieved and the external gap reduced to enable the country to service its foreign debt.
6. Given the present condition of industry, there can be no major expansion of industrial output.

It follows from these points that the private sector's consumption and investment must expand relative to the public sector's over the 1984–90 period in a manner not harmful to the balance of payments if the country is to have any hope of reducing inflation while at the same time avoiding a major recession due to lack of aggregate demand. What is suggested here, therefore, is a policy mix designed to gradually contract the government sector and expand private sector demand toward existing industrial capacity, capacity presently underutilized and incapable of finding export markets.

In terms of government policy tools, several possiblities exist for implementing this strategy:

1. The central government could control real investment and/or consumption.
2. Real credit from the banking system to the government could be controlled.
3. Nominal credit from the banking system to the government could be controlled.

Clearly, the problems encountered in the late 1970s through attempting to control inflation through preannounced devaluations rule out exchange rate policy as a viable anti-inflationary tool.[6]

In a country with inflation well over 100 percent per annum, the idea of targeting real variables such as government consumption, investment, or bank credit to the government makes little sense, simply because the real magnitudes of these variables will not be known until after the fact (once their inflationary impact has established their levels).

While, in principle, inflationary impact of government policy action might be forecast and these forecasts used to establish real targets, it remains a sad fact that economists simply lack the technical ability to produce precise forecasts (at least within 20 percent) in a hyperinflationary environment such as Argentina's. Yet forecasts of this type would be necessary to target either the level of real government expenditures or real bank credit to the public sector.

Here the problem is being able to predict the public's inflationary expectations and the manner and extent to which these expectations interact with socioeconomic variables to produce inflation. While one can deduce this information from historical data and show how the historical patterns were established, the instability that characterizes Argentina makes any estimate of future inflationary expectations a futile task.

This leaves nominal bank credit to the government as the only remaining policy tool. The optimal control model assumes that the central bank authorities in cooperation with the government will be able to gradually reduce the expansion in nominal credit downward over time. The IMF, of course, would be greatly supportive of this action.

It is implicitly assumed that the government undertakes various reforms in financial and exchange rate markets that include:

1. Maintaining exchange control with a basic rate of exchange that retains its real level, that is, that evolves in real terms according to domestic inflation less than international inflations;

2. Establishing the short-term passive bank interest rates at levels that are only slightly negative, while establishing the active rates at neutral levels;
3. Maintaining sufficient monetary efficiency to allow short-term active non-bank rates to establish themselves at a slightly higher positive level than that of the international market.

The Marcelo Diamond and Daniel Naszewski contend that the above reforms are politically acceptable and essential for any real economic recovery.[7] Although these reforms are not explicitly introduced into the forecasting model, they are implicit in the model's construction.

Forecasts of the Economy: 1984-90

With the estimated macroeconomic equations, policy guidelines, and policy tools already outlined, a series of forecasts of the Argentinian economy were run for the 1984–90 period. In each case, the constraint placed by the model on government policy is that the rate of inflation had to be reduced on a year-to-year basis.

The main forecast assumes that nominal bank credit to the government can and will be reduced in percentage increments over the period in question. The initial range set is:

1. 1984: 100 percent
2. 1985: 90 percent
3. 1986: 80 percent
4. 1987: 70 percent
5. 1988: 50 percent
6. 1989: 40 percent
7. 1990: 30 percent

These compare to the historical rates of 510 percent in 1983, 222 percent in 1982, 284 percent in 1981, 155 percent in 1980, and 148 percent in 1979.

The second assumption concerns the value of dummy variables over the forecast period. The forecast assumes the Radicals will remain in power. Therefore:

1. *DUMP* was set at 0 (reflecting a shift to the policy orientation of the 1960s), while *DUMPB* was set at 1 (also reflecting the policy orientation of the 1960s).

2. *DUMW* was set at 1 (indicating continuance of austerity).
3. *DUMZ* was set at 0 (reflecting a return to pre-Malvinas conditions).
4. *DUMC* was left at 1 (reflecting government consumption holding its relatively high 1983 level).

The third assumption was that nominal external public debt would be held constant at 1983 levels.

Table 14-2 presents the results of the forecasts with gross domestic product optimized, given the above credit and debt constraints. It indicates that:

1. Real GDP can grow without a recession, although only averaging 2.8 percent in real terms over the 1983–90 period.
2. Government expenditures expand at an average annual rate of 1.5 percent compared with a 2.7 percent average annual rate for the private sector.
3. While private sector investment in 1990 is still only slightly over one-half its 1980 level, it expands at an average annual rate of 5.5 percent.
4. Due to inflation eroding away the value of bank credit to the government, real bank credit to the government contracts at 5.8 percent per annum.
5. Both the current account of the balance of payments and the external gap in national accounts move from large deficits in 1983 to moderate surpluses in the late 1980s.
6. Real central government deficit is reduced considerably.
7. Military expenditures, on the assumption that the policy orientations of the civilian and military regimes of the 1960s will remain the same in the 1980s and that there will be no further Malvinas-type situations, fall sharply in 1984, but gradually expand so that by the end of 1987, they have regained their 1982 levels. In real terms, military expenditures are forecast to expand at 2.3 percent per annum, slightly below the overall expansion of the economy.

To determine in this policy context the impact of alternative rates of growth in nominal public sector external debt (in dollars), two runs were made. The first, shown in table 14-3, has nominal debt increasing at a 5 percent average annual rate (0 percent in real terms assuming world inflation at 5 percent). The second, shown in table 14-4, has nominal public sector external debt falling at an average annual rate of 5 percent per annum.

Table 14-2
Argentina: Macroeconomic Forecasts, Moderate Austerity Program I: Non-Peronist Regime, 1984-90
(millions of 1970 pesos)

Macro Variable	1983 Actual	Simulation Forecast							Average Annual Growth		1980 Actual
		1984	1985	1986	1987	1988	1989	1990	1980-90	1983-90	
Gross Domestic Product	101440	103250	105750	108600	111680	115110	119150	123130	1.0	2.8	111142
Government expenditures	33361	32993	33472	33969	34502	35159	36102	37015	5.1	1.5	22415
Consumption	23939	23708	23859	24041	24249	24524	24971	25480	7.1	0.9	9537
Investment	9422	9285	9614	9928	10253						
Private expenditures	63046	66132	67134	68547	70155	71852	73619	75718	-2.0	2.7	92317
Consumption	57453	59254	60144	61399	62826	64333	65903	67767	-1.3	2.4	77329
Investment	5593	6878	6990	7148	7328	7518	7716	7951	-6.1	5.2	14988
Government expenditures/private expenditures	0.529	0.499	0.499	0.496	0.492	0.489	0.490	0.489	7.2	-1.1	0.243
Bank credit											
Public[a]	38.0	41.8	46.5	51.8	57.9	66.9	83.5	102.2	10.2	15.2	38.8
Public[a]	16.4	14.4	13.7	13.3	12.9	12.2	11.2	10.8	-1.7	-5.8	12.8
Private	22.5	27.4	32.8	38.6	45.0	54.6	72.3	91.3	9.2	22.2	38.0
Current account balance of payments[b]	-2057	-2792	-2223	-1695	-1158	-537	236	806	—	—	-4767
Domestic savings	19900	12135	13595	15005	16450	18097	20120	21727	1.2	1.3	19242
Government domestic debt[c]	1.00	0.96	0.92	0.88	0.80	0.85	0.74	0.69	3.9	-5.2	0.47
External public debt[d]	20501	20501	20501	20501	20501	20501	20501	20501	5.1	0.0	12524
Government deficit/GDP	-5.3	-2.7	-1.8	-1.8	-1.7	1.7	-1.3	-1.4	-7.0	-17.3	-2.9
External GAP	-4013	-4028	-3009	-2071	-1131	-56	127	2242	—	—	-6201
Consumer inflation (%)	433	167	122	101	87	68	42	38	—	—	87.6
Military expenditures[e]	100.5	86.8	89.9	94.4	99.3	104.7	110.7	117.8	2.0	2.3	96.2

Notes: [a] Central bank credit in billions of 1980 pesos.
[b] Current account balance of payments in millions of U.S. dollars.
[c] Government domestic debt in millions of 1980 pesos.
[d] External public debt in millions of U.S. dollars.
[e] Military expenditures in millions of 1974 pesos.

Table 14-3
Argentina: Macroeconomic Forecasts, Moderate Austerity Program II: Non-Peronist Regime, 1984-90
(millions of 1970 pesos)

	1983				Simulation Forecast					Average Annual Growth		1980
Macro Variable	Actual	1984	1985	1986	1987	1988	1989	1990	1980-90	1983-93	Actual
Gross Domestic Product	101440	102540	103860	105170	106460	107890	109760	111410	0.1	1.3	111142
Government expenditures											
Consumption	33361	33047	33559	34076	34620	35382	36228	37140	5.2	1.5	22415
Investment	23939	23892	24217	24570	24949	25398	26025	26721	7.6	1.6	12878
	9422	9154	9342	9506	9607	9883	10203	10419	0.9	1.4	9537
Private expenditures											
Consumption	63046	65974	66386	66908	67407	67831	68192	68770	-2.9	1.2	92317
Investment	57453	59114	59479	59543	60386	60763	61084	61596	-2.2	1.0	77329
	5593	6861	6906	6965	7021	7068	7109	7173	-7.1	3.6	14988
Government expenditures/private expenditures	0.529	0.501	0.506	0.509	0.514	0.520	0.531	0.540	8.3	0.3	0.243
Bank credit											
Public[a]	38.0	41.8	46.5	51.8	57.9	66.9	83.5	102.2	10.2	15.2	38.8
Private	16.4	14.4	13.7	13.3	12.9	12.3	11.1	10.9	-1.6	-5.7	12.8
	22.5	27.4	32.8	38.6	45.0	54.6	72.3	91.3	9.2	22.2	38.0
Current account balance of payments[b]	-2571	-3742	-4173	-4693	-5257	-5791	-6232	-6936	-3.8	—	-4767
Domestic savings	19900	11150	11526	11764	11956	12276	12897	13026	-3.8	-5.9	19242
Government domestic debt[c]	1.00	0.97	0.92	0.88	0.85	0.80	0.73	0.69	3.9	-5.2	0.47
External public debt[d]	20501	21526	22602	23732	24919	26165	27474	28847	8.7	5.0	12524
Government deficit/GDP	-5.3	-2.7	-1.9	-1.8	-1.8	-1.7	-1.4	-1.5	-6.4	-16.5	-2.9
External GAP	-4013	-4864	-4723	-4707	-4735	-4676	-4414	-4566	03.0	-1.9	-6201
Consumer inflation (%)	433	167	122	102	87	68	42	38	—	—	87.6
Military expenditures[e]	100.5	86.8	88.8	91.0	93.3	95.6	98.1	101.4	0.5	0.1	96.2

Notes: [a]Central bank credit in billions of 1980 pesos.
[b]Current account balance of payments in millions of U.S. dollars.
[c]Government domestic debt in millions of 1980 pesos.
[d]External public debt in millions of U.S. dollars.
[e]Military expenditures in millions of 1974 pesos.

Table 14-4
Argentina: Macroeconomic Forecasts, Moderate Austerity Program III: Non-Peronist Regime, 1984-90
(millions of 1970 pesos)

Macro Variable	1983 Actual	Simulation Forecast							Average Annual Growth		1980 Actual
		1984	1985	1986	1987	1988	1989	1990	1980-90	1983-90	
Gross Domestic Product	101440	103950	107570	111770	116770	121240	126790	132240	1.8	3.9	111142
Government expenditures											
Consumption	33361	32939	33391	33876	34408	35010	36022	136945	5.1	1.5	22415
Investment	23939	23523	23518	23565	23653	23818	24164	24579	6.7	0.4	12878
	9422	9415	9872	10311	10755	11252	11858	12366	2.6	4.0	9537
Private expenditures											
Consumption	63046	66290	67867	70097	72653	75360	78158	81280	-1.3	3.7	92317
Investment	57453	59394	60795	62775	65045	67450	69934	72707	-0.6	3.4	77329
	5593	6895	7072	7322	7608	7911	8223	8573	-5.4	6.3	14988
Government expenditures/private expenditures	0.529	0.497	0.492	0.483	0.474	0.465	0.461	0.455	6.5	-2.1	0.243
Bank credit											
Public[a]	38.0	41.7	46.5	51.8	57.9	66.9	83.5	102.1	10.2	20.3	38.8
Private	16.4	14.4	13.7	13.3	12.9	12.3	11.1	10.0	-1.6	-5.7	12.8
	22.5	27.4	32.8	38.6	45.0	54.6	72.3	91.3	9.2	22.2	38.0
Current account balance of payments[b]	-2571	-1841	-3693	1018	2370	3766	5274	6544	—	—	-4767
Domestic savings	19900	13119	15566	17947	20333	22889	25785	28225	3.9	5.1	19242
Government domestic debt[c]	1.00	0.97	0.92	0.88	0.85	0.80	0.74	0.69	3.9	-5.2	0.47
External public debt[d]	20501	19476	18502	17577	16698	15863	15070	14317	1.3	-5.0	12524
Government deficit/GDP	-5.3	-2.7	-1.7	-1.6	-1.6	-1.5	-1.2	-1.3	-7.7	-18.2	-2.9
External GAP	-4013	-3192	-1378	3133	1971	3727	5703	7286	—	—	-6201
Consumer inflation (%)	433	167	122	102	87	68	42	38	—	—	87.6
Military expenditures[e]	100.5	86.8	91.2	97.5	104.9	112.8	121.5	131.2	3.2	3.9	96.2

Notes: [a] Central bank credit in billions of 1980 pesos.
[b] Current account balance of payments in millions of U.S. dollars.
[c] Government domestic debt in millions of 1980 pesos.
[d] External public debt in millions of U.S. dollars.
[e] Military expenditures in millions of 1974 pesos.

The results clearly indicate the benefits that would accrue to the country through successful efforts to reduce its external indebtedness:

1. The growth of GDP averages 1.3 percent from 1983 to 1990, with increased external debt, but rises to 3.9 present with reduced external indebtedness.
2. The main adverse effect of external public debt is felt in increased balance of payments deficits that are not offset by corresponding increases in government expenditures. That is, while increased external debt stimulates government expenditures, it simultaneously creates increased leakages out of the income stream into imports, with the net effect being deflationary.
3. The crowding-out effect on the private sector of increased public external indebtedness, together with the lower rate of GDP growth, would reduce private expenditures from a 3.7 percent average annual growth with external debt contracting to 1.2 percent, with external debt expanding at 5.0 percent per annum (table 14.3).

Clearly, real benefits to the economy in general and the private sector in particular are to be derived from efforts on the part of the public sector to constrain or reduce its external debt. Given the current economic situation in Argentina, however, there appears to be little hope that substantial progress will be made in this area. Holding the nominal external public debt at a constant level is probably the best the country could hope for.

Next, the effect of alternative stabilization programs on the economy in general and on military expenditures in particular was examined. The first simulation was a mild austerity program, with bank credit to the public sector set at a constant 100 percent per annum as shown in, table 14-5. The second was a severe austerity program with bank credit reduced at about twice the rate of the original moderate program in table 14-2. The results in tables 14-5 and 14-6 indicate that there are tangible benefits to be derived from austerity:

1. Real GDP increases from an average annual rate of growth of 0.8 percent to 1.3 percent with severe austerity.
2. Private consumption, however, increases only 0.1 percent per annum as a result of severe austerity.
3. Interestingly enough, the government (through severe control of credit to itself) is able, through reducing inflation, to gain a

Table 14-5
Argentina: Macroeconomic Forecasts, Mild Austerity Program I: Non-Peronist Regime, 1984-90
(millions of 1970 pesos)

Macro Variable	1983 Actual	Simulation Forecast							Average Annual Growth			1980 Actual
		1984	1985	1986	1987	1988	1989	1990	1980-90	1983-90	
Gross Domestic Product	101440	103250	105660	108290	110500	113880	117430	120490	0.8	2.5	111142
Government expenditures											
Consumption	33361	32999	33438	33861	34272	34677	35375	35136	4.8	1.0	22415
Investment	23939	23708	23847	23995	24135	24266	24519	24663	6.7	0.4	12878
	9422	9284	9590	9866	10136	10411	10856	11073	1.5	2.3	9537
Private expenditures	63046	66132	67144	68528	70062	71676	73238	75340	-2.0	2.6	92317
Consumption	57453	59294	60152	61382	62744	64178	65564	67431	-1.4	2.3	77329
Investment	5593	6878	6991	7146	7318	7499	7673	7908	-6.2	5.1	14988
Government expenditures/private expenditures	0.529	0.499	0.498	0.484	0.489	0.484	0.483	0.474	6.9	-1.6	0.243
Bank credit											
Public[a]	38.0	41.7	46.0	49.8	52.9	55.5	63.7	65.9	5.4	8.2	38.8
Private	16.4	14.4	13.9	13.7	13.7	13.6	12.6	13.2	0.3	-3.1	12.8
	22.5	27.4	32.1	36.1	39.3	41.9	51.2	52.7	3.3	12.9	38.0
Current account balance of payments[b]	-2571	-2792	-2263	-1796	-1335	-863	-114	243	—	—	-4767
Domestic savings	19900	12135	13505	14766	16014	17285	19194	20244	0.5	0.2	19242
Government domestic debt[c]	1.00	0.97	0.93	0.90	0.88	0.87	0.84	0.83	5.9	-2.6	0.47
External public debt[d]	20501	20501	20501	20501	20501	20501	20501	20501	5.1	0.0	12524
Government deficit/GDP	-5.3	-2.7	-1.8	-1.9	-1.9	-2.0	-1.6	-2.0	-3.6	-13.2	-2.9
External GAP	-4013	-4028	-3077	-2249	-1439	-624	665	1263	—	—	-6201
Consumer inflation (%)	433	167	130	120	116	115	75	96	—	—	87.6
Military expenditures[e]	100.5	86.8	90.0	94.2	98.8	103.6	108.6	114.2	1.8	1.9	96.2

Notes: [a]Central bank credit in billions of 1980 pesos.
[b]Current account balance of payments in millions of U.S. dollars.
[c]Government domestic debt in millions of 1980 pesos.
[d]External public debt in millions of U.S. dollars.
[e]Military expenditures in millions of 1974 pesos.

Table 14-6
Argentina: Macroeconomic Forecasts, Severe Austerity Program I: Non-Peronist Regime, 1984-90
(millions of 1970 pesos)

Macro Variable	1983 Actual	Simulation Forecast							Average Annual Growth			1980 Actual
		1984	1985	1986	1987	1988	1989	1990	1980-90	1983-90		
Gross Domestic Product	101440	103250	105850	108950	112490	116510	121400	126290	1.3	3.2		111142
Government expenditures	33361	32993	33509	34098	34815	35759	37262	38991	5.7	2.3		22415
Consumption	23939	23708	23871	24095	24406	24873	25721	26877	7.6	1.7		12878
Investment	9422	9284	9639	10002	10408	10886	11541	12113	2.4	3.7		9537
Private expenditures	63046	66132	67124	68564	70242	72060	73859	75933	-1.9	2.7		92317
Consumption	57453	59254	60135	61413	62904	64519	65564	66117	-1.3	1.7		77329
Investment	5593	6878	6989	7150	7338	7541	7743	2975	-6.1	5.2		14988
Government expenditures/private expenditures	0.529	0.499	0.499	0.497	0.496	0.496	0.505	0.513	7.8	-0.4		0.243
Bank credit												
Public[a]	38.0	41.7	4710	54.3	64.8	82.2	117.0	165.2	15.6	23.3		38.8
	16.4	14.4	13.5	12.8	12.0	10.8	9.1	8.6	-3.9	-8.8		12.8
Private	22.5	27.4	33.6	41.5	52.9	71.3	107.9	156.6	15.2	31.9		38.0
Current account balance of payments[b]	-2571	-2792	-2181	-1575	-922	-193	724	1366	—	—		-4767
Domestic savings	19900	12135	13693	15289	17024	18969	21407	23303	1.9	2.3		19242
Government domestic debt[c]	1.00	0.97	0.92	0.86	0.80	0.73	0.62	0.54	1.4	-8.4		0.47
External public debt[d]	20501	20501	20501	20501	20501	20501	20501	20501	5.1	0.0		12524
Government deficit/GDP	-5.3	-2.7	-1.7	-1.5	-1.4	-1.1	-0.6	-0.0	-16.1	-28.6		-2.9
External GAP	-4013	-4028	-2934	-1863	-722	541	2123	3215	—	—		-6201
Consumer inflation (%)	411	167	110	84	60	38	14	9	—	—		87.6
Military expenditures[e]	100.5	86.8	90.0	94.6	100.2	105.7	112.7	120.8	2.3	2.7		96.2

Notes:
[a]Central bank credit in billions of 1980 pesos.
[b]Current account balance of payments in millions of U.S. dollars.
[c]Government domestic debt in millions of 1980 pesos.
[d]External public debt in millions of U.S. dollars.
[e]Military expenditures in millions of 1974 pesos.

larger share of resources. With severe austerity, the public sector achieves a 2.3 percent average annual increase, compared with 1 percent with mild austerity.

4. Similarly, long-run military expenditures increase from an average annual growth of 1.8 percent with mild austerity to 2.3 percent under a severe austerity program.

Politically, however, the stimulating effect a severe austerity program might have on the economy might well not be worth the cost. As noted, the private sector would not have a marked improvement in standards of living to compensate for the possible short-run increase in unemployment a program of this type could generate.

A summary of the results is given in table 14-7.

In all, table 14-2's forecasts under moderate austerity with constant levels of nominal external debt are superior in terms of the policy goals outlined above, such as inflation reduction, private sector expansion, and balance of payments improvement. Furthermore, holding the level of nominal public external debt at its 1983 level (or thereabouts) should, with the balance of payments improvements generated by the policy mix assumed, be perfectly feasible.

The budgetary implications of the moderate austerity program with nominal external public debt held constant (table 14-8), increasing at 5 percent (table 14-9), and declining at 5 percent per annum (table 14-10) show the share of defense in the government's budget ranging from 11.5 percent with decreasing debt to 9.8 percent with increasing debt. Clearly (everything else being equal), increased external indebtedness will force down the defense sector's share of the overall budget. This reduction, however, cannot be considered very significant, particularly in light of the analysis previously indicating that defense expenditures (everything else being equal) were relatively insensitive to debt service obligations of the government.

For a basis of comparison as to what might happen to defense expenditures if a Peronist type of government assumed power in 1987 (arbitrarily chosen) forecasts were made using the various debt and austerity assumptions outlined above. The results in table 14-11 clearly show the reduction in defense expenditures that a political change of this nature might imply. Here, there is the assumption that the Peronists would advocate the populist programs that characterized them in the 1973-76 period.

Finally, the occurrence of a Malvinas situation was simulated under moderate austerity assumptions in table 14-12 to indicate the likely expansion in defense expenditures caused by external developments.

Table 14-7
Argentina: Macroeconomic Forecasts, Non-Peronist Regime, 1990 Values
(millions of 1970 pesos)

	Mild Austerity: External Public Debt Average Annual Growth			Moderate Austerity: External Public Debt Average Annual Growth			Severe Austerity: External Public Debt Average Annual Growth		
Macro Variable	5.0%	0.0%	-5.0%	5.0%	0.0%	-5.0%	5.0%	0.0%	-5.0%
Gross Domestic Product	108780	120490	129603	114102	123130	132240	114583	126290	135402
Government expenditures	35861	35861	35666	37140	37015	36945	39115	38990	27270
Consumption	25904	24663	23762	26721	25480	24579	28118	26877	25976
Investment	9957	11073	11904	10419	11535	12366	10997	12113	1294
Private expenditures	68392	75340	80902	68770	75718	81280	68985	75933	81495
Consumption	61261	67431	72371	61596	67767	72707	61787	67958	72898
Investment	7131	7908	8531	7173	7951	8573	7197	7975	8597
Government private expenditures	0.524	0.474	0.441	0.540	0.489	0.455	0.567	0.513	0.477
Bank credit									
Public[a]	65.9	65.9	65.9	102.2	102.1	102.1	165.2	165.2	165.2
Private	13.2	13.2	13.2	10.9	10.9	10.9	8.6	8.6	8.6
	52.7	52.7	52.7	91.3	91.3	91.3	156.6	156.6	156.6
Current account balance of payments[b]	-7499	243	5981	-6936	806	6544	-6377	1366	7103
Domestic savings	11543	20244	26742	13206	21727	28225	14601	23303	29801
Government domestic debt[c]	0.83	0.83	0.83	0.69	0.69	0.69	0.54	0.54	0.54
External public debt[d]	28847	20501	14317	28847	20501	14317	28847	20501	14317
Government deficit/GDP	-2.2	-2.0	-1.9	-1.5	-1.4	-1.3	-0.5	-0.5	-0.5
External gap	-5545	1263	6308	-4566	2242	7286	-3593	3215	8259
Consumer Inflation (%)	96	96	96	38	38	86	9	9	9
Military expenditures[e]	98.4	114.8	128.2	101.4	117.8	131.2	105.3	102.4	135.1

Notes: [a]Central bank credit in billions of 1970 pesos.
[b]Current account balance of payments in millions of U.S. dollars.
[c]Government domestic debt in millions of 1980 pesos.
[d]External public debt in millions of U.S. dollars.
[e]Military expenditures in millions of 1974 pesos.

Table 14-8
Argentina: Budgetary Forecasts, Moderate Austerity Model I, with Nominal External Public Debt Held Constant: Non-Peronist Regime, 1984-90
(percentages)

Budgetary Item	1983 Actual	Simulation Forecast							Average Annual Growth		1980 Actual
		1984	1985	1986	1987	1988	1989	1990	1980-90	1983-90	
Share of debt service	37.1	30.7	30.0	30.0	30.0	29.5	29.0	29.3	-3.3	6.0	16.3
Share of defense	14.2	13.0	13.6	13.4	13.1	12.7	12.0	10.8	-3.8	-4.0	19.0
Share of domestic security	4.2	4.4	4.5	4.6	4.6	4.6	4.7	4.6	1.3	-3.8	6.8
Share of general administration	4.4	7.0	7.1	7.1	7.0	7.0	6.9	6.7	6.2	0.5	6.4
Share of social services	17.4	23.7	24.3	24.3	24.3	24.3	24.5	24.4	4.9	-1.6	28.6
Share of education	7.6	9.8	10.6	10.1	9.5	8.6	7.4	5.3	-5.0	-8.9	13.4
Share of health	1.4	4.0	4.1	4.1	4.1	4.1	4.2	4.2	17.0	4.5	2.7
Share of housing	1.1	3.4	3.2	3.1	3.1	3.1	3.1	3.2	16.5	20.4	0.5
Share of social security	5.3	5.2	5.2	5.6	6.0	6.6	7.4	8.6	7.2	-0.6	9.1
Other	2.0	1.3	1.2	1.4	1.6	1.9	2.4	3.1	16.0	0.7	2.9
Share of economic development	20.5	18.3	18.2	17.6	17.2	16.5	16.1	15.5	-3.9	-2.6	20.2
Other	2.2	2.9	2.3	3.0	3.8	5.4	6.8	8.7	21.7	12.4	2.7
Total	(100.0)	(100.0)	(100.0)	(100.0)	(100.0)	(100.0)	(100.0)	(100.0)	—	—	(100.0)

Table 14-9
Argentina: Budgetary Forecasts, Moderate Austerity Model II, with Nominal External Public Debt Increasing 5 Percent per Annum: Non-Peronist Regime, 1984-90
(percentages)

Budgetary Item	1983 Actual	Simulation Forecast							Average Annual Growth		1980 Actual
		1984	1985	1986	1987	1988	1989	1990	1980-90	1983-90	
Share of debt service	37.1	32.2	32.7	34.3	36.1	37.8	39.3	41.5	1.6	9.8	16.3
Share of defense	14.2	12.9	13.3	13.0	12.6	12.1	11.2	9.8	-5.2	-6.4	19.0
Share of domestic security	4.2	4.4	4.4	4.3	4.3	4.2	4.1	3.9	-1.1	-5.4	6.8
Share of general administration	4.4	7.0	7.1	7.0	7.0	6.9	6.7	6.5	5.7	0.2	6.4
Share of social services	17.4	22.9	22.7	21.8	20.9	20.1	19.3	18.2	0.6	-4.4	28.6
Share of education	7.6	12.5	12.8	12.0	11.3	10.5	9.6	8.0	0.7	-5.0	13.4
Share of health	1.4	3.8	3.7	3.6	3.4	3.2	3.0	2.8	10.4	0.4	2.7
Share of housing	1.1	3.4	3.3	3.3	3.3	3.4	3.5	3.8	19.4	22.5	0.5
Share of social security	5.3	5.0	4.8	4.9	5.1	5.3	5.5	6.0	1.8	-4.1	9.1
Other	2.0	1.2	0.9	0.9	0.9	1.0	1.2	1.6	5.5	-5.8	2.9
Share of economic development	20.5	18.3	18.1	17.6	17.1	16.6	16.2	15.6	-3.8	-2.6	20.2
Other	2.2	2.3	1.7	2.0	2.0	2.3	3.2	4.5	10.8	5.2	2.7
Total	(100.0)	(100.0)	(100.0)	(100.0)	(100.0)	(100.0)	(100.0)	(100.0)	—	—	(100.0)

Table 14-10
Argentina: Budgetary Forecasts, Moderate Austerity Model III, with Nominal External Public Debt Declining 5 Percent per Annum: Non-Peronist Regime, 1984-90
(percentages)

Budgetary Item	1983 Actual	Simulation Forecast							Average Annual Growth		1980 Actual
		1984	1985	1986	1987	1988	1989	1990	1980-90	1983-90	
Share of debt service	3.71	29.2	26.6	25.1	23.9	22.6	21.1	20.2	-8.3	2.2	16.3
Share of defense	14.2	13.1	13.8	13.7	13.5	13.2	12.5	11.5	-3.0	-4.9	19.0
Share of domestic security	4.2	4.5	4.7	4.8	4.9	5.0	5.1	5.2	3.1	-2.6	6.8
Share of general administration	4.4	7.1	7.2	7.2	7.2	7.1	7.0	6.8	6.4	0.6	6.4
Share of social services	17.4	24.4	26.8	26.5	27.2	27.8	28.6	29.0	7.6	0.1	28.6
Share of education	7.6	10.0	12.0	10.7	10.2	9.4	8.3	6.3	-2.6	-7.3	13.4
Share of health	1.4	4.2	4.5	4.6	4.8	4.9	5.1	5.2	20.6	6.8	2.7
Share of housing	1.1	3.3	3.1	3.0	2.9	2.9	2.8	2.8	14.3	18.8	0.5
Share of social security	5.3	5.4	5.7	6.3	7.0	7.8	9.0	10.4	10.1	1.3	9.1
Other	2.0	1.5	1.5	1.9	2.3	2.8	3.4	4.3	11.6	4.0	2.9
Share of economic development	20.5	19.1	19.9	20.3	20.7	21.1	21.5	21.8	0.9	0.8	20.2
Other	2.2	2.6	1.0	2.4	2.6	3.2	4.2	5.5	14.0	7.4	2.7
Total	(100.0)	(100.0)	(100.0)	(100.0)	(100.0)	(100.0)	(100.0)	(100.0)	—	—	(100.0)

Table 14-11
Argentina: Forecast of Military Expenditures at Three Annual Growth Rates for External Debt, 1984-90
(millions of 1974 pesos)

	1984	1985	1986	1987	1988	1989	1990	1983-90	1980-90	1975-90	1970-90
Non-Peronist Regime											
Mild austerity											
External debt Growth											
5.0%	86.8	88.8	90.9	92.8	94.5	96.0	98.4	-0.3	0.2	4.0	1.9
0.0	86.8	90.0	94.2	98.8	103.6	108.6	114.8	1.9	1.8	5.1	2.7
-5.0	86.8	91.2	97.4	104.4	111.7	119.3	128.1	3.5	2.9	5.9	3.2
Moderate austerity											
External debt Growth											
5.0%	86.8	88.8	91.0	93.3	95.6	98.1	101.4	0.1	0.5	4.2	2.0
0.0	86.8	90.0	94.4	99.3	104.7	110.7	117.8	2.3	2.0	5.3	2.8
-5.0	86.8	91.2	97.5	104.9	112.8	121.4	131.2	3.9	3.2	6.0	3.4
Severe austerity											
External debt Growth											
5.0%	86.8	88.8	91.2	93.9	97.0	100.6	105.3	0.7	0.9	4.5	2.2
0.0	86.8	90.0	94.6	100.2	105.7	112.7	120.8	2.7	2.3	5.4	2.9
-5.0	86.8	91.2	97.7	105.5	114.3	123.9	135.1	4.3	3.5	6.2	3.5
Peronist Regime, 1987-90											
Mild austerity											
External debt Growth											
5.0%	86.8	88.8	90.9	73.5	75.2	76.6	79.1	-3.4	-1.9	2.5	0.8
0.0	86.8	90.0	94.2	79.5	84.3	89.3	95.5	-0.7	-0.1	3.8	1.7
-5.0	86.8	91.2	97.4	85.1	92.4	100.0	108.8	1.1	1.2	4.7	2.4
Moderate austerity											
External debt Growth											
5.0%	86.8	88.8	91.0	74.0	76.3	78.8	82.1	-2.8	-1.6	2.8	1.0
0.0	86.8	90.0	94.4	80.0	85.4	91.4	98.5	-0.3	0.2	4.0	1.9
-5.0	86.8	91.2	97.5	85.6	93.5	102.2	111.9	1.5	1.5	4.9	2.6
Severe austerity											
External debt Growth											
5.0%	86.8	88.8	91.2	74.7	77.7	81.3	86.0	-2.2	-1.1	3.1	1.2
0.0	86.8	90.0	94.5	80.7	86.9	93.9	102.4	0.3	0.6	4.3	2.1
-5.0	86.8	91.2	97.7	86.2	95.0	104.6	115.8	2.0	1.9	5.2	2.7

Average Annual Growth applies to the last four columns.

Table 14-12
Argentina: Forecast of Military Expenditures in Falklands Type Cases at Three Annual Growth Rates for External Debt, 1983-90
(millions of 1974 pesos)

	Actual	Forecast					
	1983	1984	1985	1986	1987	1988	1989	1990
Non-Peronist Regime								
Moderate austerity								
External debt Growth								
5.0%	100.5	86.8	88.8	91.0	93.3	147.5	150.0	156.6
0.0	100.5	86.8	90.0	94.4	99.3	156.6	162.6	169.7
−5.0	100.5	86.8	91.2	97.5	104.9	164.7	173.3	183.1
Peronist Regime, 1987-90								
Moderate austerity								
External debt Growth								
5.0%	100.5	86.8	88.8	90.9	73.5	127.1	128.6	131.0
0.0	100.5	86.8	90.0	94.2	79.5	136.2	141.2	147.4
−5.0	100.5	86.8	91.2	97.4	85.0	443.3	151.9	160.8

Conclusions

Forecasts under a wide range of alternative austerity and external debt assumptions indicate that Argentina has good prospects for pulling out of the current crisis. While it is impossible to predict the precise economic program the government will enact, it is possible to narrow down the scope of change available to the authorities.

The simulations indicated in table 14-2 that the government will most likely be able to generate a nonrecessionary 2.8 percent increase in real gross domestic product over this period, led by the private sector expanding at an average annual rate of 2.7 percent. This can occur in an environment of falling inflation, improving balance of payments, an increased share of income for the private sector, and falling government deficits.

The implications for defense expenditures are that after a sharp fall in 1984, military expenditures should increase steadily, reaching an annual growth rate of 2.3 percent per annum over the 1984-90 period.

Based on these assumptions, the share of defense in the government's budget should decline from 14.2 percent in 1983 to 10.8 percent by 1990. (See table 14-5.)

In summing up, the analysis presented in the first part of this book demonstrated the primary importance of economic variables in accounting for variations in military expenditures across diverging types of developing countries. The parts on Venezuela and Argentina confirmed that many of these variables operate over time in individual countries to set rough limits within which defense allocations are likely to fall. Political variables were then seen to narrow these limits to the extent that it was possible to make fairly realistic forecasts of future defense allocations.

However, whether the economically centered approach to defense expenditures developed in this study can be productively applied to assessing likely budgetary developments in other parts of the world remains to be seen. Considering that perceived external threats may be both more unstable and more important in Asia, Africa, and the Middle East, it may be the case that economic variables contribute only marginally to changes in defense allocations over time for many countries in these areas. Clearly it will take a number of detailed case studies of these countries before a general conclusion can be made about the validity of economic variables in accounting for Third World military expenditures.

Notes

1. R.P. smith, "The Demand for Military Expenditure in Argentina," *The Economic Journal* (December 1980), pp. 811-820.

2. Data for the model is from World Bank, *Argentina: Economic Memorandum, vol. 2, Statistical Appendix* (Washington, D.C.: International Bank for Reconstruction and Development 1985), and International Monetary Fund, *International Financial Statistics Yearbook* (1985).

3. Cf. P. Rao and R. Miller, *Applied Econometrics* (Belmont, Calif.: Wadsworth, 1971), chap. 7

4. World Bank, *Argentina: Economic Memorandum, Vol. I, The Main Report* (Washington, D.C.: International Bank for Reconstruction and Development, 1985); "The Real Kiel Plan for Argentina," *Latin America Regional Reports, Southern Cone* (August 2, 1985), p. 5.

5. In particular, M. Diamond and D. Naszewski; "Argentina's foreign Debt: Its Origin and Consequences" in M. Wionczek, ed., *Politics and Economics of External Debt Crisis: The Latin American Experience* (Boulder, Colorado: Westview, 1985) pp. 231-76.

6. Cf. David Felix, "On Financial Blowups and Authoritarian Regimes in Latin America," mimeo (St. Louis, Missouri: Department of Economics, Washington University, October 1983).

7. Diamond and Naszewski, *op. cit.*, p.267.

Bibliography

Ames, Barry and Ed Goff. "Education and Defense Expenditures in Latin America 1948-1968" In Craig Liske, ed., *Comparative Public Policy*, pp. 210-23. New York: Wiley, 1976.

Amsden, Alic H. "Kaldor's The Military and Development—A Comment". *World Development* (August 1977): 757.

Anderson, Martin. "Dateline Argentina: Hello, Democracy". *Foreign Policy* (Summer 1984): 154-172.

Arms Control and Disarmament Agency. *World Military Expenditures and Arms Transfers, 1972-82*. Washington, D.C.: ACDA 1984.

Ayers, Ron. "Arms Production as a Form of Import Substituting Industrialization: The Turkish Case". *World Development* (1983): 813-24.

Baloyra, E., "Oil Policies and Budgets in Venezuela, 1938-68". *Latin American Research Review* (Summer 1974): 28-72.

Baran, Paul and P. Sweezy. *Monopoly Capital*. New York: Monthly Review Press, 1966.

Behrman, Tere and James Hanson, eds. *Short Term Macroeconomic Policy in Latin America*. Cambridge, Mass.: Ballinger, 1979.

Benoit, Emilie. *Defense and Economic Growth in Developing Countries*. Lexington, Mass: D.C. Heath, 1973.

_____. "Growth and Defense in Developing Countries." *Economic Development and Cultural Change* (January 1978): 271-280.

Blejer, M. "Liberalization Policies in Southern Cone Countries." *The Journal of InterAmerican Studies* (November, 1983): 431-444.

Brown, C. "Latin America Arms: For War? The Experience of the Period 1971-80." *Inter-American Economic Affairs* (Summer 1983): 61-66.

Burt, R. *Defense Budgeting*. IISS Adelphi Paper, No. 112 (Winter 1974-75).

Caiden, Naomi and Aaron Wildavsky. *Planning and Budgeting in Poor Countries*. New York: John Wiley, 1974.

Caputo, David. "New Perspectives on the Public Policy Implications of Defense and Welfare Expenditures in Four Modern Democracies: 1950-1970." *Policy Sciences* (1975): 423-446;

Chenery, H. and P. Eckstein. "Development Alternatives for Latin America." *Economic Development Report No. 29* (Project in Quantitative Research in Economic Development, Harvard University, 1967).

Collier D. "Overview of the Bureaucratic-Authoritarian Model." In D. Collier, ed., *The New Authoritarians in Latin America*. pp. 19-32. Princeton, N.J.: Princeton University Press, 1979.

Cox, Robert. "Argentina: Souring on the Democratic Dream." *Harper's Magazine* (May 1985): 49-58.

Dabelko, David and James M. McCormick. "Opportunity Costs of Defense: Some Cross-National Evidence." *Journal of Peace Research* (April 1977): 145-54.

Diamond, M. and D. Naswewski. "Argentina's Foreign Debt: Its Origin and Consequences." In M. Wionczek, ed., *Politics and Economics of External Debt Crisis: The Latin American Experience*, pp. 231-276. Boulder: Westview Press, 1985.

Dickson, Thomas. "An Economic Output and Impact Analysis of Civilian and Military Regimes in Latin South America." *Development and Change* (July 1977): 325-346;

Eckstein, O. "Discussion." In D. Abshire and R. Allen, eds., *National Security: Political, Military and Economic Strategies in the Decades Ahead*. pp. 21-23. New York: Praeger, 1963.

Economist Intelligence Unit. *Quarterly Economic Review of Argentina* (various issues).

Evans, Michael K. *Macroeconomic Activity: Theory, Forecasting and Control*. New York: Harper and Row, 1969.

Felix, David. "On Financial Blowups and Authoritarian Regimes in Latin America." Mimeo, Department of Economics Washington University (October 1983).

Frederiksen, P.C. and R.E. Looney. "Defense Expenditures and Economic Growth in Developing Countries: Some Further Empirical Evidence." *Journal of Economic Development* (July 1982): 113-125.

——. "Defense Expenditures and Economic Growth in Developing Countries." *Armed Forces and Society* (Summer 1983): 633-645.

——. "Defense Expenditures and Economic Growth in Developing Countries: A Reply." *Armed Forces and Society* (Winter 1985): 298-301.

——. "Another Look at Defense Spending and Economic Growth in Developing Countries." *Defense Analysis* (September 1985) pp. 205-210.

Giannaros, D. and J. Lee. "Private Savings Behavior and Estimation of Structural Change: The Case of Korea." Paper presented at the 20th Atlantic Economic Conference, Washington, D.C., September 1985.

Gilpin, Robert. *War and Change in World Politics*. Cambridge: Cambridge University Press, 1981.

Goode, Richard. *Government Finance in Developing Countries*. Washington, D.C.: Brookings Institute, 1984.

Gouldner, A. *The Coming Crisis of Western Sociology*. New York: Basic Books, 1970.

Graham-Tooll, Andrew. "Argentina: The State of Transition 1983-1985." *Third World Quarterly* (July 1985): 573-593.

Hall, B. and R. Hall. *Time Series Processor, Version 3.5 User's Manual*. Stanford, Ca.: B. Hall and R. Hall, 1980.

Harkavy, Robert. *The Arms Trade and International Systems*. Cambridge, Mass: Ballinger, 1975.
Hayes, Margaret Daly. "Policy Consequences of Military Participation in Politics: An Analysis of Tradeoffs in Brazilian Federal Expenditures." In Craig Liske, ed., *Comparative Public Policy*, pp. 21-52. New York: Wiley, 1976.
Heare, Gertrude. *Trends in Latin American Military Expenditures, 1940-1970*. Washington, D.C.: Department of State, 1971.
Hicks, Norman and Anne Kubisch. "Cutting Government Expenditures in LDCs." *Finance and Development* (September 1984): 37-39.
Hirschman, Albert O. "The Political Economy of Import Substituting Industrialization in Latin America." *Quarterly Journal of Economics* (February, 1968): 1-32.
Hollenhorst, J. and G. Ault. "An Alternative Answer to: Who Pays for Defense?" *American Political Science Review* (September 1971): 760-763.
Inter American Development Bank. *Economic and Social Progress in Latin America*. Washington: InterAmerican Development Bank, annually.
International Monetary Fund. *Government Financial Statistics Yearbook* (various issues).
International Monterey Fund. *International Financial Statistics Yearbook* (various issues).
Jackman, R. "Politicians in Uniform: Military Governments and Social Change in the Third World." *American Political Science Review* (December 1976): 1078-97.
Jones, Randall. "A Model for Predicting Expropriation in Latin America Applied to Jamaica." *Colombia Journal of World Business* (Spring 1980): 74-80.
Kaldor, Mary. "The Military in Development." *World Development* (June 1976): 459-82.
Katz, J. ed. *Arms Production in Developing Countries*. Lexington, Mass: Lexington Books, 1984.
Klepak, H.A. *Continuity and Change in the Argentine Army Since the Falklands*. Weybridge, England: Ian Allan, Ltd., 1985.
Klett, C. James. *Applied Multivariate Analysis*. New York: McGraw-Hall, 1972.
Landau, Luis. "Saving Functions for Latin America." In H. Chenery, ed., *Studies in Development Planning*, pp. 299-321. Cambridge, Mass: Harvard University Press, 1971.
Latin America Regional Reports. *Southern Cone* (various issues).
Lim, David. "Another Look at Growth and Defense in Less Developed Countries." *Economic Development and Cultural Change* (January 1983): 377-384.
Looney, R.E. and P.C. Frederiksen. "The Impact of Public Enterprise on Economic Growth in Latin America: The Case of Defense Industries." Paper presented at the North American Economics and Finance Association Third International Meeting, Mexico City, June 26-27, 1985.

McGowan, Patrick J. and Charles W. Kegley, eds. *Threats, Weapons and Foreign Policy.* Sage International Yearbook of Foreign Policy Studies, Vol. 5. Beverly Hills, Cal.: Sage, 1980.

McKinlay, R.D. and A.S. Cohen. "A Comparative Analysis of the Political and Economic Performance of Military and Civilian Regimes." *Comparative Politics* (October 1975): 1–30.

──────. "The Economic Performance of Military Regimes: A Cross-National Aggregate Study." *British Journal of Political Science* (July 1976): 291–310.

──────. "Performance and Instability in Military and Non-Military Regime Systems." *American Political Science Review* (September 1976): 850–864.

Miller, Steven. "Arms and Third World: Indigenous Weapons Production." *PSIS Occasional Paper no. 3.*" University of Geneva Programme for Strategic and International Security Studies, December 1980.

Most, B. "Authoritarianism and Growth of the State in Latin America: An Assessment of Their Impacts on Argentina Public Policy, 1930–1970." *Comparative Political Studies* (July 1980): 123–144.

Neuman, Stephanie. "International Stratification of Third World Military Industries." *International Organization* (Winter 1984): 167–198.

Nordlinger, Eric. "Soldiers in Mufti: The Impact of Military Rule Upon Economic and Social Change in the Non-Western States." *American Political Science Review* (December 1970): 1131–1148.

O'Donnell, G. *Modernization and Bureaucratic-Authoritarianism: Studies in South American Politics, Politics of Modernization Series No. 9.* Berkeley, Calif.: Institute of International Studies, University of California Press, 1973.

──────. "Reflections on the Patterns of Change in the Bureaucratic-Authoritarian State." *Latin American Research Review* (1978): 3–38.

──────. "Reply to Remmer and Merkx." *Latin American Research Review* (no. 2, 1982): 41–50.

Peroff, Kathleen and Margaret Podolak-Warren. "Does Spending on Defense Cut Spending on Health? A Time Series Analysis of the U.S. Economy, 1929–74." *British Journal of Political Science* (January 1979): 21–39.

Philip, George. "The Fall of the Argentine Military." *Third World Quarterly* (July 1984): 624–639.

Pluta, Joseph. "The Performance of South American Civilian and Military Governments from a Socio-Economic Perspective." *Development and Change* (July 1979): 461–484.

Prindyck, J.R. and D. Rubinfeld. *Econometric Models and Economic Forecasts.* New York: McGraw Hill, 1976.

Pryor, F.L. *Public Expenditures in Communist and Capitalist Nations.* Homewood, Ill.: Richard D. Irwin, 1968.

Rao, P. and R. Miller. *Applied Econometrics.* Belmont, Cal.: Wadsworth, 1971.

Remmer, K. "Evaluating the Policy Impact of Military Regimes in Latin America." *Latin American Research Review* (No. 2, 1978): 39–54.

Remmer, K. and G. Merkx. "Bureaucratic Authoritarianism Revisited." *Latin American Research Review* (no. 2, 1982): 3–40.

Richards, Gorden. "The Rise and Decline of Military Authoritarism in Latin America: The Role of Stabilization Policy." *SAIS Review* (Summer-Fall 1985): 155–171.

Robinson, A. "The End of the Illusion in Latin America." *Euromoney* (September 1982): 341–47.

Russett, B.M. "Some Decisions in the Regression of Time Series Data." In J.F. Herndon, ed., *Mathematical Application in Political Science*, pp. 31–52. Charlottesville: University of Virginia Press, 1971.

———. *What Price Vigilance?* New Haven: Yale University Press, 1970.

SAS User's Guide: Statistics, 1982 Edition. Cary, N.C.: SAS Institute, 1982.

Schmitter, P. "Corporatism and Public Policy in Authoritarian Portugal." *Sage Professional Paper in Contemporary Sociology.* Beverly Hills, Cal. Sage, 1975.

Schmitter, P. ed. *Military Rule in Latin America: Function, Consequences and Perspectives.* pp. 58–116. Beverly Hills, Cal.: Sage, 1973.

———. "Foreign Military Assistance, National Military Spending and Military Rule in Latin America." In P. Schmitter, ed., *Military Rule in Latin America: Function, Consequences and Perspectives.* pp. 117–88. Beverly Hills, Cal.: Sage, 1973.

———. "Military Intervention, Political Competitiveness and Public Policy in Latin America, 1950–67." In M. Janowitz and J. van Doorn, eds., *On Military Intervention*, pp. 425–506. Rotterdam: Rotterdam Unversity Press, 1971.

Shibik, Martin and Paul Bracken. "Strategic Purpose and the International Economy." *Orbis* (Fall 1983): 567–589.

Smith, Ronald P. "Military Expenditure and Investment in OECD Countries, 1954–1973." *Journal of Comparative Economics* (March 1980): 19–32.

Smith, R.P. "The Demand for Military Expenditure in Argentina." *The Economic Journal* (December 1980): 811–820.

Stockholm International Peace Research Institute. *World Armaments and Disarmament SIPRI Yearbook.* Philadelphia: Taylor and Francis, various issues).

Tait, Alan and Peter S. Heller. *International Comparisons of Government Expenditure, Occasional Paper 10.* Washington, D.C.: International Monetary Fund, 1982.

Taylor, L. *Structuralist Macroeconomics: Applicable Models for the Third World.* New York: Basic Books, 1983.

Terhal, P. "Foreign Exchange Costs of the Indian Military, 1950–72." *Journal of Peace Research* (1982): 251–259.

Tuomi, H. and R. Vayrynen, eds. *Militarization and Arms Production*, pp. 163–192. New York: St. Martin's Press, 1983.

———. *Transnational Corporations, Armaments and Development.* New York: St. Martin's Press, 1982.

United Nations Secretary General. *Economic and Social Consequences of the Arms Race and Military Expenditure.* U.N. Document No. A/8469/Rev. 1, 1971.

Valentine, Cecilian M. *The Political, Economic and Labor Climate in Venezuela*. Philadelphia: The Wharton School, 1979.

Vener, J. "Budgetary Tradeoffs Between Education and Defense in Latin America; A Research Note." *Journal of Developing Areas* (October 1983): 77-92.

Weaver, Terry. "Assessing the Impact of Military Rule: Alternative Approaches." In P. Schmitter, ed., *Military Rule in Latin America*, pp. 58-116. Beverly Hills, Cal.: Sage, 1973.

Whynes, David K. *The Economics of Third World Military Expenditure*. London: Macmillan Press, 1979.

The World Bank. *Argentina: Economic Memorandum, Volume 2, Statistical Appendix*. Washington: IBRD, 1985.

_____ . *World Bank Program on Special Assistance to Member Countries* (Washington, D.C.: World Bank, 1984.

_____ . *Sub-Saharan Africa: Progress Report on Development Prospects and Programs*. Washington, D.C.: World Bank, 1983.

_____ . *IDA in Retrospect*. Washington, D.C.: World Bank, 1983.

_____ . *Focus on Poverty 1983*. Washington, D.C.: World Bank, 1983.

_____ . *World Development Report*. Washington, D.C.: World Bank, various issues.

Wulfetal, Herbert, et. al. *Transnational Arms Production Technology*. Hamburg: University of Hamburg Institut fur Friedensforschun un Sicherheitspolitik, 1980.

Index

AD (Democratic Action party), 119, 122
Administration, public. *See* Public administration expenditures, Argentinian
Agriculture's share in gross national product, domestic arms production and, 33
Aid, foreign, 58n.17
Alfonsin, R., 211-212, 214-215, 243
Algeria: arms production in, discriminant analysis of, 40; defense burden in, discriminant analysis of, 10; per capital military expenditures in, 23
Alliances to major power blocs, 99
Allocation policy analysis. *See* Budgetary trade-offs
Ames, B., 76-77, 98, 102n.26, 177n.1, 225, 245n.18, 249, 260n.8
Amsden, A.H., 53, 57n.9
Anderson, M., 217n.3
Argentina, 209-308; Alfonsin government, initial reforms of, 211-213; Alfonsin government, record of, 214-217; alliances to major power blocs, 99; arms production in, discriminant analysis of, 44; budgetary priorities, impact of increased external debt servicing on, 237-239, 261-276, 283, 289; budgetary priorities, impact of regime type on, 219, 222-223, 226-245, 266, 267; budgetary trade-offs in, 81, 83, 86, 97, 100, 247, 250-260, 283-284, 289; classifications of, 98; defense burden in, discriminant analysis of, 10; ideology and level of state economic intervention, 98; investment in, 281, 282, 288, 293-301; Malvinas War, cost of, 213-214; military rule in, consequences of, 247-260; per capita military expenditures in, 23

Argentina, military expenditures in: impact of external debt servicing on, 237-239, 262, 266-268, 272; impact of political change on level of (1961-81), 228-245; impact of recent developments on, 211-218; in macroeconomic forecasting model, 283, 288-289; oil price increases and, 142, 144; optimal control forecast of, 293-307
Armed forces: Argentinian, under Alfonsin government, 211-212; military expenditures and, in arms-producing vs. non-arms-producing countries, 61-63, 69; regime type and size of, 75
Arms production, domestic, 31-49; conditions associated with, 33, 35-46, 68; conditions associated with, in Latin American countries, 39-46; conditions associated with, in non-Latin American countries, 38-46; cost of, 51; countries included in study, 48n.8; defined, 48n.5; economies of scale and, 31, 32, 46; foreign exchange availability and, 46-47, 69-75; international movement for political-military autonomy and, 47-48; in Latin America, budgetary trade-offs and, 98-102; in Latin America, impact of growth of, 51-58, 101; linkage between defense and civilian sectors in, 51, 52; linkage of military expenditures to overall expenditures and, 59-70; methodology in analysis of, 32-35; socioeconomic variables and, 32-34; stages associated with, 46; as tool for economic stabilization, 52, 56, 101
Arms purchases, Argentinian, 213-214
Arms supplier, political influence of, 51

Ault, G., 72, 102n.5
Austerity: Argentinian military expenditures and, impact on optimal control forecasts of, 294–301; patterns of, 107–111; Venezuelan military expenditures and, 111–116
Authoritarianism, new forms in Latin America of, 220–222, 225, 259, 260
Autonomy, international movement for political-military, 47–48
Ayres, R., 46, 49n.11

Balance of payments: domestic arms production and, 32–34, 68; in macroeconomic forecasting model of Argentinian economy, 280–282, 287; per capita military expenditures and, 12, 20
Baloyra, E., 149n.5
Baran, P., 260n.2
Beagle Channel dispute, 215, 216
Behrman, T., 206n.2
Benoit, E., 4, 53, 57n.6, 58n.17, 73–74, 103n.12, 152, 177n.,3
Binding constraint on growth, 58n.18
Blejer, M., 244n.9
Bolivia: alliances to major power blocs, 99; arms production in, discriminant analysis of, 44; budgetary trade-offs in, 82, 83, 92, 100; classifications of, 98; defense burden in, discriminant analysis of, 10
Borrowing, public foreign: domestic arms production and, 33, 35–42; Venezuelan, historical patterns of military expenditures and, 130–140; Venezuelan, housing and community service expenditures and, 159, 162. See also Debt, external public
Borrowing, Venezuelan public domestic, 160, 162, 173, 175
Bracken, P., 49n.14
Brazil: alliances to major power blocs, 99; arms production in, discriminant analysis of, 44; budgetary trade-offs in, 76, 81, 83, 85, 100; classifications of, 98; defense burden in, discriminant analysis of, 10; military expenditures in, oil price increases and, 142, 144; military expenditures in, Venezuelan military expenditures' response to, 140–142; regime type and budgetary priorities of, 224–225
Brown, C., 149n.1
Budgetary priorities: external debt servicing in Argentina and, 237–239, 261–276, 283, 289; regime type and,

previous empirical examinations of, 222–226; regime type and, in Argentina, 219, 222–223, 226–245, 266, 267
Budgetary process in Latin America, 59–60
Budgetary trade-offs, 71–104; Argentinian, 81, 83, 86, 97, 100; Argentinian, in macroeconomic forecasting model, 283–284, 289; Argentinian, military rule and, 247, 250–260; of arms-producing vs. non-arms-producing countries, 98–102; austerity patterns and, 108–111; conceptual issues regarding, 151–154; empirical results of analysis of, 80–97, 100; literature on, 71–78; methodology of analysis of, 78–80; per capita income and, 80; regime type and, 74–77, 79, 247, 250–260; theory of, 247–249; in U.S., 72–73; Venezuelan, 80, 83, 84, 100, 151–177; Venezuelan, allocation categories, 153; Venezuelan, assessment of non-defense expenditures, 154–164; Venezuelan, budget analysis (1973–82), 156–163; Venezuelan, determinants of military expenditures, 164–166; Venezuelan, distributed lag impacts experienced by non-defense sectors, 166–176; Venezuelan, longer-term determinants of non-defense expenditures, 163–164; Venezuelan, optimal control forecast of, 179–207
Burdens, defense. See Defense burden, determinants of Third World
Bureaucratic authoritarian model, 220–221, 225, 259, 260
Burma: arms production in, 40; defense burden in, 10
Burt, R., 70n.1

CAB. See Current account balance
Caiden, N., 1152n.1
Cameroon: arms production in, 40; defense burden in, 10
Campo de Mayo, 216–217
Capital, domestic arms production and net inflow of external, 38–42
Caputo, D., 249, 260n.7
Car, arms production in, 40
CBCGP. See Central bank credit to government
Central African Republic, defense burden in, 10
Central bank credit to government: in Argentina, 279, 287; in Argentina, optimal control forecast of, 293–301;

real and nominal, as policy tool, 291; Venezuelan budgetary expenditures forecast (1983-90) and, 199-205; Venezuelan health expenditures and, 169, 170; Venezuelan military expenditures and, 130-140, 164-166

Central bank credit to private sector in Venezuela, 184, 192

Chad: arms production in, 40; defense burden in, 10

Chenery, H., 58n.18, 193, 207n.8

Chile: alliances to major power blocs, 99; arms production in, discriminant analysis of, 44; budgetary trade-offs in, 81, 83, 87, 100; classifications of, 98; defense burden in, discriminant analysis of, 10

Civilian regime, budgetary effect of, 74-77, 79, 222-226. *See also* Regime type

Cluster analysis, use of, 6

Cohen, A.S., 53, 57n.10, 223-224, 244n.12, 245n.15

Collier, D., 244n.3

Colombia: arms production in, 44; defense burden in, 10; military expenditures in, oil price increases and, 142, 143; military expenditures in, Venezuelan military expenditures in response to, 140-142; per capita military expenditures in, 23

Communications expenditures in Venezuela, 155

Community services expenditures: budgetary trade-offs and, 83-97; Venezuelan, 155, 159-160, 162, 173, 174; Venezuelan, in optimal control model, 185, 195

Compensatory fiscal policy, 67-68, 69

Constraints, Venezuelan economic, 179-182. *See also* Resource constraints, financial

Consumer price index estimates in optimal control model for Venezuela, 183, 188-189

Consumption, private: in macroeconomic forecasting model of Argentinian economy, 282, 288; Venezuelan, estimates in optimal control model of, 184, 192

Consumption, public: determinants of share in gross domestic product, 64-67; domestic arms production and, 33, 35-38; in macroeconomic forecasting model of Argentinian economy, 282, 288; military expenditures in arms-producing vs. non-arms-producing countries and, 61-63, 69; per capita military expenditures and, 12, 19, 20, 22, 23-27; as policy tool, 291; Venezuelan, education expenditures and, 161, 162-163; Venezuelan, estimates in optimal control mdel of, 183, 191-192; Venezuelan, military expenditures and, 112-113, 115, 130-140; Venezuelan, public services expenditures and, 156, 158; Venezuelan, social security expenditures and, 169, 171

COPEI (Social Christian party), 119, 122

Costa Rica: alliances to major power blocs, 99; arms production in, discriminant analysis of, 44; budgetary trade-offs in, 83, 93, 100; classifications of, 98; defense burden in, discriminant analysis of, 10

Cox, R., 102n.32

Credit. *See* Central bank credit to government

Current account balance: Argentinian, optimal control forecast of, 293-301; domestic arms production and, 35-45; domestic arms production in Latin American countries and, 39, 42, 43, 44-45; domestic arms production in non-Latin American countries and, 38-42; government deficit and, 19-23, 27; per capita military expenditures and 19, 22, 24, 27

Dabelko, D., 53, 57n.11

Debt as percent of GDP, external public: domestic arms production and, 33; per capita military expenditures and, 12, 15; as variable in analysis of Third World defense burden, 6-12

Debt servicing, impact on budgetary priorities in Argentina, 261-276; empirical testing of, 261-275; in macroeconomic forecasting model, 283, 289; military expenditures and, 237-239, 262, 266-268, 272; regime types and, 219, 222-223, 226-245; trend in levels of debt servicing, 267

Debt, external public: Argentinian, impact of alternative rates of growth in, 293-297; Argentinian, optimal control forecasts of budget with varying, 300, 303-306; domestic arms production and, 35-38; domestic arms production in Latin American countries and, 39, 42, 43, 44-45; domestic arms production in

Debt, external public *(continued)*
non–Latin American countries and, 42, 44; per capita military expenditures and, 12, 16–18, 19, 22, 23–27, 29; as variable in defense burden analysis, 6–12; variable for domestic arms production analysis, 32–34; Venezuelan, budgetary expenditures given expanding, 201, 202–203; Venezuelan, community services expenditures and, 173, 174; Venezuelan, estimates in optimal control model of, 183, 191; Venezuelan, health expenditures and, 169, 170; Venezuelan, military expenditures and, historical patterns, 130–140
Debt, public domestic, 280, 287
Defense burden, determinants of Third World, 3–30; economic growth, impact on, 4–5; factor and discriminant analysis of, 4–12; financial resource constraints and, 5–12; per capita military expenditures, analysis of, 12–27; on regional basis, 23–28, 29. *See also* Budgetary trade-offs; Military expenditures
Defense sector, reduction during economic austerity of, 108
Deficit, government: Argentinian, in macroeconomic forecasting model, 284, 287; Argentinian, optimal control forecast of, 293–301; current account balance and, 19–23, 27; financing of public consumption from, domestic arms production and, 64–67; per capita military expenditures and, 19, 24, 25; Venezuelan, central government investment and, 184, 192; Venezuelan, community services expenditures and, 173, 174; Venezuelan, historical patterns of military expenditures and, 130–140
del Rio, A.B., 206n.2
Democratic Action party of Venezuela, 119, 122
Developing countries. *See* Latin America; Third World; specific countries
Development. *See* Economic growth and development
Development programs, financial resource constraints and cuts in, 5
Deviation from trends in Venezuelan real military expenditures, determinants of, 142–148
DGP. *See* Debt, external public
Dickson, T., 76, 102n.22, 222, 244n.10, 292, 308n.5

Discriminant analysis: of domestic arms production, results of, 35–46; of Third World defense burdens, 10–12
Disinflation, 221
Domestic arms production. *See* Arms production, domestic
Domestic security expenditures, Argentinian: budgetary trade-offs and, 250–252, 254, 256, 259; external debt servicing and, impact on, 262, 266, 267, 269, 272; in macroeconomic forecasting model, 283, 287; optimal control forecasts of, with varying external public debt, 302–304
Dominican Republic: alliances to major power blocs, 99; arms production in, discriminant analysis of, 44; budgetary trade-offs in, 82, 83, 89, 100; classifications of, 98; defense burden in, discriminant analysis of, 10

Eckstein, O., 248, 260n.4
Eckstein, P., 58n.18, 193, 207n.8
ECNIA, 19, 22, 24
Econometric time series model for optimal control forecast, 182–188
Economic growth and development: Argentinian, external debt servicing and, 265, 267, 271, 275; Argentinian, impact on military expenditures of, 211–218; Argentinian, in macroeconomic forecasting model, 283, 289; Argentinian, military regime and, 251, 257–259; Argentinian, optimal control forecasts with varying external public debt, 302–304; binding constraint on, 58n.18; defense burden and, 4–5; domestic arms production and, 51–58, 101; foreign exchange constraint on, 55–56; regulation of, 52. *See also* Budgetary trade-offs
Economic policies of authoritarian regimes, similarity of, 222
Economic service expenditures: budgetary trade-offs and, 83–97; Venezuelan, 160, 162, 173, 175; Venezuelan, forecasts of, 201, 202
Economy of scale, domestic arms production and, 31, 32, 46
Ecuador: arms production in, 43, 44; budgetary trade-offs in, 81, 83, 88, 100; classifications of, 98; defense burden in, discriminant analysis of, 10; military expenditures of, 140–142, 143
Education expenditures: Argentinian, budgetary trade-offs with defense of,

251–258; Argentinian, forecasts with varying external public debt, 302–304; Argentinian, impact of external debt servicing on, 263–264, 267, 269–270, 273; Argentinian, in macroecnomic forecasting model, 284, budgetary trade-offs and, 83–97; military expenditures and, 75, 76–77, 78, 249; Venezuelan, 155, 161, 162–163, 166, 168; Venezuelan forecasts of, 201, 202; Venezuelan, in macroeconomic forecasting model, 185, 195

Egypt: arms production in, 40; defense burden in, 10

El Salvador: alliances to major power blocs, 99; arms production in, discriminant analysis of, 44; budgetary trade-offs in, 83, 96, 97, 100; classifications, 98; defense burden in, discriminant analysis of, 10

Elasticity of military expenditures in Venezuela, 131, 137–139

Emulation effect, 140–142

Ethiopia: arms production in, 40; defense burden in, 10

Evans, M.K., 207n.7

Exchange rate market, reforms in, 291–292

Expanding-sum game, 153–154

Expenditures. *See* Budgetary priorities; Budgetary trade-offs; specific types of expenditures

Export instability index, domestic arms production and, 33

Export price index, 279, 287

Export volume index, 279, 287

Exports: domestic arms production and, 33, 35–38, 39, 42–45; in macroeconomic forecasting model of Argentinian economy, 281, 282, 288; military expenditures and, 198–199; per capita military expenditures and, 12, 20; Venezuelan, estimates in optimal control model of, 183, 189–190

Fabricaciones Militares (Argentina), 216

Factor analysis of Third World defense burdens, 6–10; showing per capita military expenditures, 12–27

Falklands War, 142

Felix, D., 308n.6

Financial markets, reforms in, 291–292

Financial resource constraint. *See* Resource constraints, financial

Fiscal policy: compensatory, 67–68, 69; domestic arms production-economic growth relationship and, 55, 56; operations in macroeconomic forecasting model of Argentinian economy, 280–282, 287; regime type and, 76; Venezuelan, optimal control forecasts (1983–90) of, 199–205. *See also* Socioeconomic programs, defense budgetary trade-offs with

Fiscal variables for domestic arms production analysis, 32–34

Foreign aid, 58n.17

Foreign exchange: availability, domestic arms production and, 46–47, 69–75; constraint on economic growth, 55–56. *See also* Debt, external public; Reserves, gross international

Frederiksen, P.C., 4–5, 30nn.1, 2, 53, 57n.12, 58nn.13, 16, 102n.29, 104n.39

Friedman, M., 192

GCNP. *See* Consumption, public
GDB. *See* Deficit, government
GDEFP. *See* Deficit, government
GDP. *See* Gross domestic product (GDP)
Gendarmeria Nacional (Argentina), 216
GEP. *See* Government expenditures
GFBP. *See* Borrowing, public foreign
Ghana: arms production in, 40; defense burden in, 10
Giannaros, D., 245n.24
Gilpin, R., 49n.14
GNPPER. *See* Gross national product
Goff, E., 76–77, 98, 102n.26, 177n.1, 225, 245n.18, 249, 260n.8
Goode, R., 70n.3, 116n.2
Gouldner, A., 260n.3
Government consumption. *See* Consumption, public
Government expenditures: Argentinian, in macroeconomic forecasting model, 281, 287; Argentinian, optimal control forecast of, 293–301; Argentinian, as percent of gross domestic product, 232–243; arms production and linkage of military expenditures to overall, 59–70; in compensatory fiscal policy, 68; Venezuelan, economic services expenditures and, 160, 162; Venezuelan, in macroeconomic forecasting model, 183, 190–191; Venezuelan, military expenditures and, historical patterns, 130–140; Venezuelan,

Government expenditures *(continued)*
military expenditures as percent of, 118, 122, 124–125; Venezuelan, public services expenditures and, 156, 158; Venezuelan, social security and welfare expenditures and, 157, 158, 169, 171
Government Finance Statistics Yearbook (IMF), 78
Government participation in economy: spending pressures and, 64; as structural factor, 64–67. *See also* Arms production, domestic; Fiscal policy
Government, Finance and Expenditures (IMF), 153
Graham-Tooll, A., 217n.2
Greece: defense burden in, 10; per capita military expenditures in, 23
Gross domestic product (GDP): Argentinian, impact of increased public external debt on, 295–297; Argentinian, in macroeconomic forecasting model, 280, 282, 285, 288; Argentinian, optimal control forecast of, 293–301; domestic arms production and, 33; military expenditures and, 4; military expenditures and, in arms-producing vs. non-arms-producing countries, 61–63, 69; per capita military expenditures and, 24–26, 27; share of public consumption in, determinants of, 64–67; Venezuelan, education expenditures and, 161, 162–163; Venezuelan, historical patterns of military expenditures and, 130–140; Venezuelan, non-defense expenditures as ratios to, 155–163; Venezuelan, private consumption and, 192; Venezuelan, social security and welfare expenditures and, 157, 158, 169, 171
Gross international reserves. *See* Reserves, gross international
Gross national product: military budgets and performance of, 117–118; per capita, per capita military expenditures and, 19, 22, 23–27; as variable for domestic arms production analysis, 32–34
Growth, economic. *See* Economic growth and development
GRP. *See* Revenues, government
Guatemala: arms production in, 44; defense burden in, 10

Hall, B., 207n.3, 245n.23
Hall, R., 207n.3, 245n.23

Hanson, J., 206n.2
Harkavy, R., 48n.3
Hayes, M.D., 72, 76, 102n.2, 177n.1, 224, 245n.17
Health expenditures: Argentinian, budgetary trade-offs with, 251, 253, 254, 256, 258; Argentinian, impact of external debt servicing on, 264, 266, 267, 270, 274; Argentinian in macroeconomic forecasting model, 284; Argentinian, optimal control forecasts with varying external public debt, 302–304; budgetary trade-offs and, 83–97; Venezuelan, 155, 157, 158, 169, 170; Venezuelan, forecasts of, 201, 202; Venezuelan, in macroeconomic forecasting model, 185, 195
Heare, G.E., 117–118, 149, 149n.4
Hegemonic power, indigenous arms production and disintegration of, 47
Heller, P.S., 154, 177n.8
Hicks, N., 116n.8
Hirschman, A.O., 57n.2
Hollenhorst, J., 72, 102n.5
Honduras: arms production in, 44; defense burden in, 10
Housing expenditures: Argentinian, budgetary trade-offs with, 251, 253, 255, 258, 259; Argentinian, impact of external debt servicing on, 264, 266, 270, 274–275; Argentinian, in macroeconomic forecasting model, 284; Argentinian, optimal control forecasts with varying external public debt, 302–304; budgetary trade-offs and, 83–97; Venezuelan, 155, 159–160, 162, 169, 172

Identities in optimal control model of Venezuelan economy, 185–186, 195–196
Import price index, 279, 287
Imports: Argentinian, in macroeconomic forecasting model, 281, 282, 288; substitution policies, 43; Venezuelan, estimates in optimal control model of, 184, 193
Imports, growth in: domestic arms production and, 33, 39, 42–45; as variable in discriminant analysis of Third World defense burden, 7–12
Income of country, budgetary reduction during austerity and, 109–111. *See also* Per capita income
"Income shift," military expenditures and, 4

Index · 321

India: arms production in, discriminant analysis of, 40; defense burden in, discriminant analysis of, 10; military claim on foreign exchange in, 49n.11; per capita military expenditures in, 23
Indigenous arms production. *See* Arms production, domestic
Indonesia: arms production in, 40; defense burden in, 10; per capita military expenditures in, 23
Inflation: in Argentina, 280, 287; domestic arms production and control of, 52; policy design in optimal control forecasting, 290-291; in Venezuela, 181, 183, 188-189, 198-199, 202, 205
Instability, causes of cyclical or short-term economic, 67
Inter American Development Bank, 206n.1
International Monetary Fund, 78, 153, 182, 217, 291
Investment, government: as policy tool, 291; Venezuelan, estimates in optimal control model of, 184, 192
Investment, private: Argentinian, 281, 282, 288, 293-301; Venezuelan, 184, 193
Israel: arms production in, 40; defense burden in, 10
Ivory Coast: arms production in, 40; defense burden in, 10

Jackman, R., 223, 245n.14
Jamaica: arms production in, 44: defense burden in, 10
Jones, R., 49n.10
Jordan: arms production in, 41; defense burden in, 10; per capita military expenditures in, 23

Kaldor, M., 53, 57n.8
Katz, J., 48n.1, 57n.3
Kegley, C.W., 48n.3
Kenya: arms production in, 41; defense burden in, 10
Klepak, H.A., 218n.17
Korea: arms production in, 40; defense burden in, 10; per capita military expenditures in, 23
Kubisch, A., 116n.8
Kuwait: defense burden in, 10; per capita military expenditures in, 23

Latin America: alternative classifications of countries in, 98, 99-100; authoritarianism in, new forms of, 220-222, 225, 259, 260; budgetary process in, 59-60; domestic arms production in, determinants of, 39-46; domestic arms production in, budgetary trade-offs and, 98-102; domestic arms production in, impact on growth of, 51-58, 101; economic climates of 1970s and 1980s, 59; economic variables affecting per capita military expenditures in, 23-27, 29; military expenditures in, determinants of, 61-63; military expenditures in, impact on Venezuelan military expenditures, 140-144; regime types and budgetary priorities in, 222-226. *See also* specific countries
Least squares regression in optimal control forecast model, 182
Lee, J., 245n.24
Liberia, defense burden in, 10
Libya: arms production in, 40; defense burden in, 10
Lim, D., 53, 58n.14, 104n.41
Loans/exports, defense burden and gross inflow of public, 6-12. *See also* Debt, external public
Longitudinal analysis of budgetary trade-offs, 75, 78
Looney, R.E., 4-5, 30nn.1, 2, 53, 57n.12, 58nn.13, 16, 102n.29, 104n.39
Lusinchi government of Venezuela, 179, 197, 206

Macroeconomic forecasting model: of Argentinian economy, 278-290; uses in forecasting, 196-197; for Venezuelan economy, 182-188
Madagascar, arms production in, 40
Malawi: arms production in, 40; defense burden in, 10
Malaysia: arms production in, 40; defense burden in, 10; per capita military expenditures in, 23
Mali, defense burden in, 10
Malvinas War, cost of, 213-214
Manufacturing, domestic arms production and share in GDP of, 33
Mauritania: arms production in, 40; defense burden in, 10
McCormick, J.M., 53, 57n.11
McGowan, P.J., 48n.3
McKinlay, R.D., 53, 57n.10, 223-224, 244n.12, 245n.15
Merkx, G., 244n.2
Mexico: alliances to major power blocs, 99; arms production in, 43, 44;

Mexico *(continued)*
  budgetary trade-offs in, 82, 83, 90, 100; classifications of, 98; defense burden in, discriminant analysis of, 10; military expenditures in, 140-142, 144; per capita military expenditures in, 23
Military authoritarianism, 221
Military capabilities, domestic arms production and, 46
Military expenditures: budgetary process in Latin America and, 59-60; determinants in Latin America of, 61-63; domestic arms production and, 32-38, 39, 59-70; economic growth and, 53-57; education expenditures and, 75, 76-77, 78, 249; exports and, 198-199; "income shift" and, 4; linkage with government expenditures and external debt, 60-67; performance of gross national product and, 117-118; share in total budget, per capita military expenditures and, 23-27; as tool in economic stabilization, 67-69. *See also* Budgetary trade-offs; Defense burden, determinants of Third World; Per capita military expenditures; specific countries
Military regimes: budgetary priorities of civilian regimes vs., 222-226; budgetary trade-offs in, 74-77, 79, 247, 250-260
Miller, R., 149n.6, 308n.3
Miller, S., 49n.15, 57n.1
Models. *See* Macroeconomic forecasting model
Money supply in macroeconomic forecasting model of Argentinian economy, 279, 287
Morocco: arms production in, 40; defense burden in, 10
Most, B., 222-223, 244n.5
Multiple discriminant function analysis (MDA) of domestic arms production, 34-35

Naszewski, D., 292, 308n.5
"Neoclassical" Model of defense, 194
Net capita inflows, per capita military expenditures and, 19, 22, 24
Neuman, S., 31, 47, 48nn.2, 5
Nicaragua, arms production in, 44
Nigeria: arms production in, 40; defense burden in, 10
Nordlinger, E., 74, 102n.14

O'Donnell, G., 219-222, 244nn.2, 259
Oil price increases, impact in Venezuela of, 118-140; on development policy, 181-182; historic defense-macroeconomic patterns and, 130-140; on military expenditures, 142, 143-144; on military expenditures, trends in, 118-129
Oil revenues, Venezuelan: as chief source of income, 107; estimating export earnings from, 189-190; non-defense expenditures and, 163
Optimal control forecasts of military expenditures in Argentina, 277-308; for 1984-90, 292-307; macroeconomic model for, 278-290; methodology of, 277-278; policy design in, 290-292
Optimal control forecasts of Venezuelan budgetary expenditures, 179-207; economic priorities and constraints and, 179-182; final forecasts (1983-90), 199-205; identities in, 185-186, 195-196; macroeconomic model for, 182-188; preliminary simulations of, 198-199; structural equation estimates in, 188-196; uses of model in forecasting, 196-197
Orinoco Heavy Oil Belt, 189

Pakistan: arms production in, 40; defense burden in, 10
Panama: arms production in, 44; defense burden in, 10
Paraguay: arms production in, discriminant analysis of, 44; budgetary trade-offs in, 82, 83, 93, 100; classifications of, 98
PCB. *See* Consumption, public
PDB. *See* Debt, external public
Peleg, I., 48n.3
Per capita income: budgetary trade-offs and, 80; domestic arms production and, 46; per capita military expenditures and, 27-29
Per capita military expenditures: analysis of determinants of, 12-29; domestic arms production and, 33; in Latin American countries, 23-27, 29; in non-Latin American countries, 27, 28; per capita income and, 27-29
Performance variables in domestic arms production analysis, 32-34
Peroff, K., 71, 78, 79, 102n.1
Peronist regime, 226-228, 230, 235
Peru: alliances to major power blocs, 99; arms production in, discriminant

analysis of, 44; budgetary trade-offs in, 82, 83, 91, 100; classifications of, 98; defense burden in, discriminant analysis of, 10; military expenditures in, 140-142, 143
Philip, G., 217n.1
Philippines: arms production in, discriminant analysis of, 40; defense burden in, discriminant analysis of, 10; per capita military expenditures in, 23
Planning, budgeting process and military, 60
Pluta, J., 75, 102n.15
Podolak-Warren, M., 71, 78, 79, 102n.1
Policy design in optimal control forecasting, 290-292
Political influence of arms supplier, 51
Population size, domestic arms production and, 33, 61-63
Prefectura Nacional Maritima (Argentina), 215-216
Prindyck, J.R., 207n.3
Priorities, Venezuelan economic, 179-182. See also Budgetary priorities
Private consumption. See Consumption, private
Pryor, F.L., 73, 103n.9, 152, 177n.3, 248, 260n.5
Public administration expenditures, Argentinian: budgetary trade-offs with defense of, 250-252, 254, 258; impact of external debt servicing on, 262, 266-268, 272; in macroeconomic forecasting model, 283, 287; optimal control forecasts of, with varying external public debt, 302-304
Public consumption. See Consumption, public
Public domestic debt, 280, 287
Public external debt. See Debt, external public
Public services expenditures: budgetary trade-offs and, 83-97; Venezuelan, 156-157, 158, 166, 167; Venezuelan, forecasts of, 201, 202; Venezuelan, in macroeconomic forecasting model, 185, 195

Rao, P., 149n.6, 308n.3
"Rational" model of defense, 194
Reforms: of Alfonsin government, initial, 211-213; in financial and exchange rate markets, 291-292

Regime changes in Venezuela, military expenditure trends and, 119-129
Regime type: budgetary priorities and, in Argentina, 219, 222-223, 226-245, 266, 267; budgetary priorities and, previous empirical examinations of, 222-226; budgetary trade-offs and, 74-77, 79, 247-260; budgetary trade-offs and, in Argentina, 247, 250-260; changes in, effect of, 259, 266, 267; civilian, 74-77, 79, 222-226; O'Donnell thesis on transition to new forms of authoritarianism, 219-222
Remmer, K., 244n.2, 245n.19
Research and development, budgetary trade-offs in, 248
Reserves: Third World domestic arms production and need for, 46-47
Reserves, gross international: domestic arms production and, 33, 35-38; domestic arms production and, in Latin American countries and, 39, 42, 43, 44-45; domestic arms production and, in non-Latin American countries and, 38-42; as variable in analysis of Third World defense burden, 6-12
Resource balance, domestic arms production and, 33
Resource constraints, financial: binding external and internal, 58n.18; measures of, 6; military expenditures-economic growth relationship and, 5-12, 53-57
Resources, allocation of. See Budgetary trade-offs
Revenues, government: as control variable in analysis of Argentinian budget priorities, 228, 229, 231, 233; in macroeconomic forecasting model of Argentinian economy, 281, 287; regime type and propensity to spend out of, 230-232, 233, 243; Venezuelan military expenditures and, 130-140, 164, 165; Venezuelan military expenditures and, linkages over time between changes in, 142-148; Venezuelan military expenditures as percent of, 112-113, 115, 118, 120-121, 122, 123; Venezuelan public services expenditures and, 156, 158; Venezuelan social security and welfare expenditures and, 157-162, 169, 171; Venezuelan, central government investment and, 184, 192; Venezuelan, estimates in optimal control

Revenues, government *(continued)*
  model of, 183, 190. *See also* Oil
  revenues, Venezuelan; Tax revenues
Richards, G., 244*n*.8
Robinson, A., 207*n*.6
Ruandu, arms production in, 40
Rubinfeld, D., 207*n*.3
Russett, B.M., 72, 73, 77, 102*n*.4, 153, 177*n*.6
Rwanda: discriminant analysis of defense burden in, 10; per capita military expenditures in, 23

Saudi Arabia: arms production in, discriminant analysis of, 41; defense burden in, discriminant analysis of, 10; per capita military expenditures in, 23
Savings variables for domestic arms production analysis, 32–34
Schmitter, P.C., 74–75, 97, 102*n*.14, 104*n*.35, 117, 149, 149*n*.3, 223, 224, 245*nn*.13, 16
Security, domestic. *See* Domestic security expenditures, Argentinian
Shibik, M., 49*n*.14
Sierra Leone: arms production in, 40; defense burden in, 10
Simulations of Venezuelan economy, preliminary optimal control, 198–199
Singapore, arms production in, 40
Size variables in domestic arms production analysis, 32–34, 46
Smith, R.P., 73, 102*n*.8, 207*n*.9, 308*n*.1
Social Christian party of Venezuela, 119, 122
Social sectors, vulnerability in economic austerity, 108–109
Social security and welfare expenditures: Argentinian, budgetary trade-offs with defense of, 251, 253, 254, 257, 258; Argentinian, impact of external debt servicing on, 264, 266, 267, 270, 274; Argentinian, in macroeconomic forecasting model, 284; Argentinian, optimal control forecasts with varying external public debt, 302–304; budgetary trade-offs and, 83–97; Venezuelan, 157–162, 169, 171; Venezuelan, forecasts of, 201, 202; Venezuelan, in macroeconomic forecasting model, 184, 195
Social services expenditures, Argentinian: budgetary trade-offs with defense of, 250–252, 254, 256, 259; impact of external debt servicing on, 263, 266, 267, 269, 273; in macroeconomic forecasting model, 283, 287; optimal control forecasts with varying external public debt, 302–304
Social services expenditures, Venezuelan, 173, 174
Socioeconomic programs, defense budgetary trade-offs with, 71–104; of arms-producing vs. non-arms-producing countries, 98–102; empirical results of analysis, 80–97; literature on, 71–78; in macroeconomic forecasting model of Venezuela, 184–185, 194–195, 201, 202; methodology of analysis of, 78–80; regime type and, 74–76, 79; in U.S., 72–73. *See also* specific types of expenditures
Socioeconomic variables affecting domestic arms production, 32–34
Somalia: arms production in, 40; defense burden in, 10
South Yemen, arms production in, 41
Spain: defense burden in, 10; per capita military expenditures in, 23
Sri Lanka, defense burden in, 10
Stability, economic: domestic arms production and, 52, 56, 101; military expenditures as tool for, 67–69. *See also* Economic growth and development
Stockholm International Peace Research Institute, 78
Substitution effects, 73, 152, 248–249. *See also* Budgetary trade-offs
Substitution policies, 43
Sudan: arms production in, 40; defense burden in, 10
Super powers, traditional ties for military support with, 47–48
Sweezy, P., 260*n*.2
Syria: arms production in, discriminant analysis of, 41; defense burden in, discriminant analysis of, 10; per capita military expenditures in, 23

Tait, A., 154, 177*n*.8
Tanzania: arms production in, 40; defense burden in, 10
Tax revenues: compensatory fiscal policy and, 68; financing of public consumption from, domestic arms production and, 64–67; in macroeconomic forecasting model of Argentinian economy, 280, 287. *See also* Revenues, government
Taylor, L., 58*n*.17
Terhal, P., 49*n*.11

Thailand: arms production in, discriminant analysis of, 40; defense burden in, discriminant analysis of, 10; per capita military expenditures in, 23

Third World: arms production, economic environments conducive to indigenous, 31–49; international movement for political-military autonomy in, 47–48. *See also* Defense burden, determinants of Third World; specific countries

Threat to socioeconomic order, bureaucratic authoritarianism and, 221, 243

Time series analysis: of budgetary trade-offs, 73, 76, 78–80; of Venezuelan military expenditures as percent of government revenues, 120–121, 122

Togo, arms production in, 40

Trade-offs, budgetary. *See* Budgetary trade-offs

Transportation expenditures in Venezuela, 155

Trend analysis of Venezuelan military expenditures: as percent of government expenditures, 122, 124–125; residuals, 123, 128–129; trend-structural analysis (1950–83), 126–127

Trinidad: arms production in, 44; defense burden in, 10

Tunisia: arms production in, 40; defense burden in, 10

Tuomi, H., 48n.1

Turkey: arms production in, 40; defense burden in, 10

Uganda: arms production in, 40; defense burden in, 10

United Nations, 72, 73

United States, costs of defense in, 72–73

United States Arms Control and Disarmament Agency, 117

Uruguay: alliances to major power blocs, 99; arms production in, discriminant analysis of, 44; budgetary trade-offs in, 83, 95, 100; classifications of, 98; defense burden in, discriminant analysis of, 10

Valentine, C.M., 149n.7

Vayrynen, R., 48n.1

Vener, J., 104n.34, 177n.1, 249, 260n.9

Venezuela, 105–207; alliances to major power blocs, 99; arms production in, 43, 44; budgetary trade-offs in, 80, 83, 84, 100, 151–177; budgetary trade-offs in, optimal control forecast of, 179–207; classifications of, 98; current economic status, 107; defense burden in, discriminant analysis of, 10; development policy since oil price increases, 181–182; economic priorities and constraints, 179–182; inflation in, 181, 183, 188–189, 198–199, 202, 205; investment in, 184, 192, 193; major macroeconomic trends in (1979–83), 180; oil production, export earning from, 189–190; per capita military expenditures in, 23

Venezuela, military expenditures in, 164–166; analysis of trends in, 118–130; austerity and, 111–116; determinants of deviation from trends in, 142–148; elasticities, 131, 137–139; factors underlying (1950–83), 117–149, 164–166; historical defense-macroeconomic patterns, 130–140; impact in other Latin American countries, 140–144; in macroeconomic forecasting model, 184, 193–195; optimal control forecasts of, 202–205

Vulnerability of sectors to budgetary reduction during economic austerity, 108–110

Wagner's Law, 3, 27–29

Weapons industry. *See* Arms production, domestic

Weaver, T., 103n.14, 177n.2

Welfare expenditures. *See* Social security and welfare expenditures

Whynes, D.K., 57n.4, 70n.2, 101, 104n.40

Wildavsky, A., 115n.1

World Armaments and Disarmament: SIPRI Yearbook, 78–79

World Bank, 108, 290

Wulf, H., 48n.3

Zaire, arms production in, 40

Zambia: arms production in, 40; defense burden in, 10

Zero-sum game, 153

Zimbabwe, defense burden in, 10

About the Author

Robert E. Looney is professor of National Security Affairs at the Naval Postgraduate School, Monterey, California. He has been a faculty member of the University of California at Davis, the University of Santa Clara, and the Monterey Institute of International Studies. He has also been a development economist for the Stanford Research Institute and has served as an economic advisor to the governments of Iran, Saudi Arabia, Mexico, Panama, and Jamaica. Dr. Looney has published numerous articles in professional journals, and is the author of *The Economic Development of Iran* (1973), *Income Distribution Policies and Economic Growth in Semi-industrialized Countries* (1975), *The Economic Development of Panama* (1976), *Iran at the End of the Century* (Lexington Books, 1977), *A Development Strategy for Iran through the 1980s* (1977), *Mexico's Economy* (1978), *The Impact of World Inflation on Semidependent Countries* (1979), *Economic Origins of the Iranian Revolution* (1982), *Saudi Arabia's Development Potential* (Lexington Books, 1982), *Development Alternatives for Mexico* (1982), *Economic Policymaking in Mexico* (1985), and *The Jamaican Economy in the 1980s* (1986).

RAYMOND H. FOGLER LIBRARY
DATE DUE

BOOKS ARE SUBJECT TO